Making Photogravures with polymer plates

A modern technique of historical photo-mechanical printing using steel-backed polymer plates, etched with water, and printed by hand with traditional intaglio processes.

Scott Barnes

First Edition

ISBN-13: 978-0615919218
ISBN-10: 0615919219

ARTandWATER Editions
www.artandwater.com
photogravurepolymer@gmail.com

Table of Contents

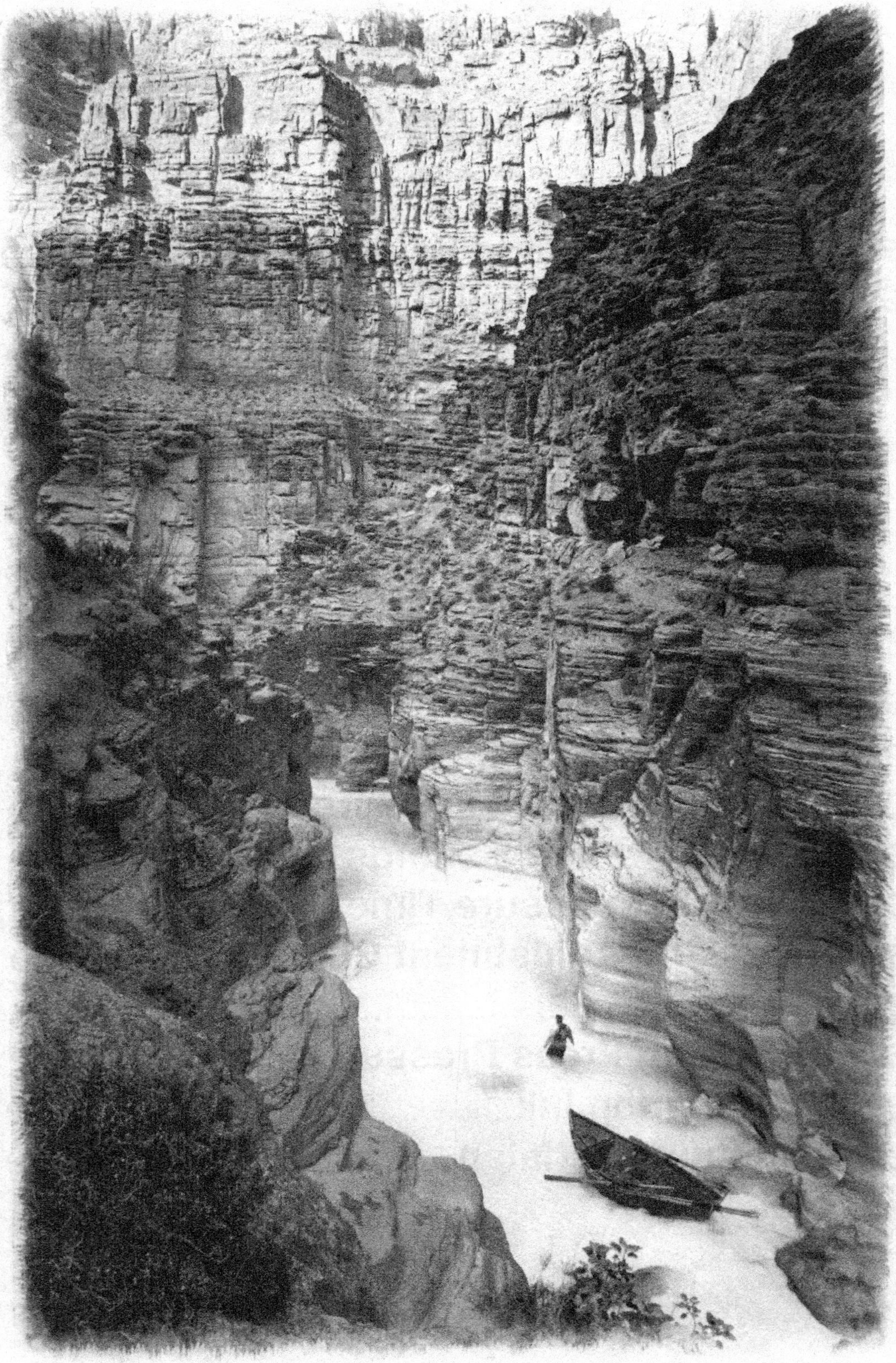

"Havasu"

photogravure

Scott Barnes

Introduction

After graduate school, I bought some of Dan Weldon's Solarplates because I was excited to make intaglio prints. I did not have the facilities of a proper print shop, and thought that the Solarplates would make a good surface for both intaglio and relief. They do, but I could not figure it out quickly, so impatiently moved on to other printmaking techniques. Knowledge on the internet was scattered and sometimes inaccurate, so I did not revisit the challenge for a few years. Eventually, I was asked by the chair of the Art Department, of the university where I teach, if I wanted to help figure out how to use polymer plates to make photogravures. He and his photographer friend were looking for some printmaking input.

I was excited to have other people helping me sort through all of the good and bad information that exists on the world wide web about this process. We recognized that the process would be full of trial and error, but some early days felt like they had more error than normal. After eliminating some misleading internet instructions, we began to see some acceptable results. The ball was rolling for me as I did more and more research on my own (making many mistakes along the way). I grew excited to report what I had found, and compare notes with the others. David Hanson and Lyle Allan have been a big help starting the research that has turned into a large body of photogravure work for me, and the eventual first draft of this book.

Learning this with other encouraging people makes it much easier. The photogravure process brings together some skill sets that are not commonly crossed. It requires skill in intaglio printmaking, traditional photography, with good understanding of digital image editing and output. Having a group of people to share ideas is important.

The intent of this book is to share the work flow that I have developed over the past three years. The methods shown are born of constant experimenting to find a balance between two things: first, finding the least expensive tools available and second, having resources that are of high enough quality to print good photographic images. Many methods, other than my own, create equally good images. I am simply sharing my workshop secrets, with the hope that more people will be encouraged to experiment with this unique and versatile method of intaglio printmaking.

The polymer plates used in this book are Printight KM73 by Toyobo. I get them from boxcarpress.com. They hold fine dot patterns that will allow for good resolution of the final print. All of the methods in this book will also work with Dan Weldon's Solarplates. I have seen exceptional images made from both brands of polymer plates.

Have fun printing. Please email me with questions or comments. photogravurepolymer@gmail.com

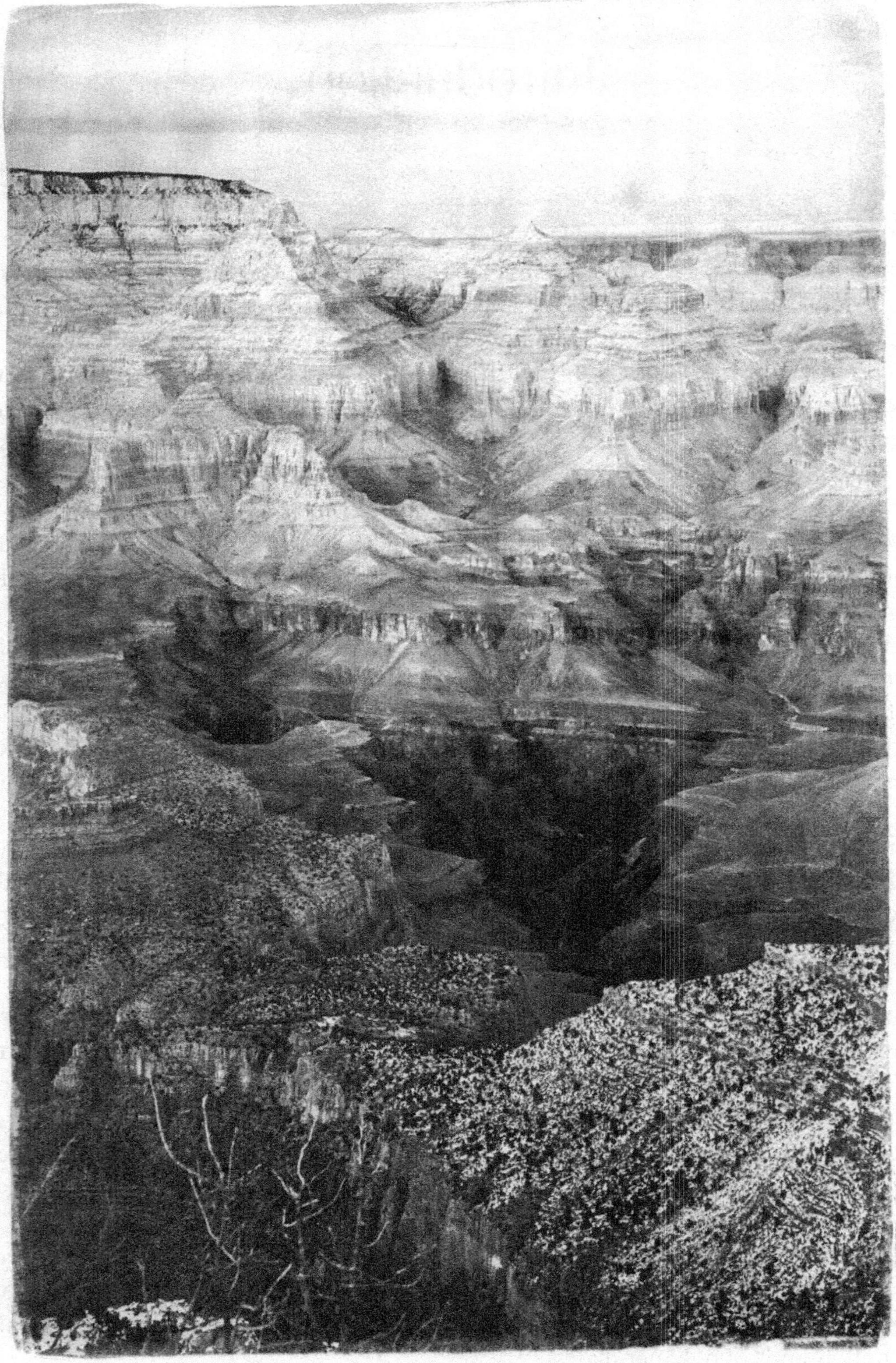

"Winter Canyon"

photogravure

Scott Barnes

Chapter 1
Equipment and Safety

Very Basic Safety Equipment:

gloves (latex, nitrile, or vinyl)
UV filtering eye glasses (get from lab supply company, not just sunglasses)
clean water supply
basic first aid kit
willingness to accept responsibility for your own safety

Disclaimer:

I am not a medical professional, and cannot offer advice on any individual's health or safety. The well-being of each person is completely up to each individual, and each person's decision whether or not to attempt any of the techniques found here is completely up to that individual. This book reveals a workflow that has developed from much trial and error. I have read the manufacturer's material safety data sheets for each product that I have used, and consulted personal physicians. I strongly suggest that you do the same. Your health is your responsibility, not mine.

A Few Basic Safety Concerns:

UV light is harmful to both skin and eyes. Minimize your exposure by making sure the UV exposure system does not have any light leaks, and leave the room while the UV exposure system is running. The UV light required for curing the photopolymers used in KM73 plates (and most photographic contact printing) is unfiltered. The exposure units emit unfiltered UV light that are much stronger than simple "blacklights" or tanning lights. The damage to eyes and skin can be significant. Long sleeve clothing and UV filtering eye glasses will minimize exposure, but will not block it completely. Do not rely on clothing or glasses as the only means of protection from ultraviolet light.

The KM73 photopolymer plates made by Toyobo are designed for the commercial printing industry. They are normally exposed and developed in expensive all-in-one units that automate the process and remove most human involvement. The manual processing shown in this book is essentially a hack of commercial supplies. It is only safer than acid etching on metal because the hazards are easier to manage. This process still involves some risks.

I have yet to read a book or set of online instructions that calls for active ventilation while processing the KM73 plates. They emit a slightly sweet odor while being washed out in water. I treat the chemistry of this particular process with the same caution and respect that I have for all photographic processes and believe that **active ventilation is needed.**

Wear gloves while processing uncured plates, particularly during the water bath washout phase. Many people do not have a reaction to the polymers in these plates, but long-term effects are not well documented. Anecdotal evidence suggests that anything is possible: immediate reaction the first time you use the plates, a delayed reaction after years of using these plates, or no reaction at all. I am in the habit of wearing gloves while handling plates: unexposed plates, during washout, while drying, through the last step of sanding the edges of an exposed and cured plate. I do not touch the plate with bare hands until I am placing it on the table to receive the first coat of printing ink.

The plate oil found in most intaglio printmaking inks does not irritate most people's skin. Typically, the pigments and modifiers are the cause of irritation and more serious threats to one's health. There are rare cases, however, where even the oil has cause problems, so you may not want to take the risk of handling any oil or ink with bare hands. Choose ink from manufacturers who list ALL of the pigments, vehicles, and modifiers on the label of each color of ink. Buy an artist's safety book and read about the hazards of various pigments. **Cadmium and lead should be avoided**. Educate yourself and make your own decision.

Be careful with solvents (paint thinners, degreasers, cleaning products). Harmful effects can range from mild skin irritation to serious medical conditions. Read the label. Wear gloves. Use adequate ventilation.

Equipment:

for **IMAGE CAPTURE:**
- Camera
- Flatbed scanner

for **IMAGE EDITING:**
- Adobe Photoshop image editing software
- Epson Stylus Pro 3800 inkjet printer
- Fixxons Waterproof Silk Screen Positive Film. (www.fixxons.com)
- Print dryer

for **TRANSPARENCY PREPARATION:**
- straight edge and razor blade (can use scissors or other cutting tool)
- baby powder (talc)
- 3" hake brush

for **PLATE MAKING:**
- KM73 photopolymer plates from Toyobo. (purchased from Boxcar Press www.boxcarpress.com)
- Ryonet RXP16x20 UV exposure unit (www.silkscreeningsupplies.com)
- Aristo Platinum Printer (discontinued UV exposure unit)
- Gralab 500 darkroom timer
- Contact Printing Frame (home made, see chapter 3)
- darkroom "safe light" (this process is not as sensitive as some, so any safelight will work)
- soft washout brush (purchased from Boxcar Press www.boxcarpress.com)
- developing tray (can use a cheap plastic tote as an alternative)
- latex gloves (can be nitrile or vinyl)
- UV glasses (that block at least 300 - 400 nm of light)
- paper towels
- hair dryer

for **PREPARING PLATE FOR PRINTING:**
- guillotine paper cutter (strong enough to cut thin steel back of KM73 plate, tin snips can be used too)
- fine bastard cut file
- sand paper (400, 600, 1200 grit)
- block of wood (to hold sand paper)

for **INKING AND WIPING THE PLATE:**
- tempered glass palette (to mix ink, any hard and smooth surface will work)
- putty knife (or scraper) from hardware store
- Gamblin Burnt Plate Oil #000
- Gamblin Burnt Plate Oil #2
- Graphic Chemical Easy Wipe
- Graphic Chemical Etching Ink (various colors, mostly different shades of black)
- magnet sheet (glued to table, which will hold the KM73 plate while inking)
- newsprint sheets
- soft plastic scraper/squeegee (from Takach Press www.takachpress.com) (can also use Bondo brand
- squeegee found in auto body repair kits)
- tarlatan
- phone book pages

for **PRINTING THE PLATE:**
- large plastic tub for soaking paper
- blotter paper (100% cotton is best, but this book shows newsprint being used)
- Rives BFK printmaking paper (100% cotton/rag, 280 gsm)
- Conrad Machine 18" Etching Press with 3 blanket system (catcher, cushion, pusher)
- wire drying rack

This list only includes websites for difficult to find items. For everything else, I suggest that you use the internet to shop for the best price that you can find.

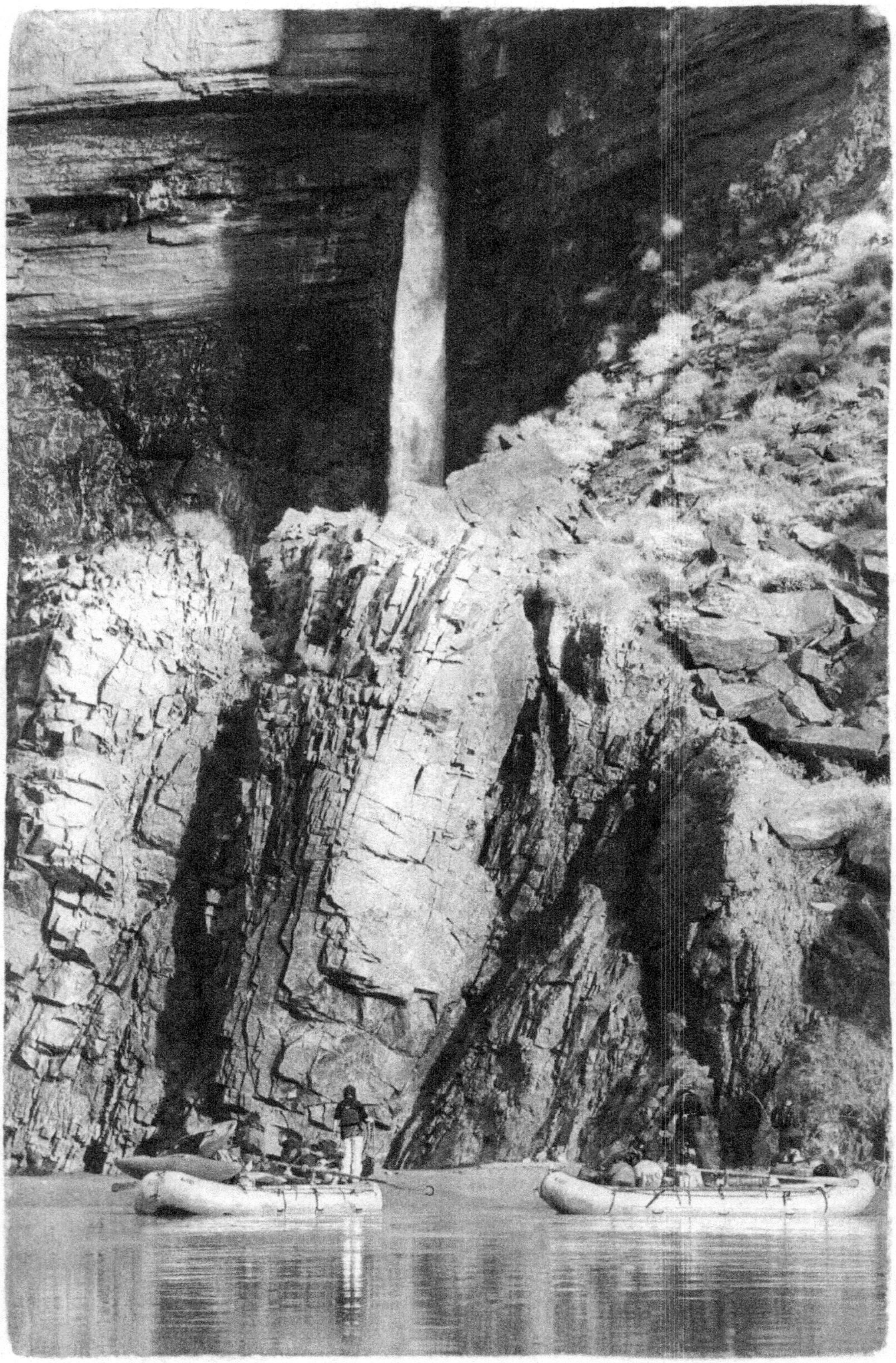

"Deer Creek"

photogravure

Scott Barnes

Chapter 2
Main Work Flow

The main work flow consists of many steps. I had considered breaking it into smaller steps, but the reality of this process is that the entire work flow in this chapter represents all the steps needed to achieve a final image. Therefore, this whole process must be seen as one continuous work flow.

Making photogravures with KM73 polymer plates takes a lot of practice. It requires physical skill that can only be learned with time, and through some trial and error. During the process of learning, I want to caution you against changing too many variables at a time. Consistency is key to finding a work flow that works.

Much has been written about making digital negatives (which can be used to create the positive transparencies for this technique), color profiles through the computer, inkjet printer, and paper. While all of that knowledge is helpful (and necessary), it only covers half of the skill base needed to make photogravures. Printing photos with this technique require just as much intaglio printmaking skill as digital photography knowledge and alternative photography skill. The alternative photography community is a tremendous resource, but consider that you must give equal time to learning from the intaglio printmaking community.

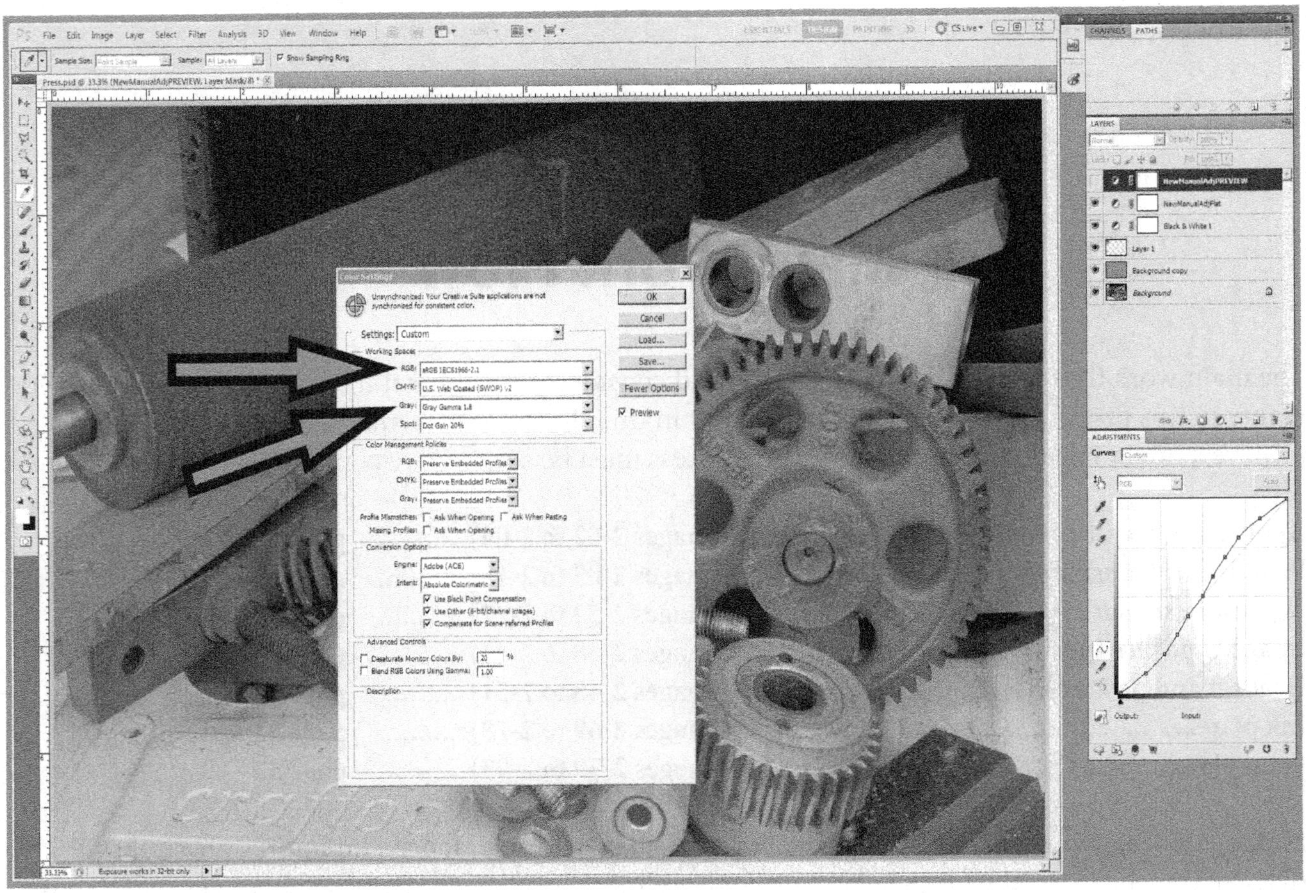

(image 2-01) Before doing anything, check the color settings. Make sure to use the same color settings throughout the entire digital work flow. Just about any setting will work, as long as it stays the same through the entire work flow (and as long as it compatible with the various devices used: camera, scanner, printer, computer's operating system, digital editing suite, etc...).

In Adobe Photoshop: Edit --> Color Settings

The two most important settings are RGB and GRAY.

In this example, RGB is set to sRGB IEC61966-2.1, which is an old standard with a small enough gamut that every device can use it. If you have an old digital camera, a very simple scanner, or are working from files from the web, this RGB profile is all you need. If you have a new digital camera, are shooting in camera raw, or are scanning negatives with a good scanner, I recommend setting the RGB to ProPhoto RGB. The gamut is larger than needed, but it will make the editing process less destructive. (more in chapter 6)

Gray Gamma 1.8 has always been my default gray setting. I've experimented with others, and they don't seem to work as well. I think that, like sRGB IEC61966-2.1, more devices are set for Gray Gamma 1.8 than other settings. ProPhoto RGB uses gray gamma 1.8. I'm sure someone, with more experience than me, disagees. But, consistency in the work flow is the first important step; more important than following one person's preference or specific expertise.

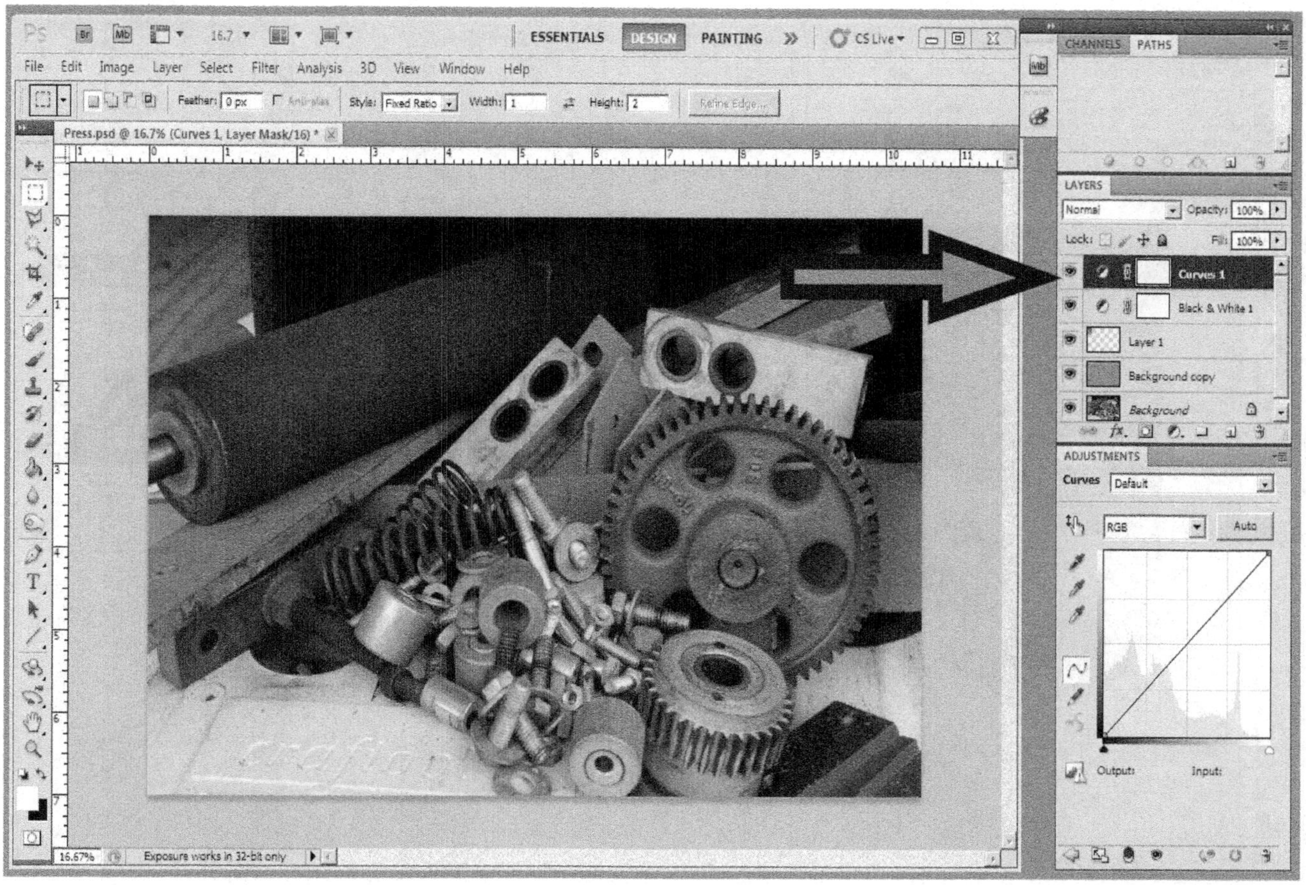

(image 2-02) Add an adjustment curve at the top of the layer stack.

This adjustment curve (see chapter 8) will compensate for the differences between the physical reality of the varying densities of the printed transparency, and the theoretical densities of the digital file. The plotted densities you see in the computer are linear. The reality of inkjet transparency ink is certainly not linear (and varies from brand to brand). Exposure to UV light is logarithmic. The adjustment curve bridges the gap.

The PC menu is different than the Mac menu. The images in this chapter show the PC menu for an Epson Stylus Pro Photo 3800 through Adobe Photoshop CS5.

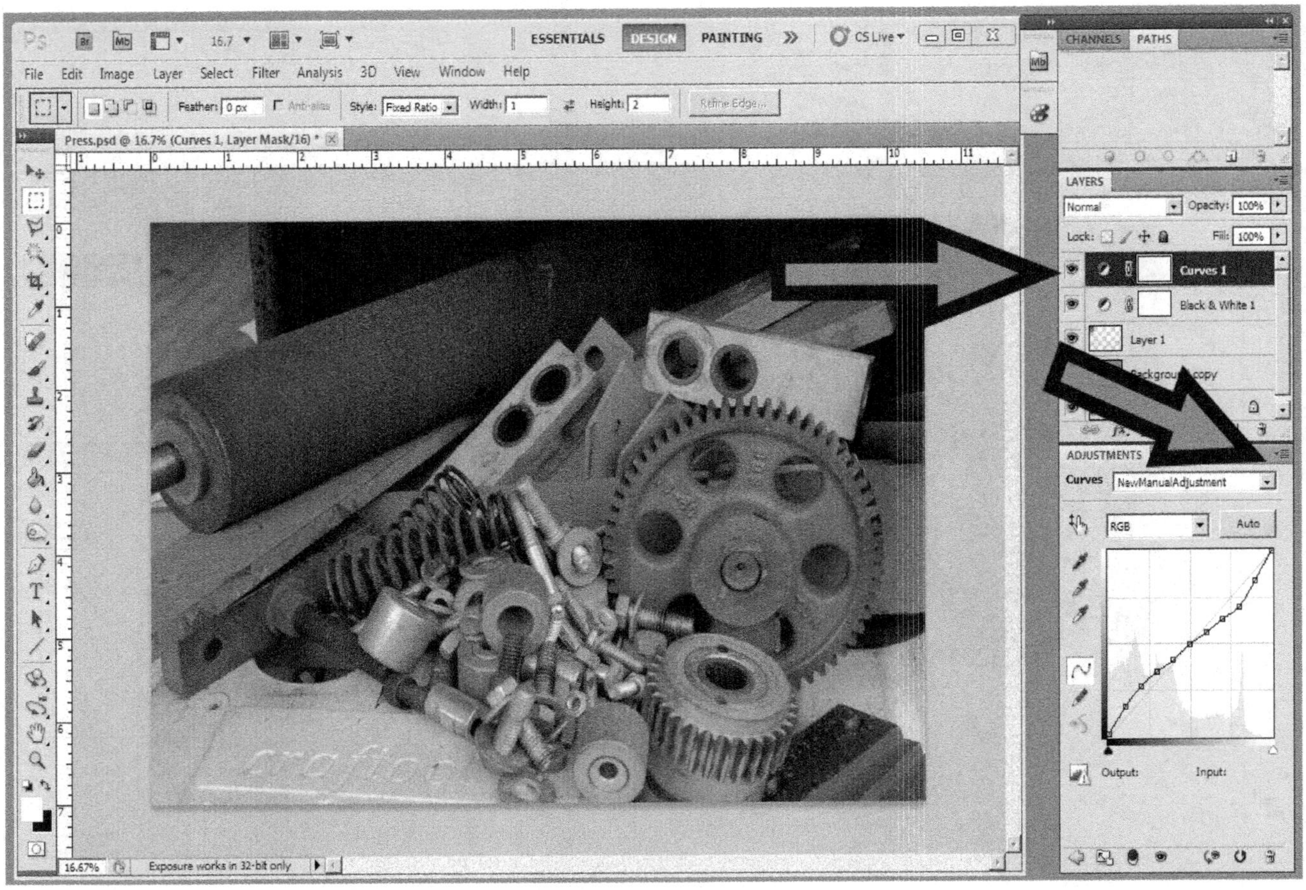

(image 2-03) Use the menu at the top of the curve window to select the adjustment curve you made in chapter 8 and make sure it is applied to your image.

If you have not yet made your own custom adjustment curve, you may try someone else's curve (as a way to get started). Since everyone's work flow is unique, be aware that a "canned" curve from someone else may not provide you with the best results.

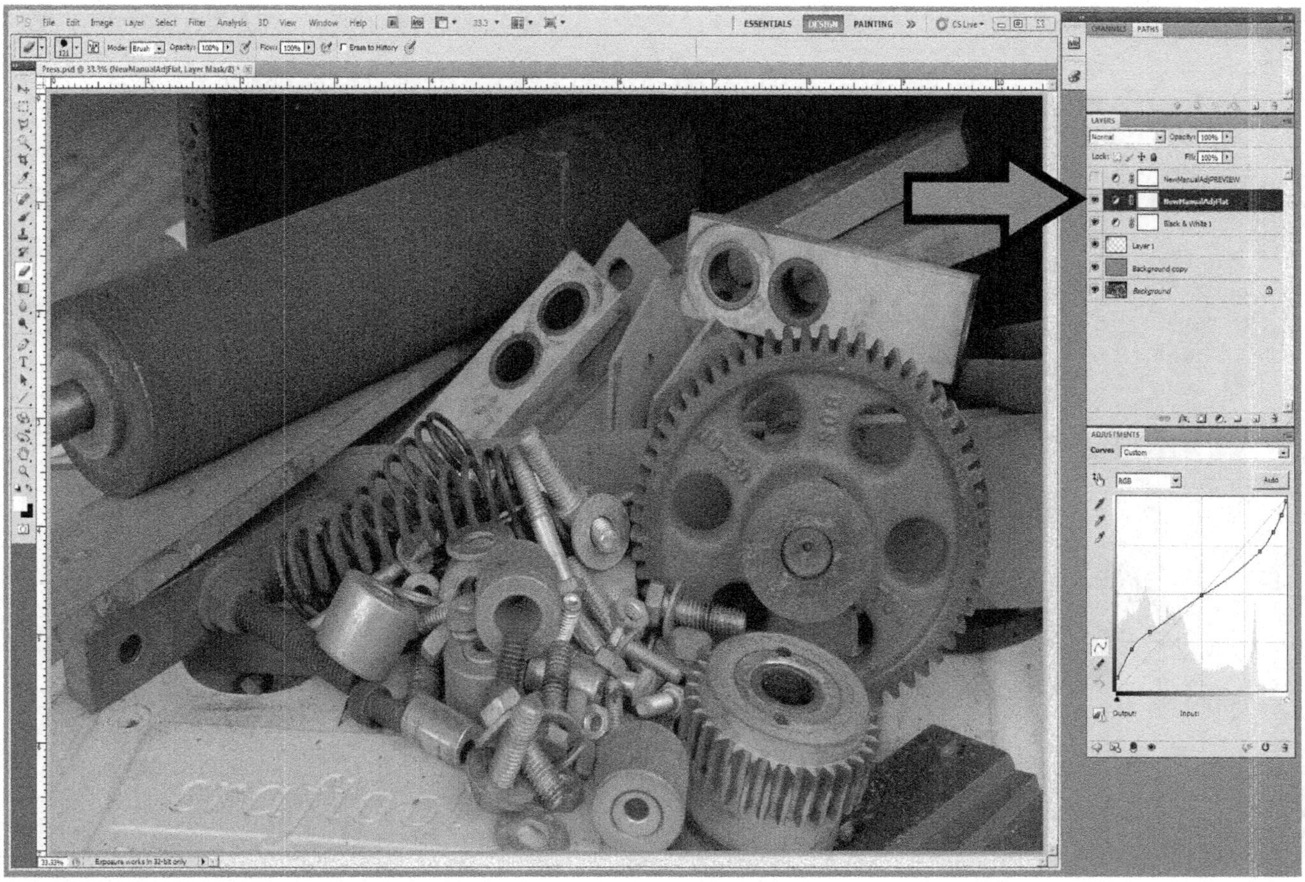

(image 2-04) Make sure that the adjustment layer is turned on, and any preview layers are turned off.

Preview layers are not covered in this book. They are can be used to soft proof your image, but only work if the process of building adjustment curves is accurate. A preview layer is only shown in this image so that you are aware of their existence in some peoples' work flows. As a soft proof layer, it should not be turned on when you are ready to print. The adjustment layer, however, does need to be turned on before printing.

Get in the habit of naming the adjustment layers. Having layers that are named "curve" and "curve-02" gets confusing.

The adjustment curve should be at the top of the layer stack. It should be turned on. It will affect everything below it in the layer stack. The image is going to look flat (significanlty less contrast). Trust the process. This transparency is designed to block UV light, not visible light.

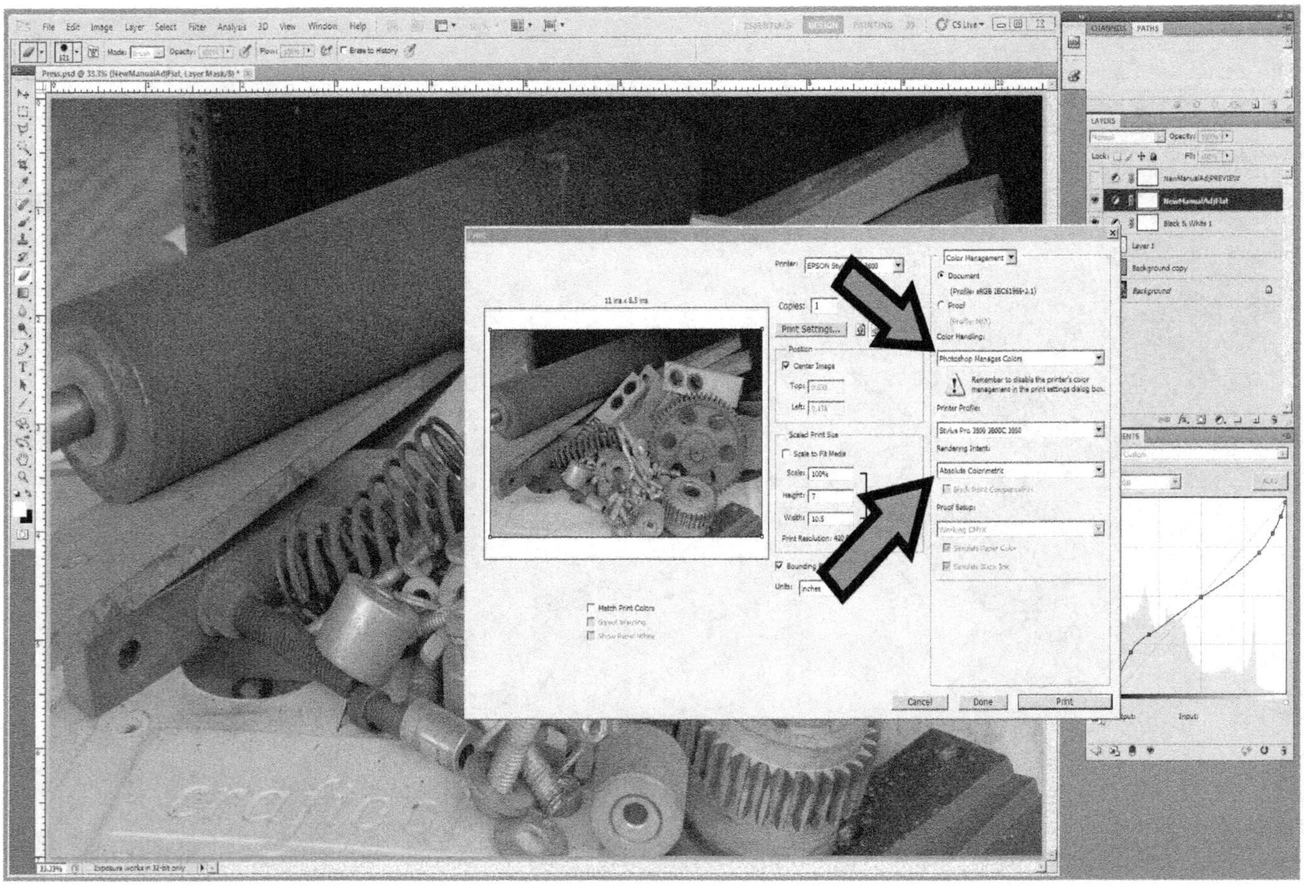

(image 2-05) In the print menu, turn off all color controls, allowing only Photoshop (or the other image editing software) to control the color. Make the rendering intent absolute colorimetric. This will make sure that out of gamut colors do not shift the rest of the colors to create a relative gray scale. When printing a digital transparency, you want to have as much control as possible, dealing in absolute terms (predictably reproducable terms). Turn off black point compensation.

This menu must be checked every time you print. It is subject to change, and is not part of what gets saved when you save a print setting (next page). Write the settings on paper to remember them.

To find this Epson Stylus Pro Photo 3800 menu in Adobe Photoshop CS5 for PC :
File --> Print

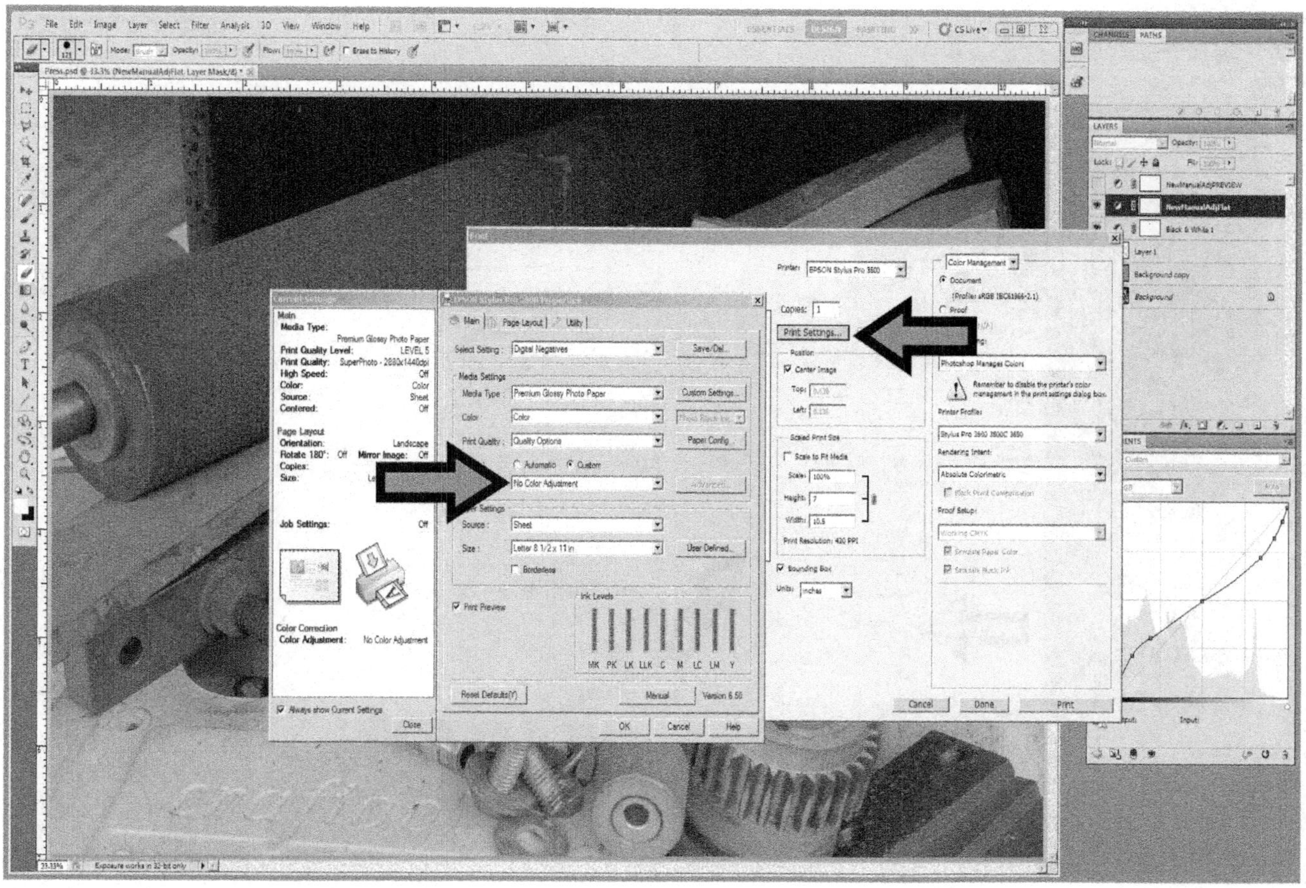

(image 2-06) In the Print Settings sub-menu, make sure that color adjustment is turned off.

The Print Settings sub-menu is the menu that dictates what the printer will do. As the printer's menu, you must turn off the color settings to allow Photoshop to control the color. Adjust paper size, source, and ink settings.

To find this Epson Stylus Pro Photo 3800 menu in Adobe Photoshop CS5 for PC :
File --> Print --> Print Settings

Check the Print Preview box to make sure it is on.

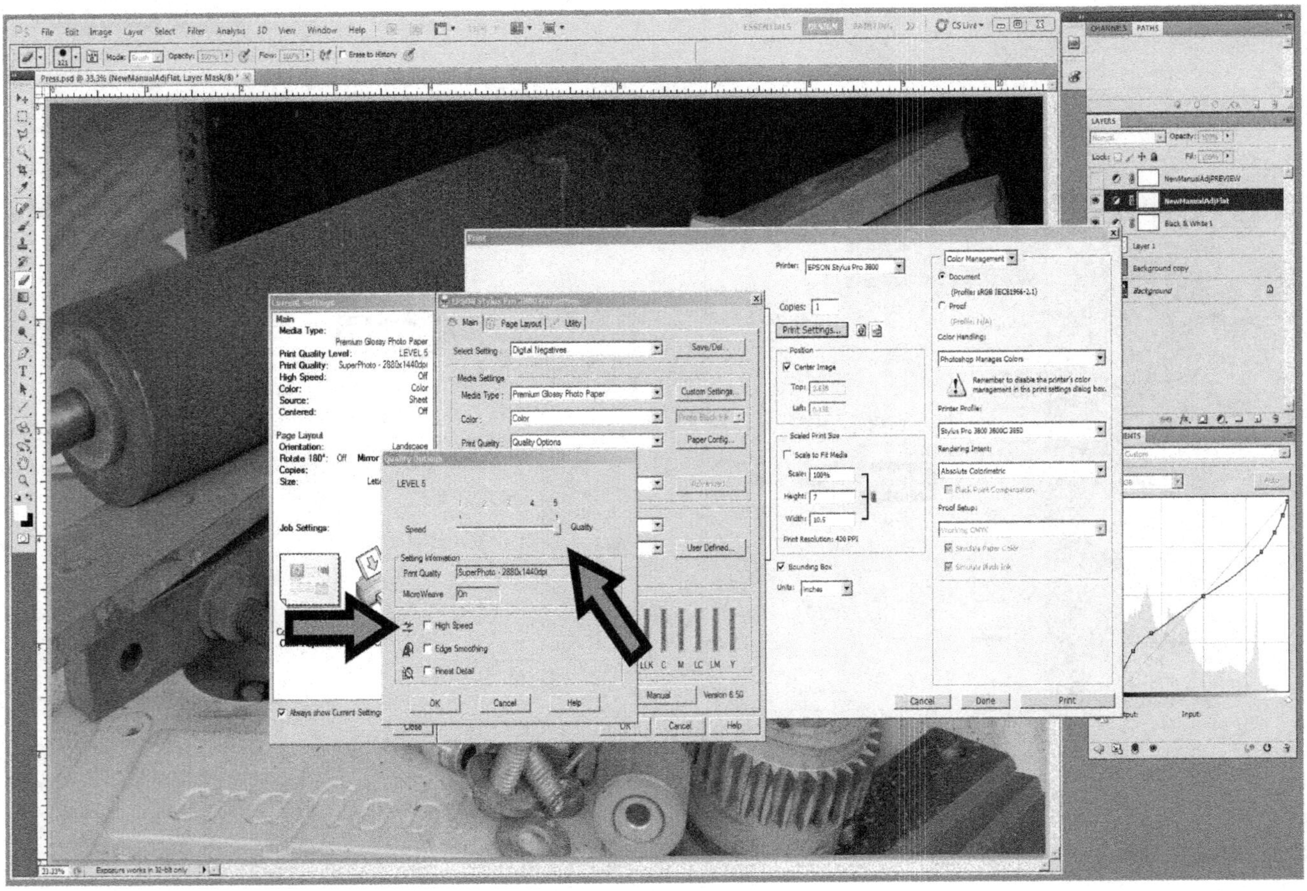

(image 2-07) In the Paper Configuration menu, find the Quality Options to control the speed at which the printer will print. Turn off high speed printing, and make sure the resolution is as high as possible.

To find this Epson Stylus Pro Photo 3800 menu in Adobe Photoshop CS5 for PC :
File --> Print --> Print Settings --> Print Quality (drop down menu) --> Quality Options

move slider to 5 (quality)
Setting Information: SuperPhoto - 2880 x 1440 dpi
MicroWeave: On
High Speed: Off
Edge Smoothing: Off
Finest Detail: Off

Write everything down. If you have doubts about what is saved in a preset and what is not, check everything. Eventually, you will learn the idiosyncrasies of your printer driver.

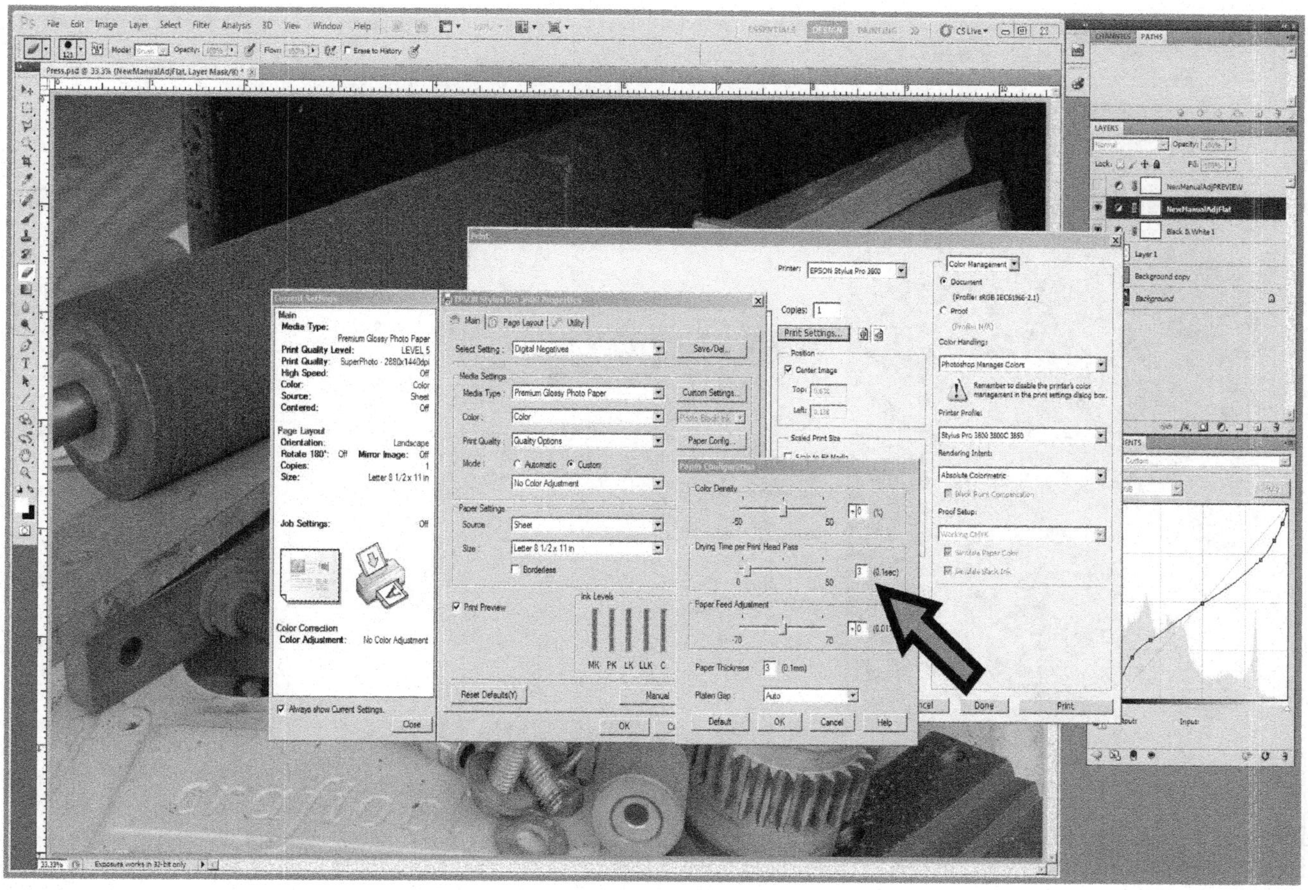

(image 2-08) Adjust the drying time per print head pass to slow down the rate of printing.

Slowing down the rate of printing will allow the ink enough time to dry before running under the guide wheels. An additional 0.3 seconds is adequate, but more will only provide additional time for the ink to dry. Not letting the ink dry between print head passes will create a situation in which the guide wheels will make marks on the wet ink.

To find this Epson Stylus Pro Photo 3800 menu in Adobe Photoshop CS5 for PC :
File --> Print --> Print Settings --> Paper Config...

Color Density: +0
Drying Time per Print Head Pass: 3 (0.1 sec)
Paper Feed Adjustment: +0
Paper Thickness: 3 (0.1mm)
Platen Gap: Auto

Save this setting, giving it a name that is easy to remember. *(My print profile is saved simply as "**Digital Negatives**" since I use it for other contact printing photographic processes)* Saving the setting will minimize the steps in future and help maintain consistency in the work flow.

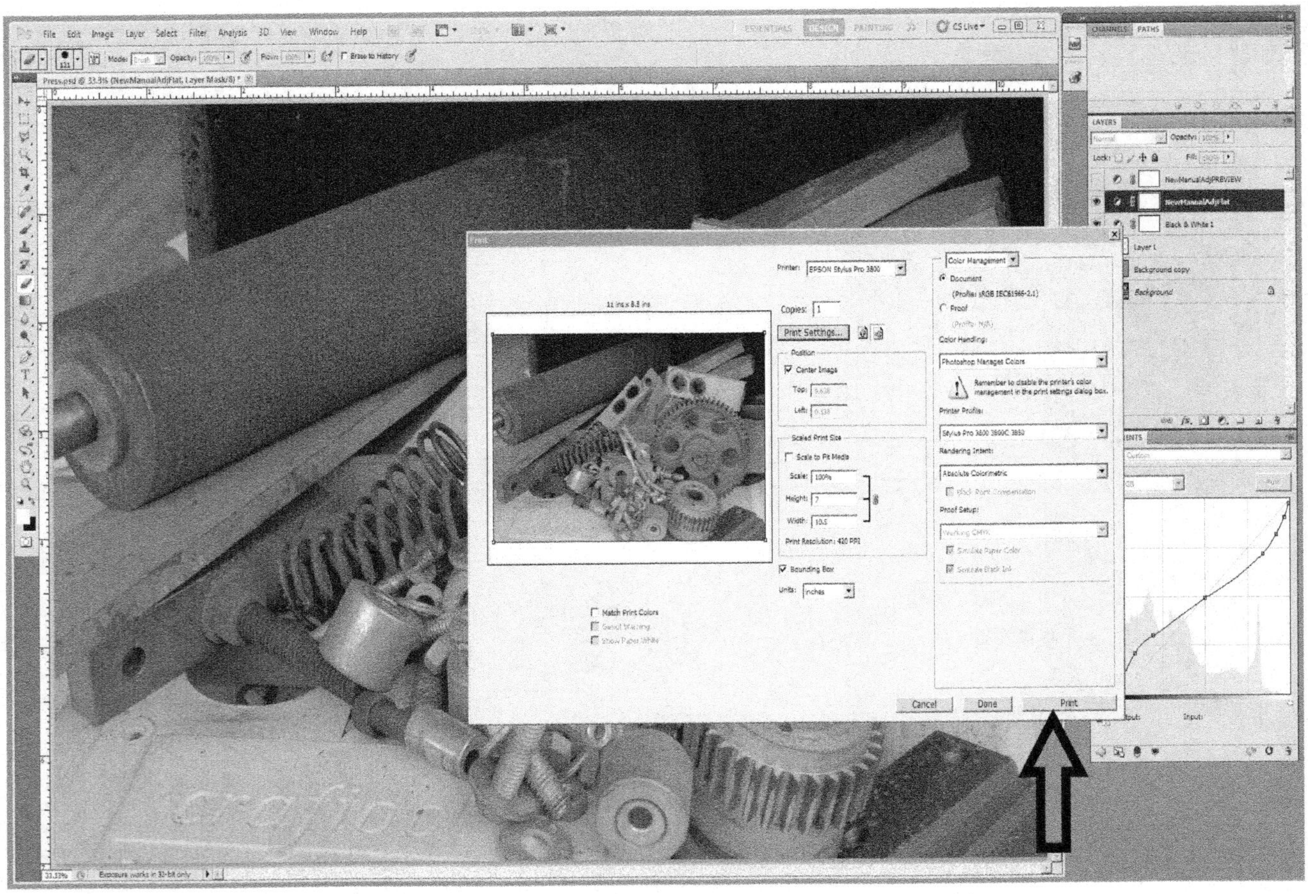

(image 2-09) Press print.

If you have th Print Preview button selected, you will have time to take the transparency media out of it's package and place it into the printer while the computer sends the job to the printer and shows the preview screen.

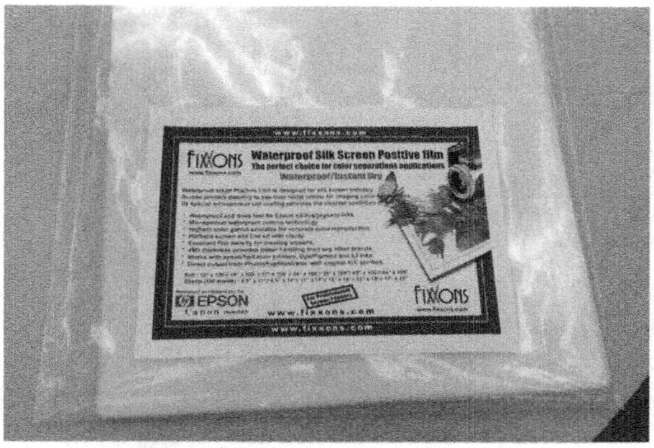

(image 2-10) Remove the transparency medium from it's package. Be careful to track which side is coated for printing.

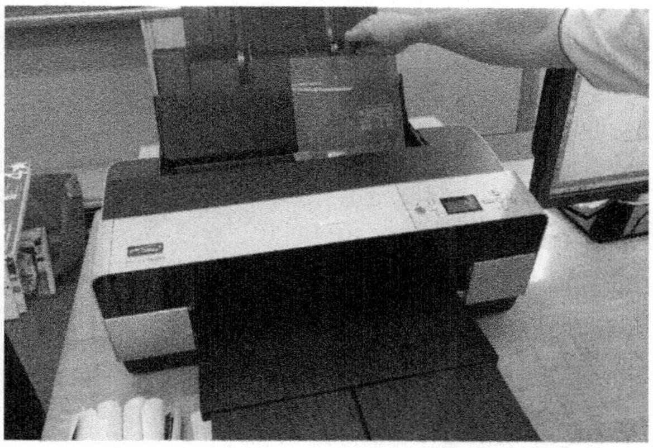

(image 2-11) Place the transparency into the printer, with the appropriate side facing the print heads. In the Epson 3800, the printable side faces up.

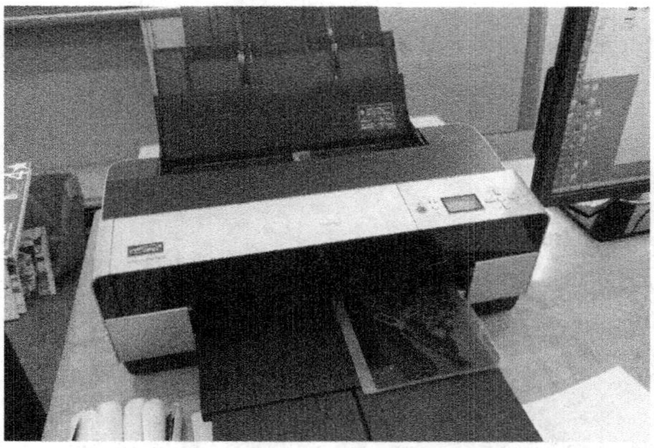

(image 2-12) Confirm the print preview by pressing Print, and let the machine print the transparency.

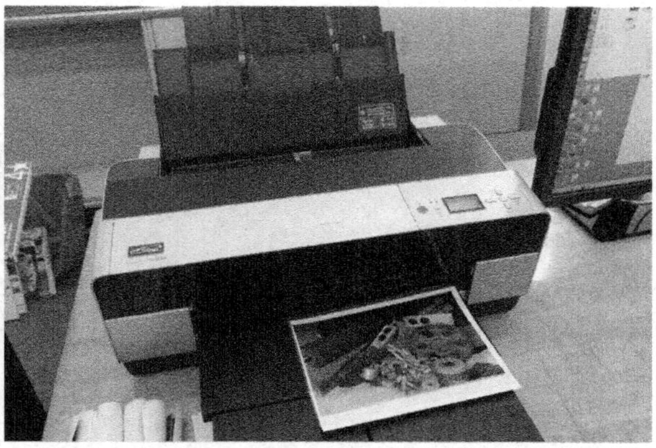

(image 2-13) Place the new transparency on a clean piece of paper so dirt and other contaminants cannot touch the back of it. White paper will also let you inspect the transparency for imperfections like banding or blurring.

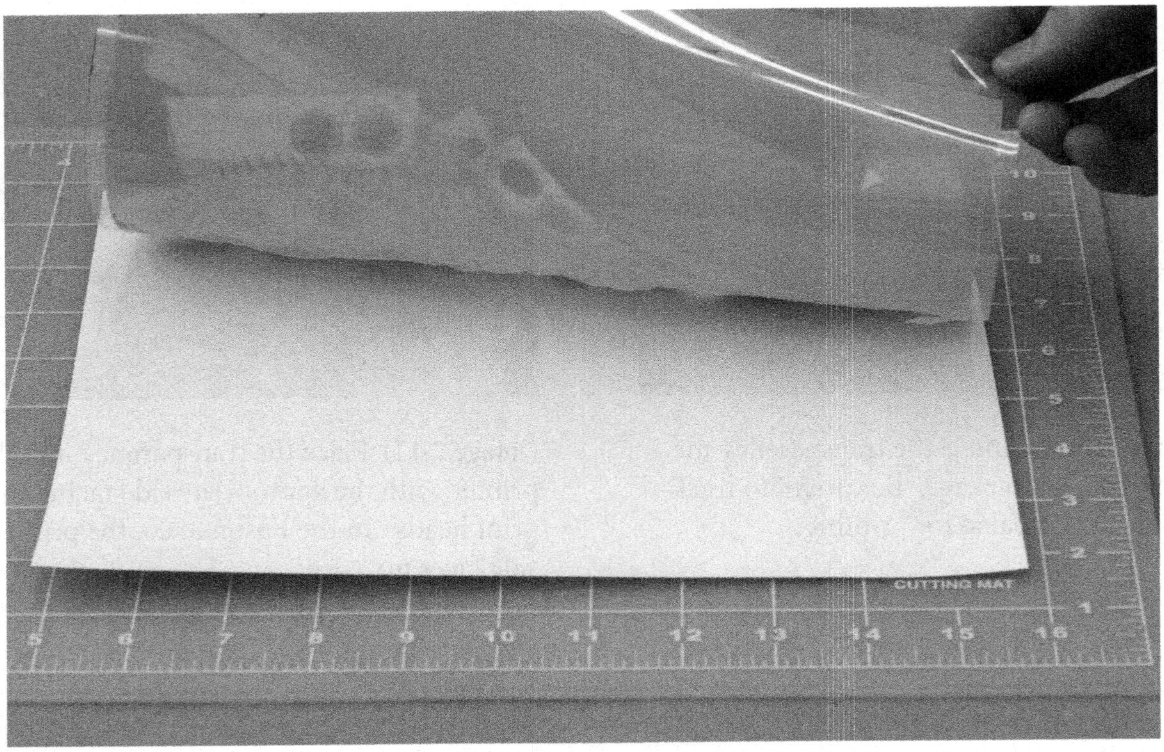

(image 2-14) A wet transparency will be cloudy, when viewed from the back, and more clear when dry.

(image 2-15) The initial cloudy appearance will typically disappear within 10 minutes. This means that the ink is dry enough for careful handling, but it is not completely dry.

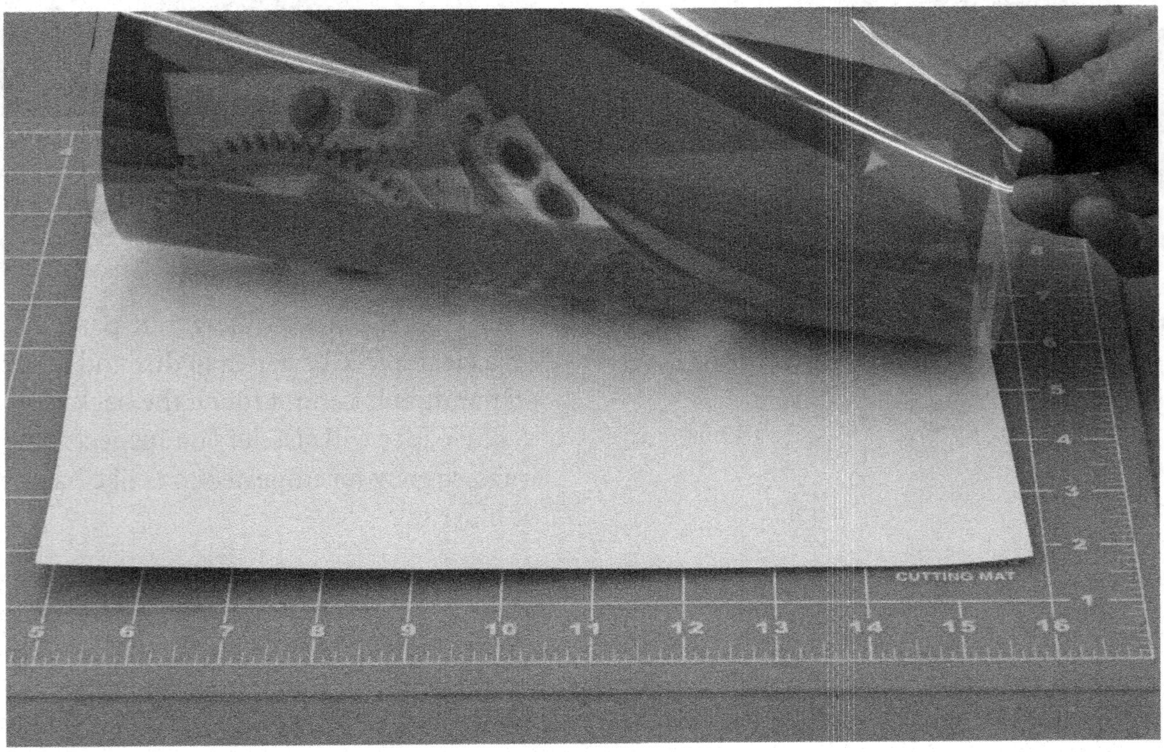

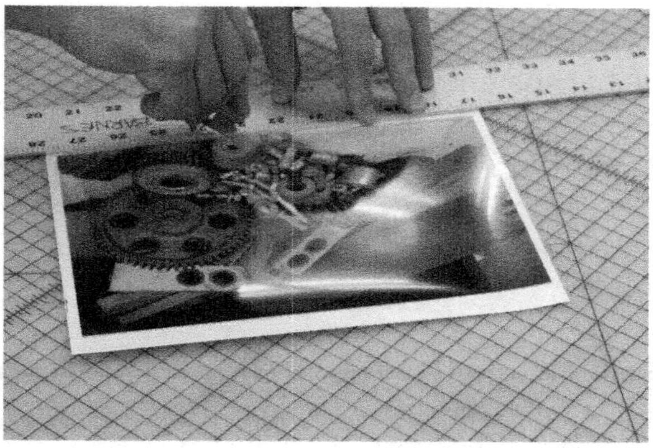

(image 2-16) Trim the transparency to the correct size.

Cut edges will make faint lines in the final work. Either leave enough clear boarder or trim the transparency to the edge of the image.

Be very careful. Inkjet transparencies are not as tough as film negatives. Wet ink will smudge easily. Dry ink scratches easily.

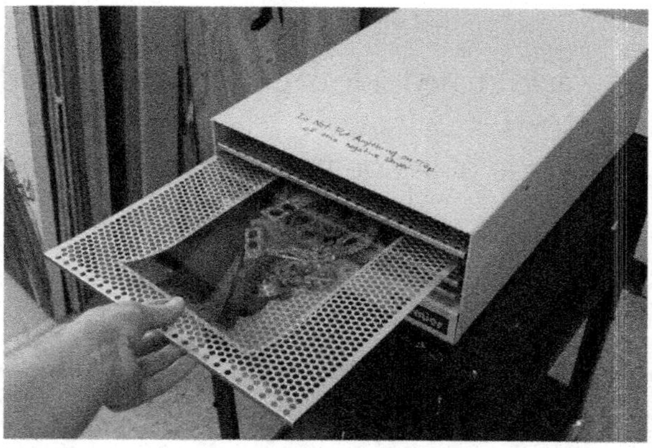

(image 2-17) Place the transparency in a print drier for an hour.

If you do not have a print drier, then you must let the transparency dry for 12 hours to make sure it is completely dry. The process can be sped up with a hair drier on a low setting. Be careful not to use a hair drier within the first 15 minute after the transparency is printed.

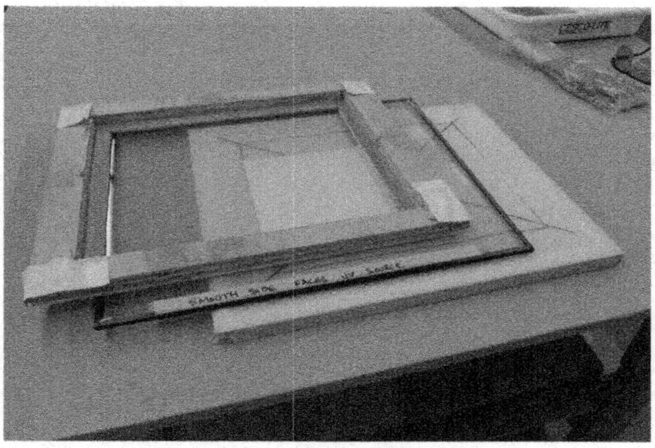

(image 2-18) Closely inspect the parts of the contact frame for damage and dirt.

See chapter 3 for more information about contact printing frames.

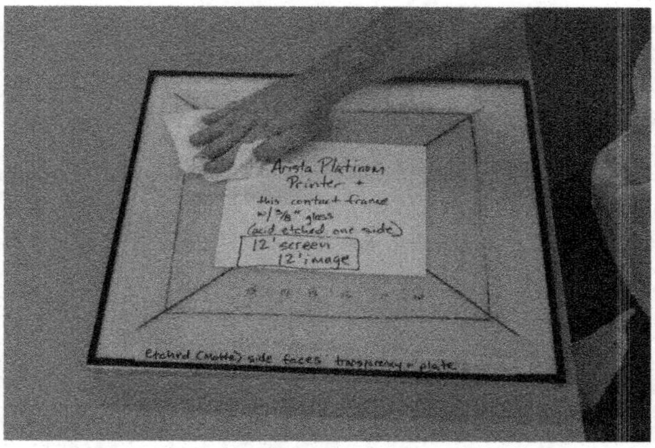

(image 2-19) Clean both sides of the glass on the contact printing frame. Even the smallest speck of dust will show up in the image.

Remember that the smooth side of the glass will go towards the UV exposure unit, and the acid etched side (matte) will face the transparency and KM 73 plate.

acid etched side of glass goes against the image transparency (or stochastic screen)

printed side of image transparency (or stochastic screen) goes against polymer side of plate

steel side of polymer plate goes against the back of the contact frame

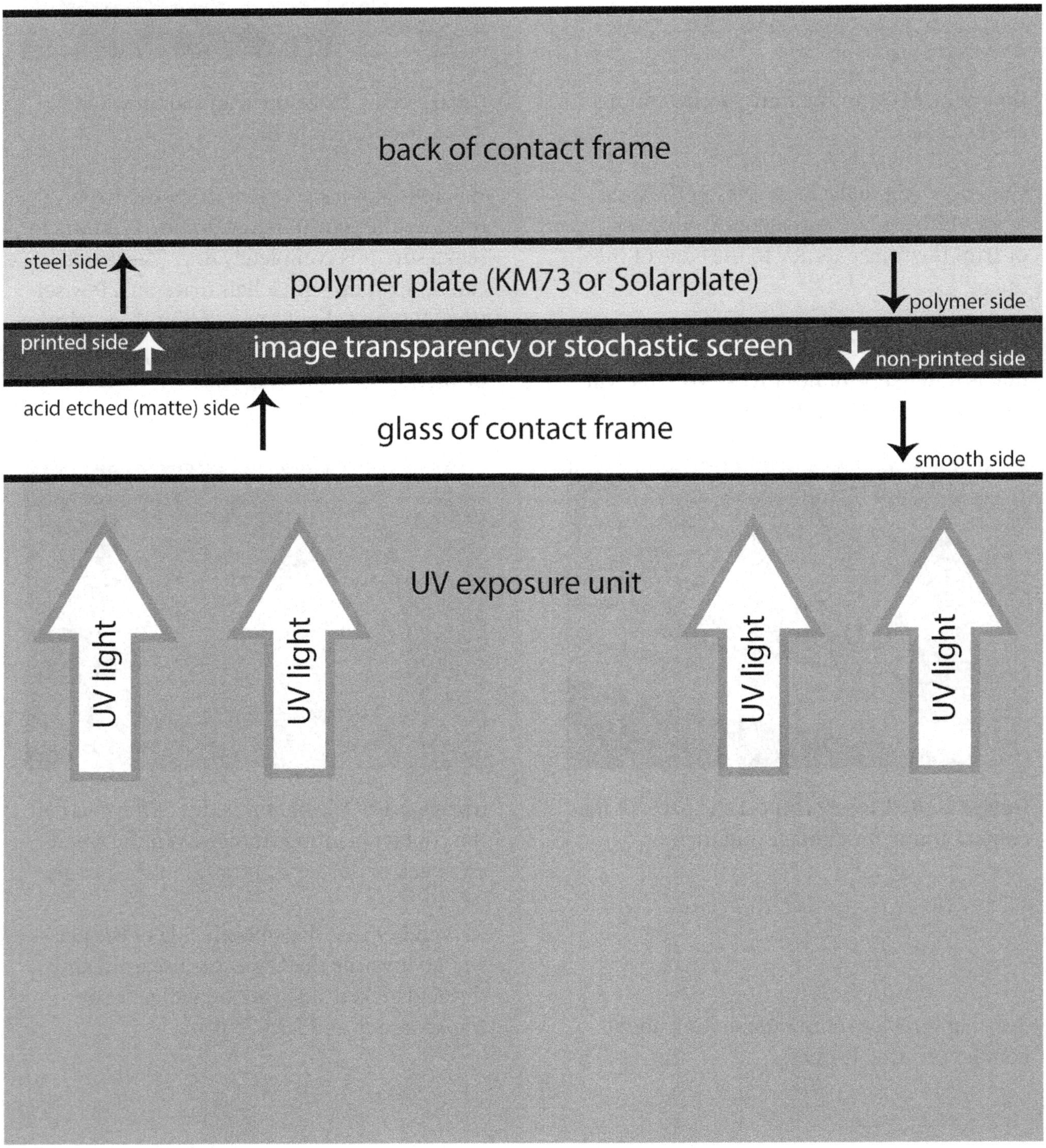

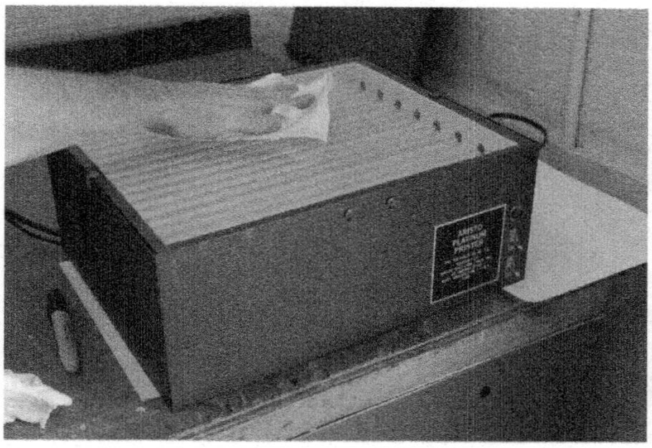

(image 2-20) Clean the glass surface of the UV exposure unit.

Turn on the safe light. Simple low wattage yellow, orange, or red incandescent bulbs can be used as safe lights for this process, but fluorescent lights should not be used.

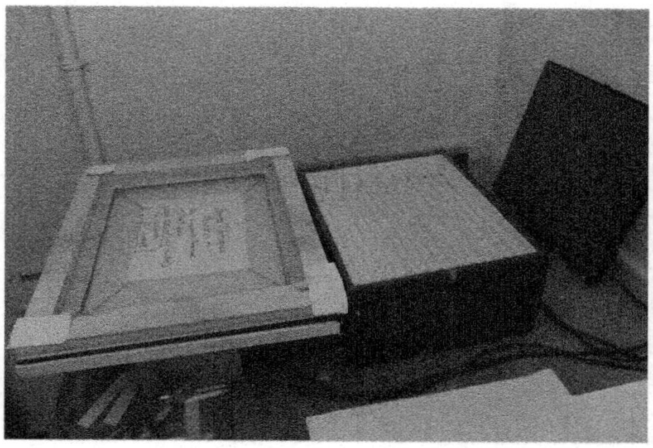

(image 2-21) Set up the contact frame and UV exposure unit.

Many people do a warm up exposure, in which they turn the UV unit on for a minute. If you do this, be sure the light source is covered, and your eyes and skin are protected from UV radiation. I place a thick black bag over the UV unit, don UV filtering eye glasses, hit the timer and leave the room while the unit is running.

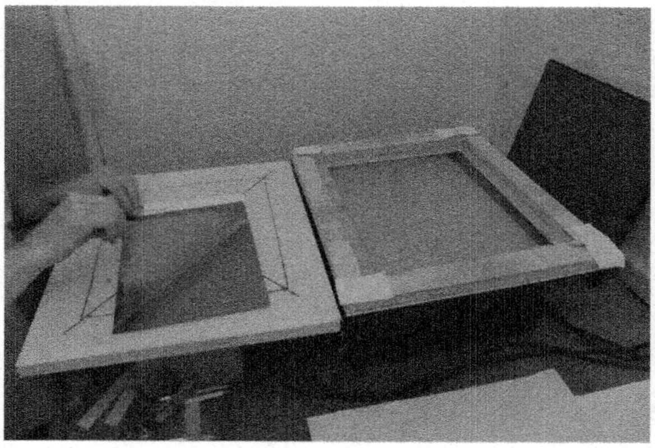

(image 2-22) Take a KM73 plate out of the light-safe bag, placing it face up on the contact frame. Remove the protective UV film from the polymer side of the plate.

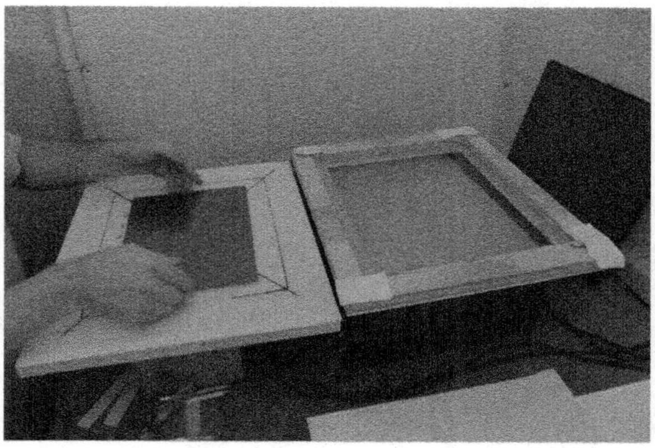

(image 2-23) Center the plate on the contact frame, making sure that the steel side is against the contact frame back, and the polymer side will face the glass. (In this example, the polymer side faces up)

The KM73 plates are steel-backed photopolymer. The steel acts as the stiff substrate, while the greenish photopolymer is the UV sensitive side.

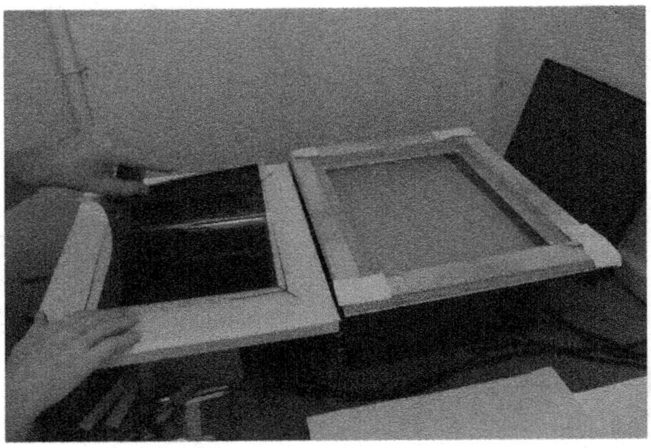

(image 2-24) Place the stocastic screen ("aquatint" screen) on top of the polymer side of the plate. Make sure that the printed side of the stochastic screen faces the polymer.

Take a close look at the stochastic screen that you have. The printed side will have a matte finish, while the non-printed side will appear glossy. If the screen is not already marked, make your own notes on the screen that are easy to read in the darkroom.

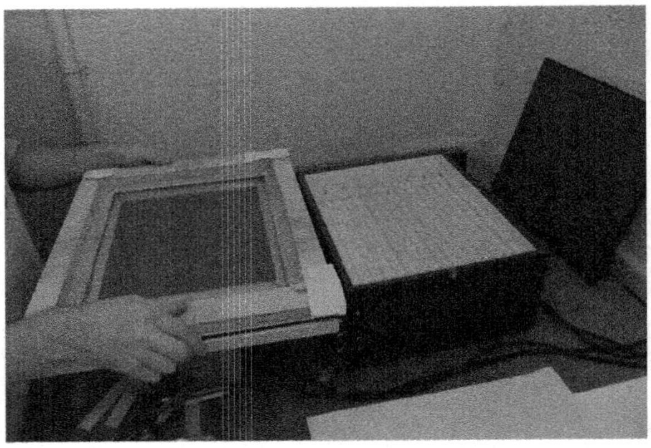

(image 2-25) Place the glass and frame on top of the stochastic screen and KM73 plate combination. Make sure the matte side of the glass (acid etched side) faces the stochastic screen.

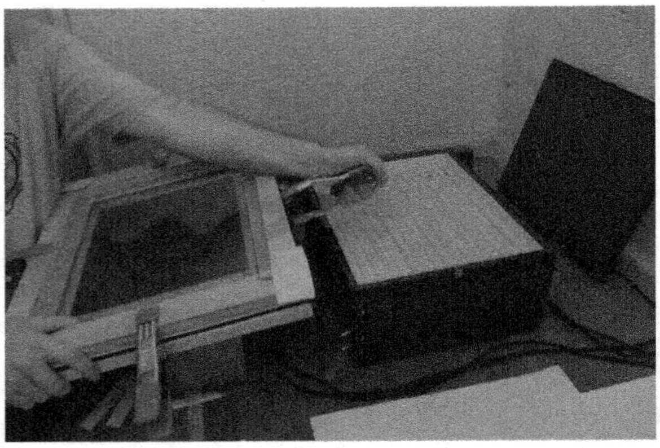

(image 2-26) Place the clamps on the contact frame, creating even positive pressure that holds the stochastic screen tightly against the KM73 plate.

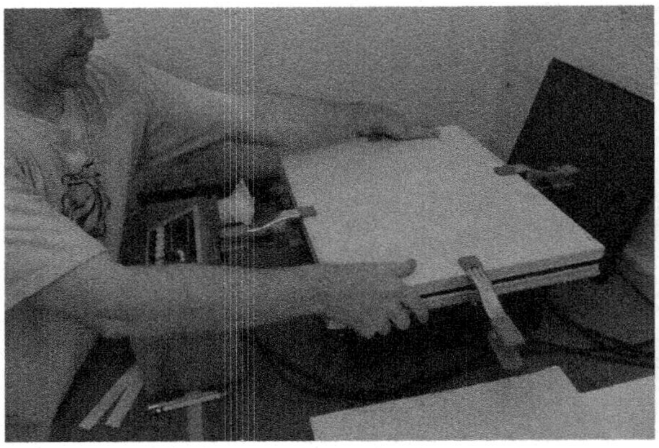

(image 2-27) Place the contact frame on top of the UV exposure unit. Make sure that it sits flat, allowing for even exposure to UV light.

Everything stacked together should be in this order:

1. **Contact frame base**
2. **KM73 plate** (steel side faces contact frame base, and polymer side faces stochastic screen)
3. **Stochastic screen** (matte printed side faces KM73 plate and glossy non-printed side faces glass)
4. **Glass** (which will face UV unit)

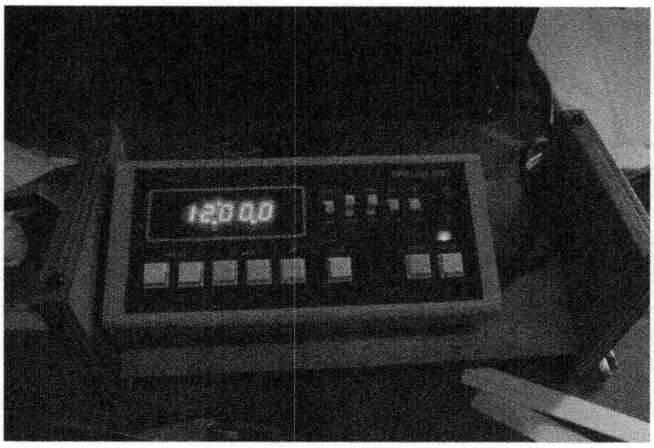

(image 2-28) Expose the KM73 plate to the stochastic screen for Base Exposure Time (chapter 5).

The UV exposure units that I use:
Aristo Platinum Printer: 10 - 16 minutes
(depending on bulb strength and glass thickness)
Ryonet RXP 16x20: 3 - 6 minutes
(depending on bulb strength and glass thickness)

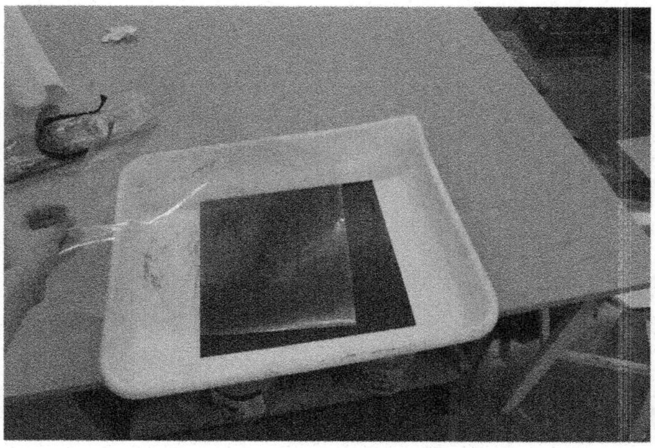

(image 2-29) While making the stochastic screen exposure, prepare the washout tray by placing a pieces of acetate over the magnet. This will make removing the steel-backed KM73 plate from the tray easier.

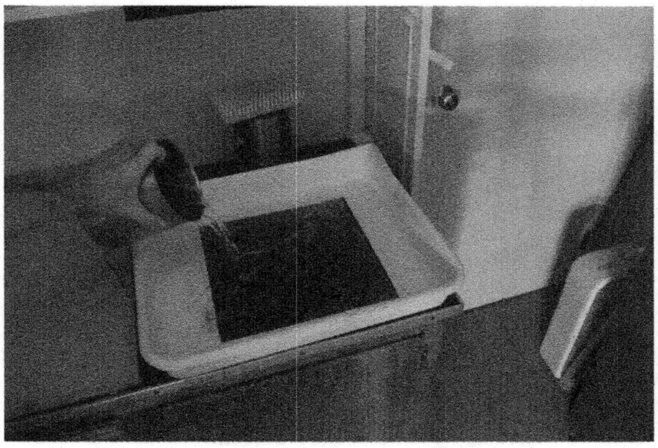

(image 2-30) Pour enough water into the washout tray to make a pool that is at least 1/2" deep.

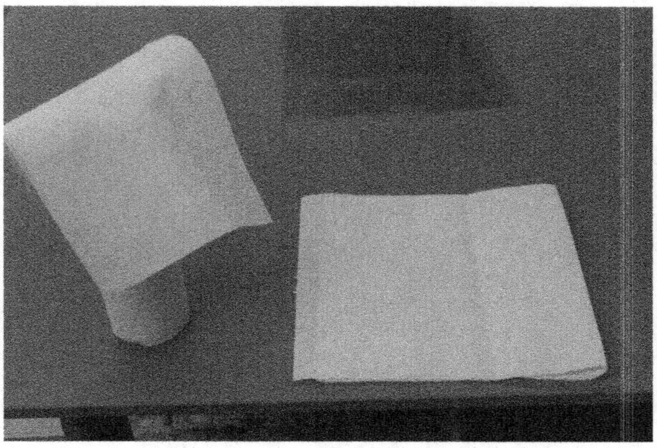

(image 2-31) Get paper towels ready so that you can immediately blot the water off the plate when finished washing out.

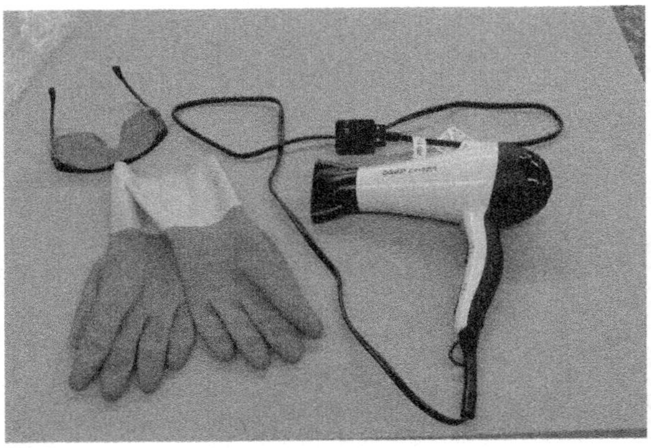

(image 2-32) Have UV filtering eye glasses, latex (or nitrile) gloves, and a hair drier within easy reach.

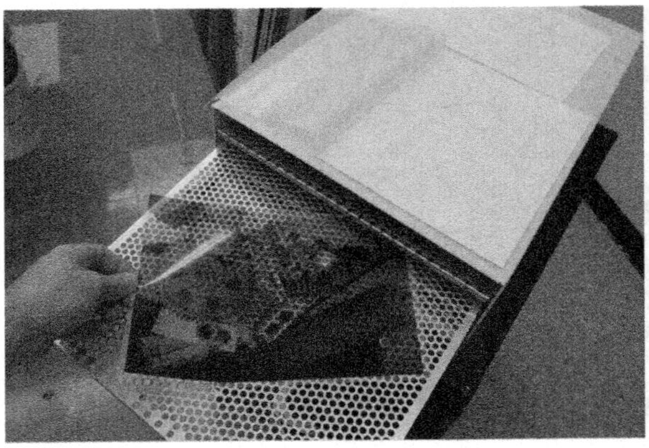

(image 2-33) Remove the transparency from the print drier.

No matter how old the transparency is, I recommend placing it in the print drier for 10 minutes before exposure. This will remove any atmospheric humidity that it has accumulated while not being used. 5 minutes with a hair drier will have the same positive effect as the print drier.

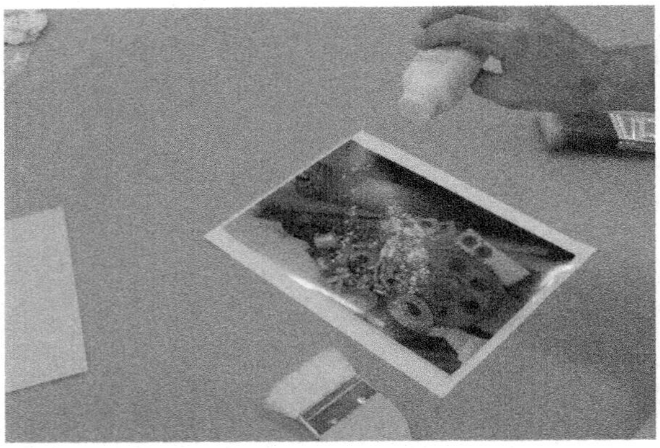

(image 2-34) Place the transparency on a clean surface, and dust some baby powder on it.

Baby powder makes a slip coat so that the plastic transparency does not stick to the polymer side of the KM73 plate. It also will let small amounts of gas escape during the exposure process.

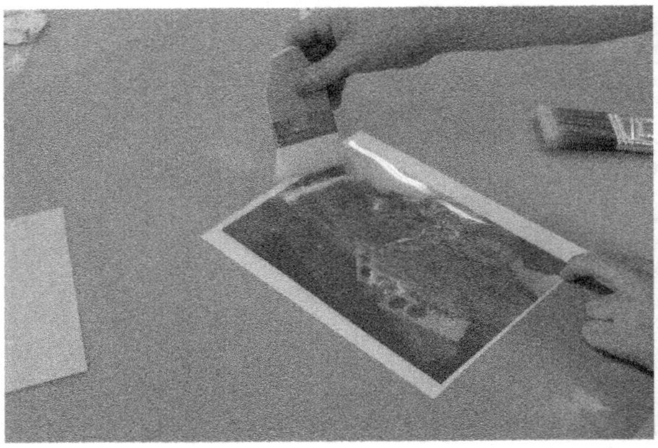

(image 2-35) Using a soft hake brush, spread the baby powder across both sides of the transparency.

Use even, gentle sweeping strokes throughout this process. The idea is to make an even slip layer on both sides, while not leaving behind any excess powder. If done correctly, it will look like you spread powder on, then removed it all.

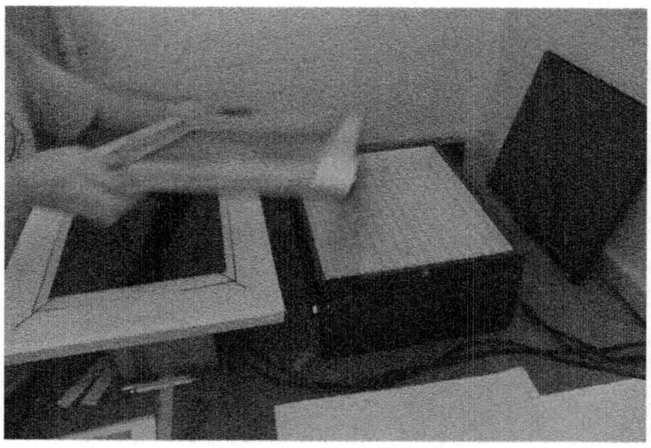

(image 2-36) When the stochastic screen exposure times (base exposure time) is finished, remove the glass from the contact frame.

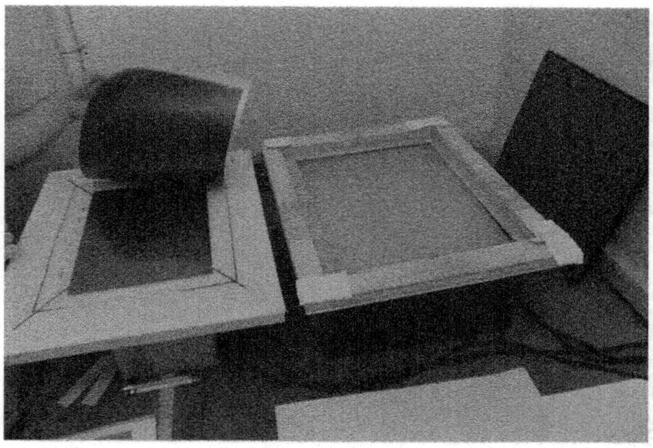

(image 2-37) Remove the stochastic screen from the KM73 plate.

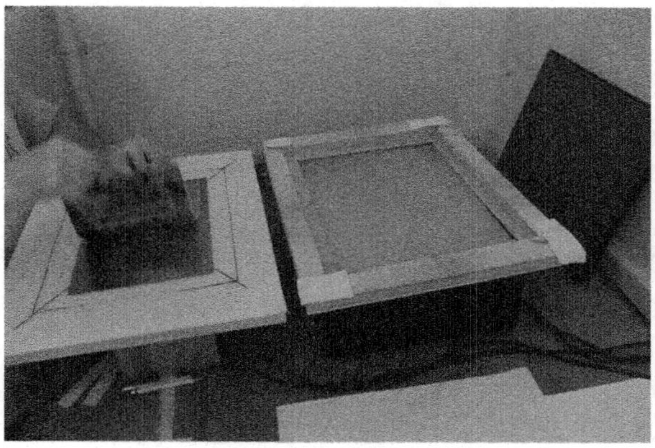

(image 2-38) Place the prepared transparency on top of the polymer side of the KM73 plate. Put the printed side of the transparency against the plate, allowing the non-printed side to face the glass and UV exposure unit.

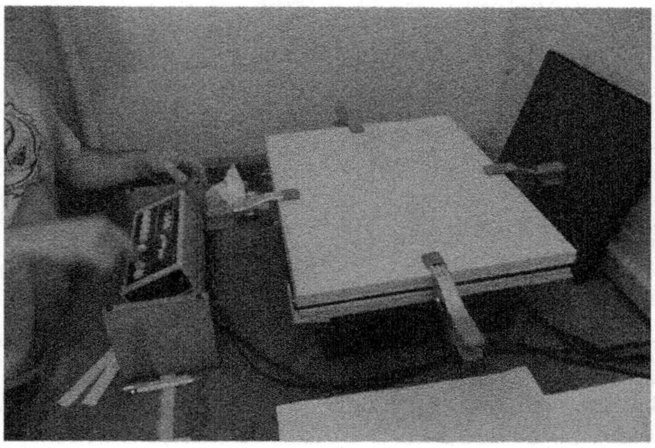

(image 2-39) Replace the glass and clamp, then put the contact frame on top of the exposure unit.

Remember the order:
UV unit
glass
transparency
KM73 polymer plate
contact frame back

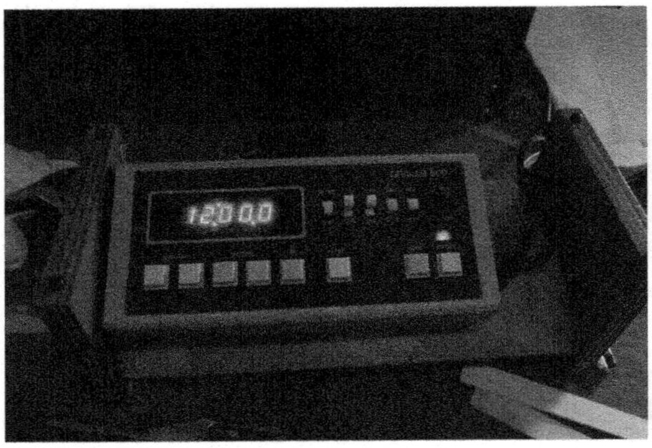

(image 2-40) Expose the transparency for the time determined in chapter 7.

Typically, I use the same time for both Base Exposure Time (chapter 5) and Image Exposure Time (chapter 7). Longer Image Exposure Time will make a lighter image, but only to a small degree.

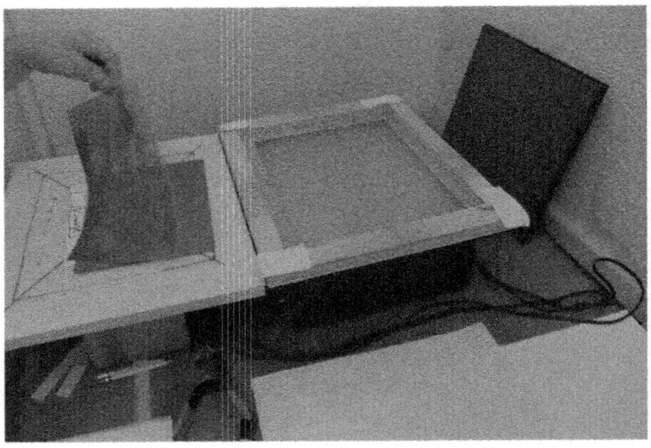

(image 2-41) When the exposure is finished, remove the transparency and put it in a safe place.

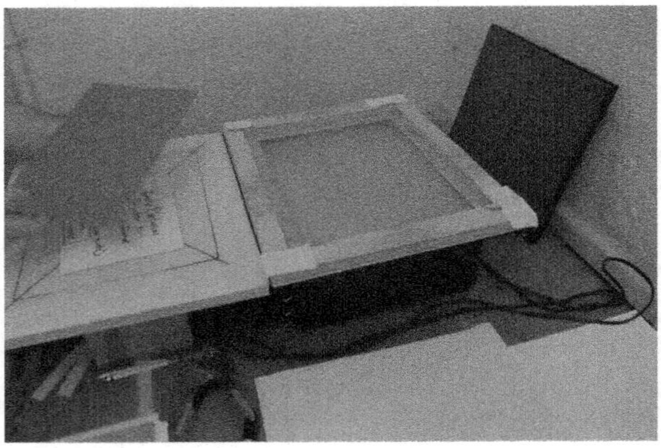

(image 2-42) Put on gloves, and gently pick up the KM73 plate that has received both the stochastic screen exposure and transparency exposure.

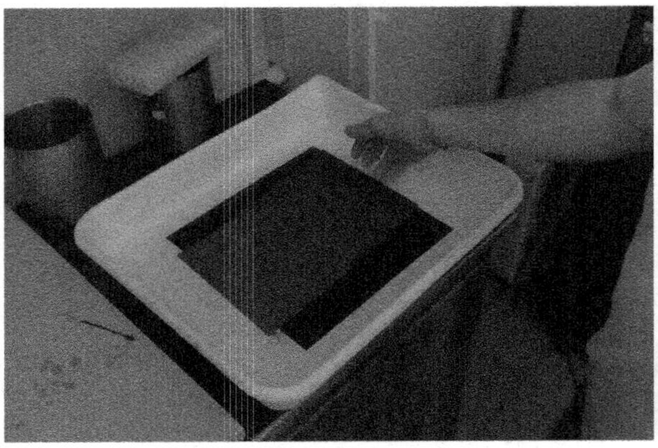

(image 2-43) Put the plate into the washout tray. The steel back of the KM73 plate will be held in place by the magnet in the tray. The sheet of acetate between the magnet and plate will be used to remove the plate from the water.

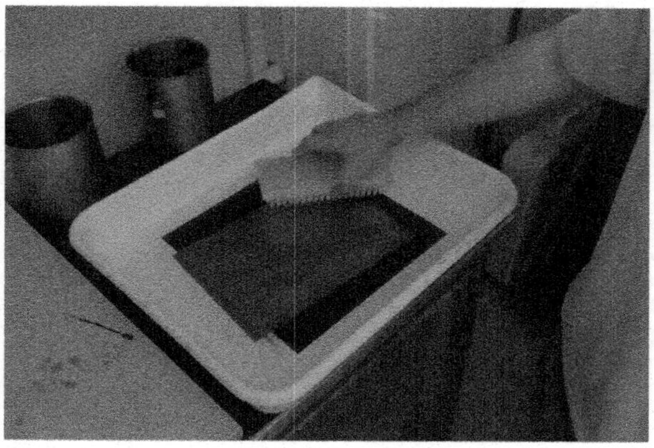

(image 2-44) Let the plate sit in the water, without any agitation, for 1 minute. After that, GENTLY brush the plate with a soft brush for 1 minute.

The pressure applied to the brush should only be the weight of your hand. Do not press on the brush. The polymer that was not cured by UV light is easily removed. The polymer that was cured is only hard enough to resist gentle scrubbing.

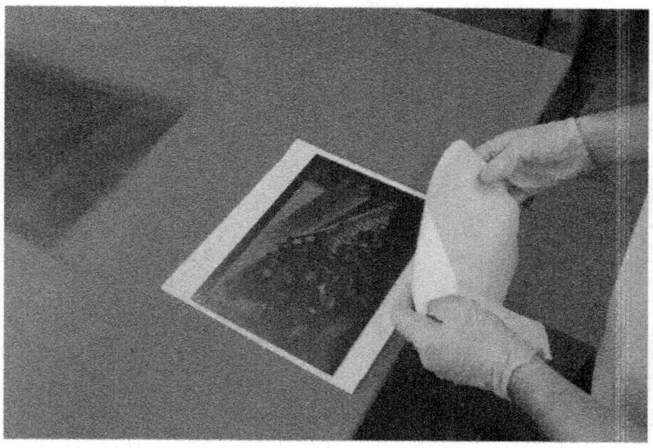

(image 2-45) After no more than 2 minutes in the washout tray, immediately bring the plate over to paper towels.

Some people use newsprint for this process because it leaves less lint that paper towels. I use paper towels carefully and have not yet had an issue.

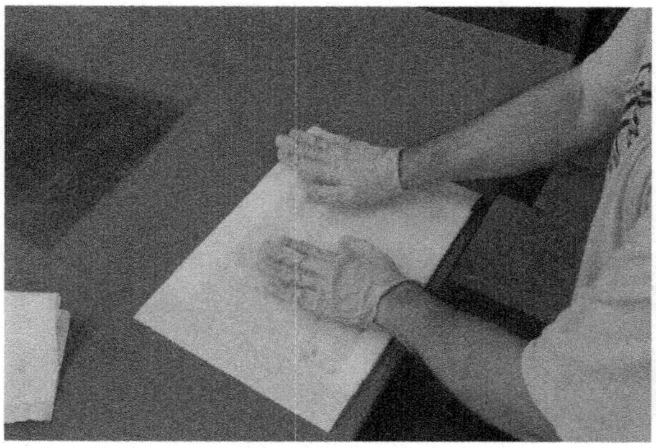

(image 2-46) Place a paper towel on top of the plate. Do not move the paper towel across the plate, or you will blur the image you have made. Quickly and gently pat the paper towel to absorb most of the water from the plate.

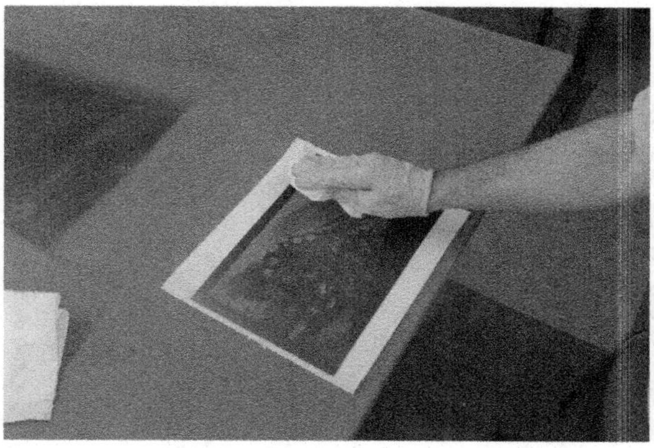

(image 2-47) Immediately remove the paper towel from the surface of the plate or it will stick to the uncured polymer. Ball up the paper towel to blot water spots, using very light pressure.

Move quickly and gently throughout this entire process. The entire paper towel step should not take more than 15 seconds.

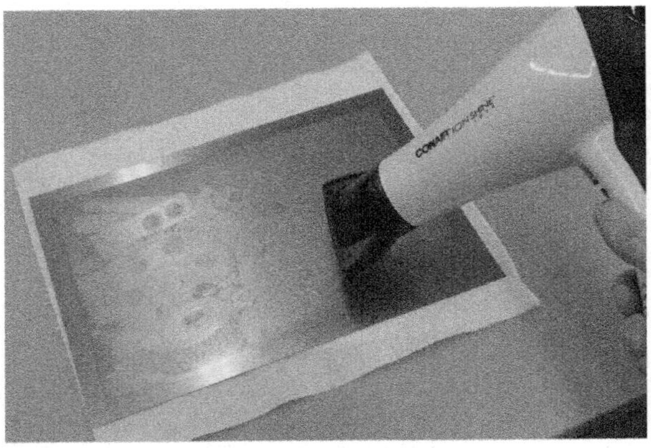

(image 2-48) You won't get every drop of water with the paper towels. That is ok. Use a hair drier (high heat) to finish drying the plate. Water will be gone within 20 seconds.

Spend 7minutes sweeping hot air from the hair drier across the surface of the KM73 plate to heat set the polymer.

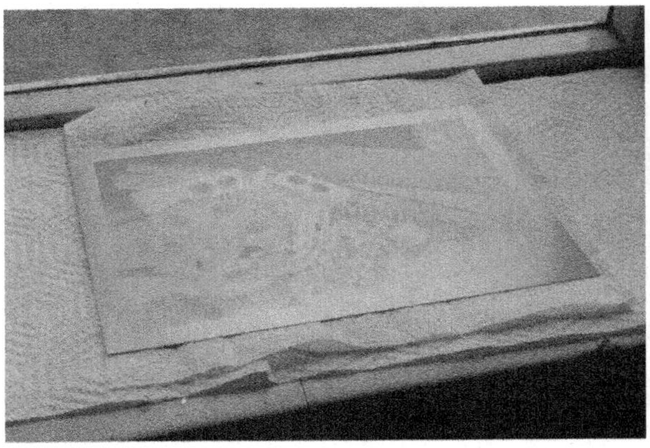

(image 2-49) Let the plate sit in a window for a couple of hours. This exposes the plate to UV light and some heat, further ensuring that the image is fully cured. The polymer will turn from green to blue (greenish blue) when it is fully cured.

I tend to make most of my plates at night, so leave them in a window that faces the sunrise, knowing that they will get a good final UV cure from the morning sun.

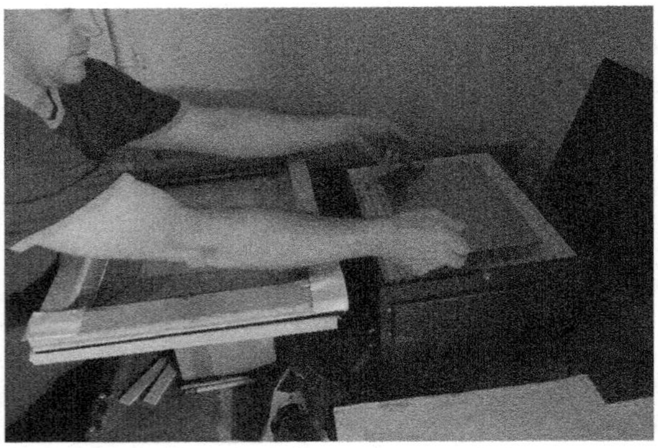

(image 2-50) Post expose the KM73 plate by putting it against the UV unit (polymer facing the UV lights). It does not need to go back in the contact frame for this step.

Placing the plate in the window (image 2-49) works well, but does take a long time. This step is quicker, and easier to measure.

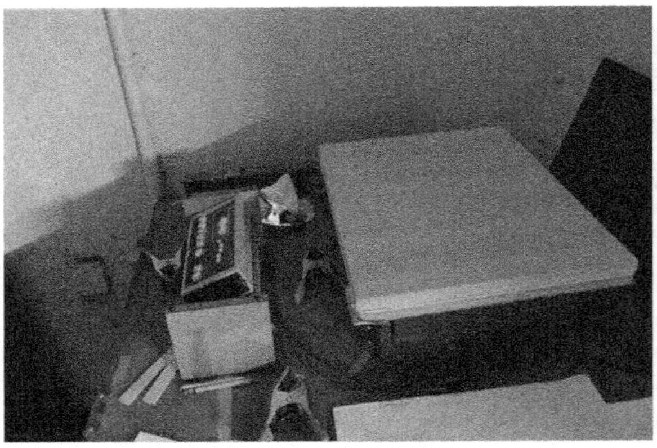

(image 2-51) Use the same time as the Base Exposure Time. Add 20% more time if you want to be sure the plate is fully cured.

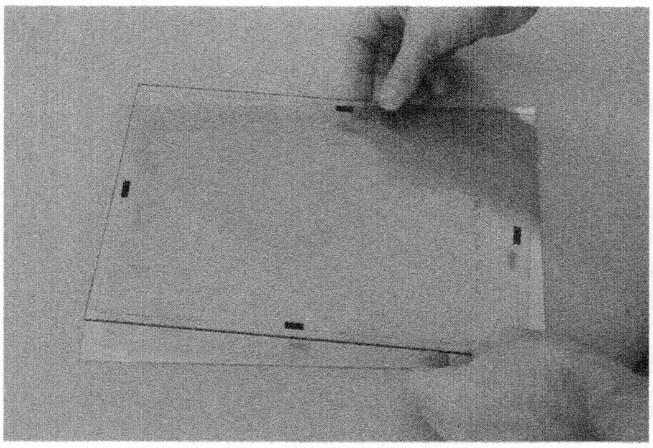

(image 2-52) When all of the exposure (and curing) steps are finished, you are ready to trim the plate and prepare the edges.

I have been using the same size for two series of prints, so have made a template out of acrylic sheet.

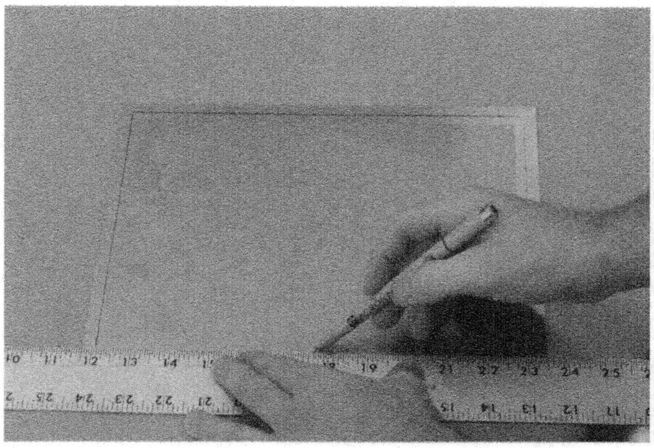

(image 2-53) Use a straight edge and marker to draw trim lines around the image.

I like to leave 1/8" - 3/8" of border on all the plates I make. It was initially an aesthetic choice, but I have since found that it makes the inking process easier too.

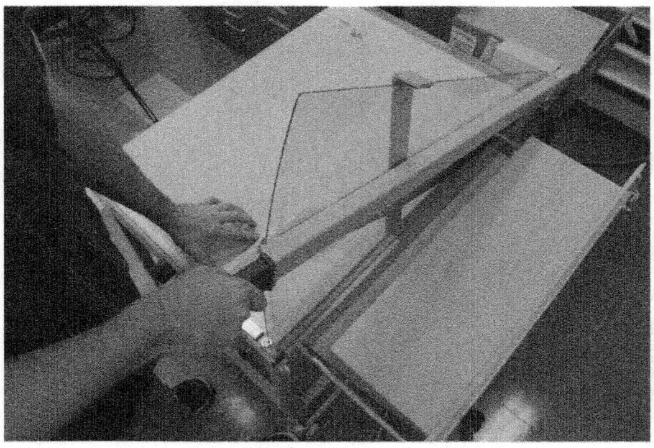

(image 2-54) Cut the plate with either a guillotine style paper cutter, or with hand-held metal shears.

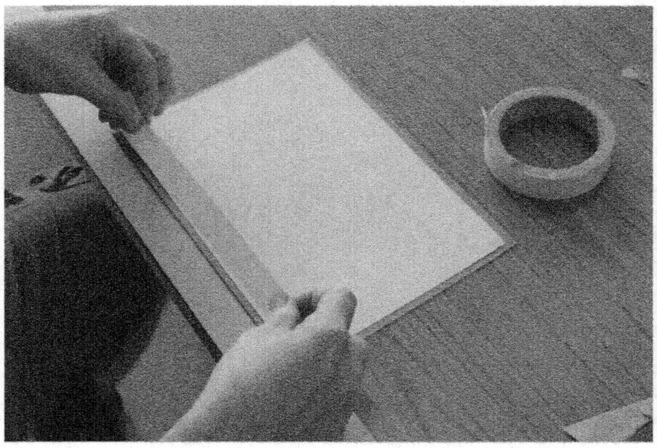

(image 2-55) Cut a piece of paper to a size that is about 1/4" smaller than the size of the plate. Tape the paper on top of the plate so that fine metal and polymer shavings do not get trapped in the image area.

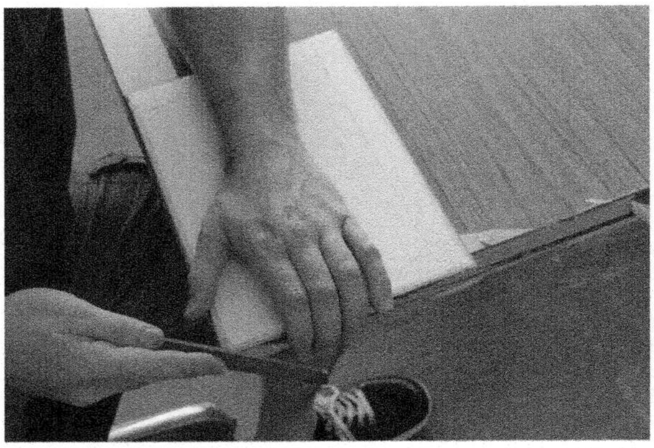

(image 2-56) Using a fine tooth file, remove metal burs and bevel the edges of the plate.

I like to round the corners and put a 45 degree angle on the edges.

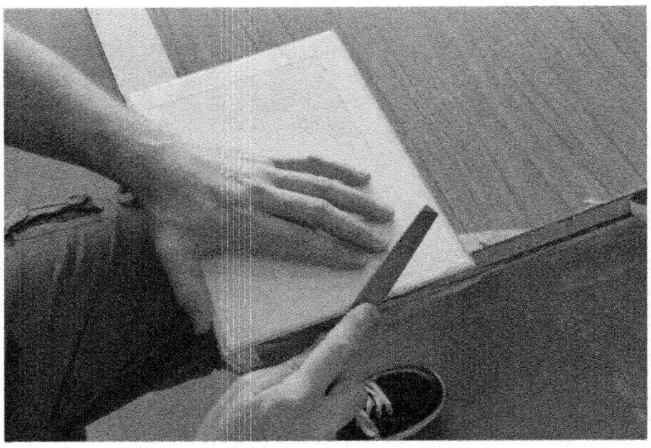

(image 2-57) Go all the way around the plate, making sure that every edge has been treated with the file. Burs and hard edges will hold ink (which will make unexpected marks on your print) and wear out tarlatan faster.

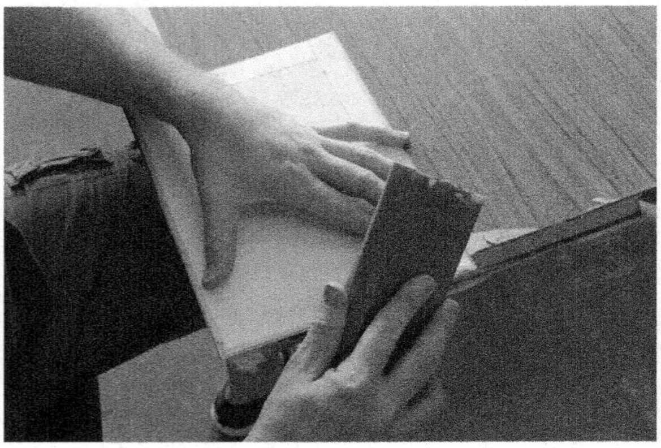

(image 2-58) Sand the edges with progressively finer sand paper to acheive a smooth finish that is easy to clean with each print pass.

I use 400, 600, then 1200 grit sand paper.

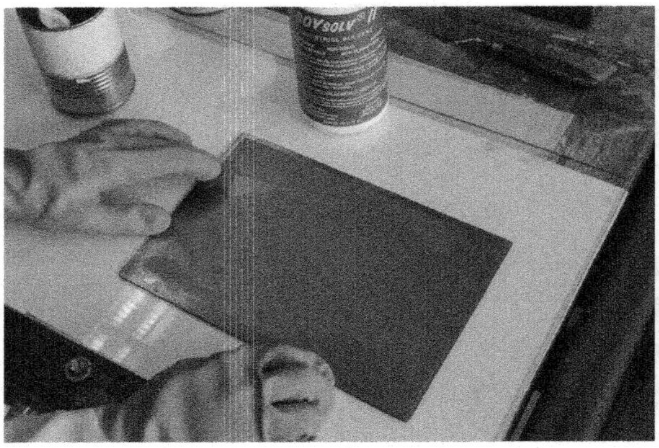

(image 2-59) Take off the paper, and use SoySolv II (or another solvent) to remove residual glue from the tape.

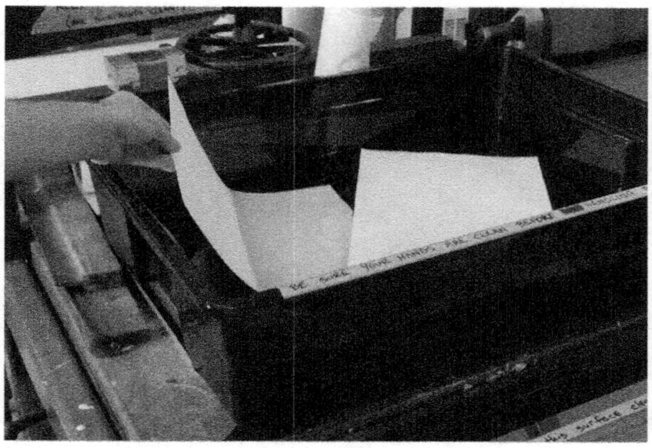

(image 2-60) When ready to print, the first thing that needs to happen is preparing paper (chapter 9) so that it is damp enough to accept ink and make even tonal transitions.

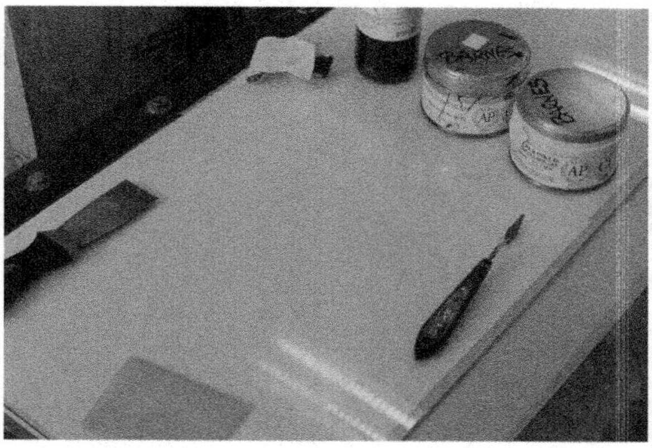

(image 2-61) Set up the inking workspace to condition the ink (chapter 11).

Make sure you have ink, palette knife and flat scraper, plastic squeegee, burnt plate oil, tack reducer.

Glass makes the best palette, but wax paper or acrylic sheet will work to.

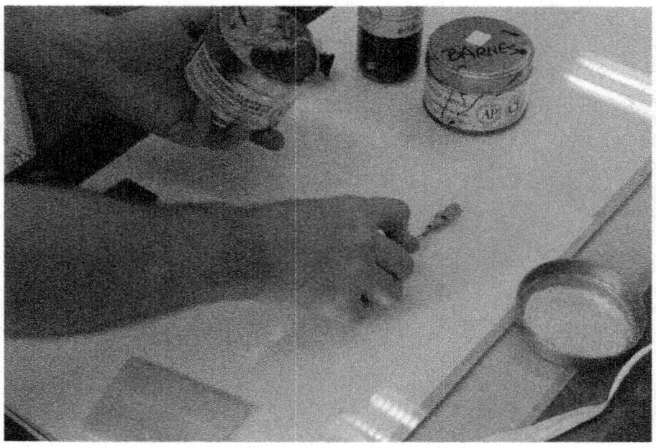

(image 2-62) Place a small amount of Graphic Chemical Easy Wipe (or any other tack reducer) on to the palatte.

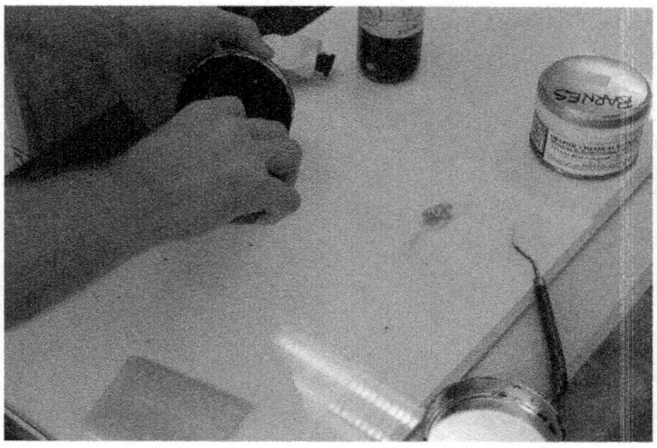

(image 2-63) Get some ink and put it on the palette.

Be sure to scrape off even layers of ink from inside the tin can. At first, you will have to remove the dried film on top of all the ink. Next, you'll scrape off an even film of fresh ink. By making sure the ink inside the can is always level and even, the part that dries out will always be level and even, making removing the dried crust easier.

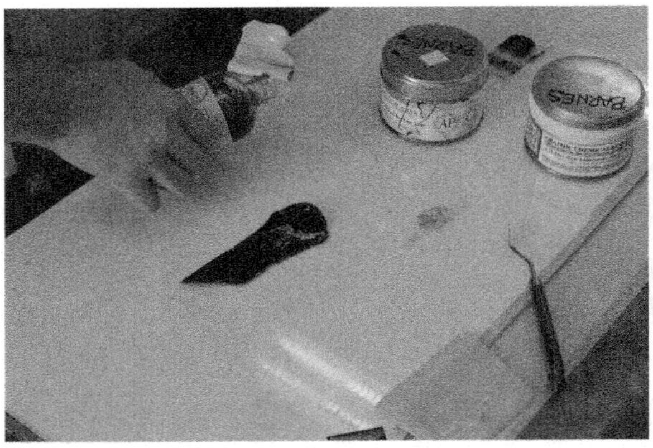

(image 2-64) Pour out a little bit of burnt plate oil on to the palette.

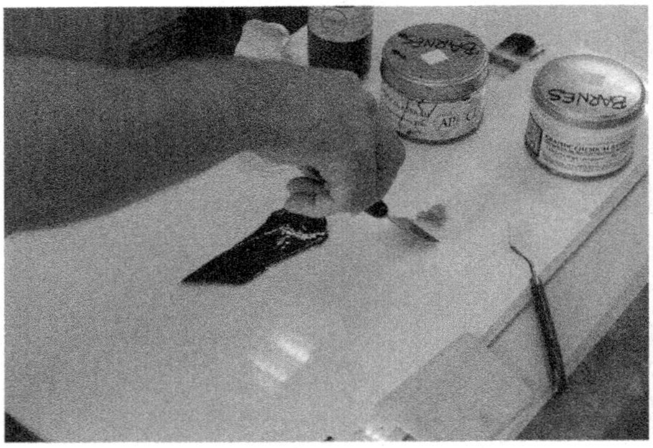

(image 2-65) Add up to 10% tack reducer into the ink.

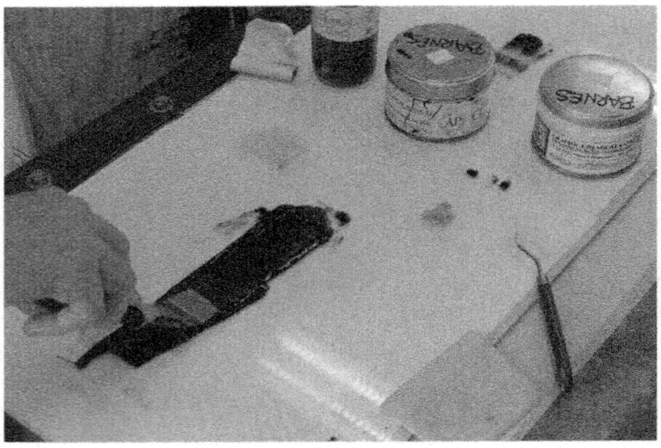

(image 2-66) Add very little burnt plate oil into the ink.

"Draw" the ink down with the flat scraper, blending the plate oil and tack reducer with the ink.

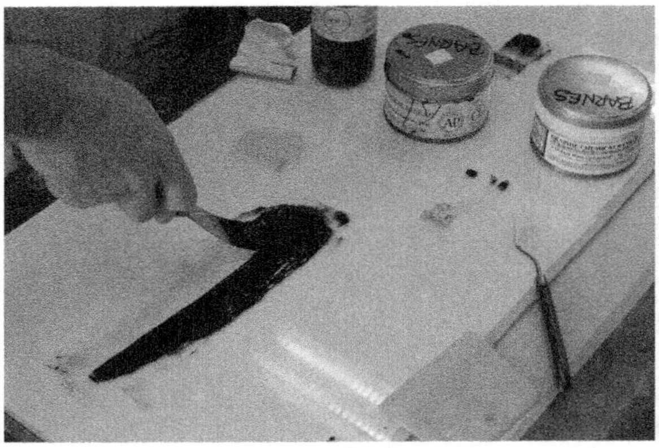

(image 2-67) When drawn down flat, inspect the ink for dust and hardened chunks of ink and remove them if necessary.

Scrape up the spread ink into a small pile. Draw the ink down again to keep mixing the ink, tack reducer, and burnt plate oil. Repeat this process of mixing for a minute or two until you feel that everything is evenly mixed, and that the ink is properly conditioned (chapter 11).

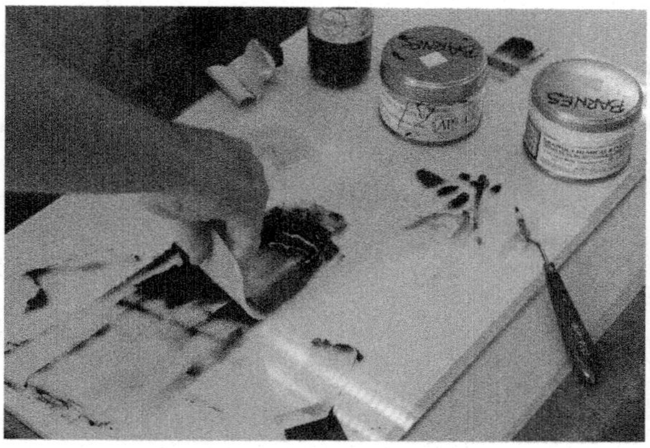

(image 2-68) Using the soft plastic squeegee, pick up a bead of ink from the palette.

Bondo brand plastic scrapers, found in the auto body repair aisle, work well for this step.

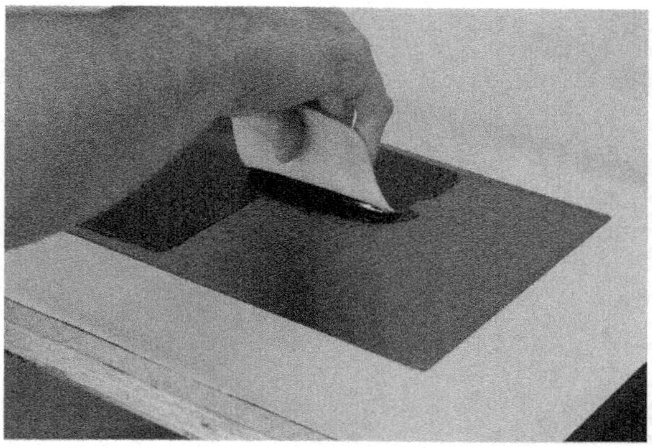

(image 2-69) Spread the ink evenly across the KM73 plate, gently pressing the ink into the aquatint matrix.

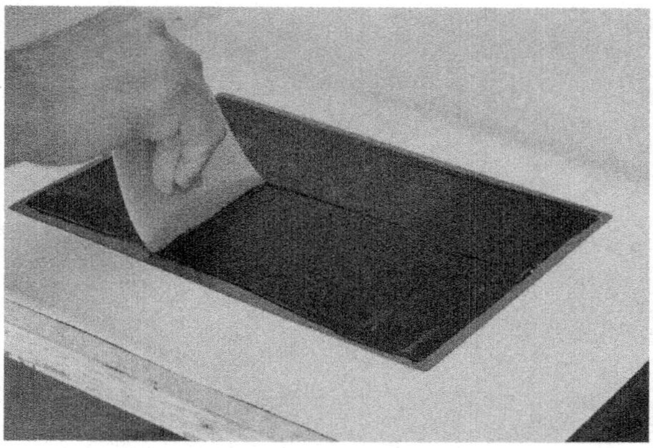

(image 2-70) Push the ink into the recesses from more than one angle to make sure everything that requires ink will receive it.

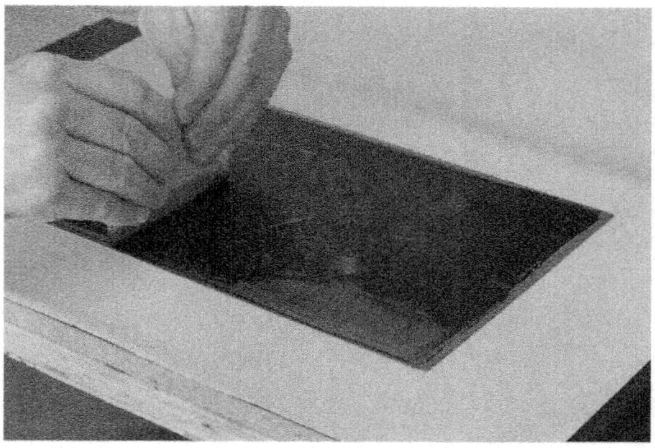

(image 2-71) Once covered with ink, begin the process of removing the excess from the plate. Do this by holding the soft plastic scraper perpendicular to the KM73 plate. Apply gentle pressure and scrape extra ink off the surface (wiping that excess onto the palette for reuse).

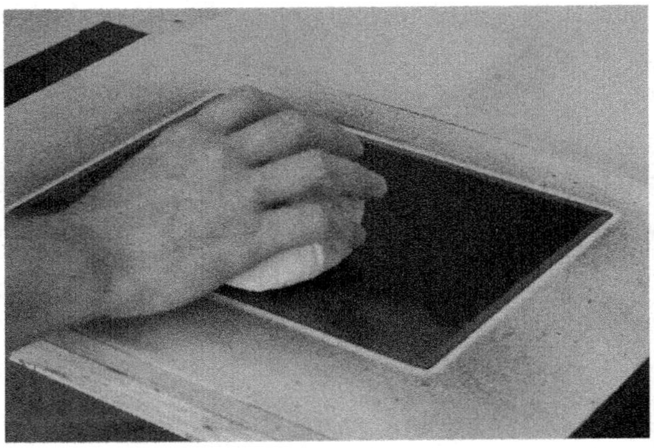

(image 2-73) When most of the excess ink is removed from the surface, use a ball of tarlatan to continue removing ink from the surface. (see chapter 12 about folding tarlatan)

The printmaker must develop a feel for the materials. This only can be achieved with a lot of practice. Beginners should remember to only use as much pressure as a resting forearm; barely more weight than required to operate the mouse on a computer.

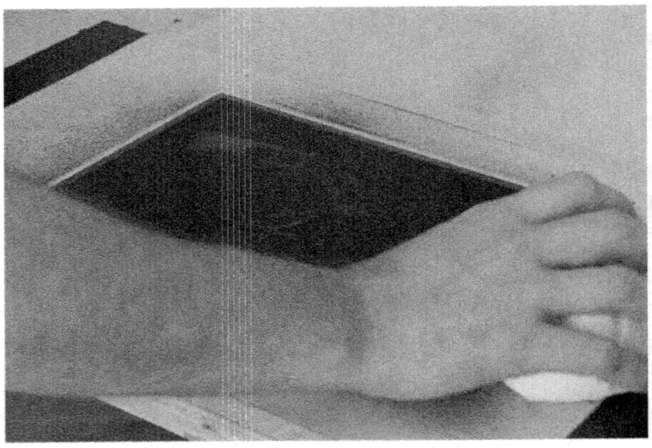

(image 2-74) Move the tarlatan flat, across the entire surface of the plate. The idea is to remove ink only from the surface, not from the recesses that make up the aquatint matrix. Stopping a wipe in the middle of the plate may change the gentle pressure of the tarlatan, allowing it to dip into one of the recesses, unintentionally removing ink.

Edges and corners that are sanded smooth make this motion easier.

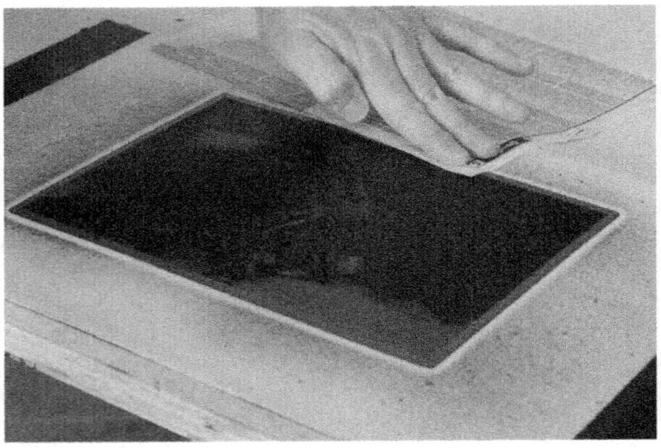

(image 2-75) When the tarlatan has removed as much ink as it can (without taking any out of the recesses), then it's time for a final wipe with tissue paper or pages from a phone book.

First, wipe the edges with the tip of a finger.

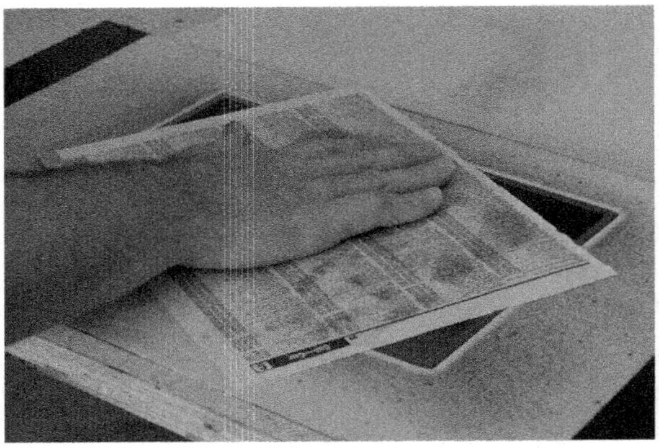

(image -276) Next, with a flat palm, wipe the entire surface of the plate. Use the same light weight approach as with the tarlatan.

Keep your hand as flat and relaxed as possible. This will polish the highlights of the image without removing ink from the shadows.

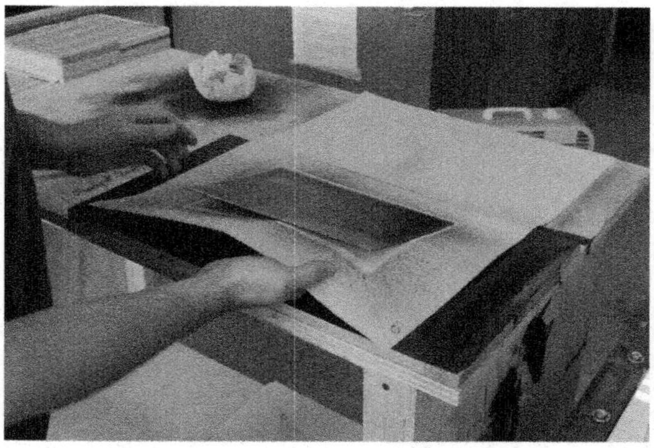

(image 2-77) Pick the plate off the magnet with the newsprint. Move the plate to the edge of the inking table.

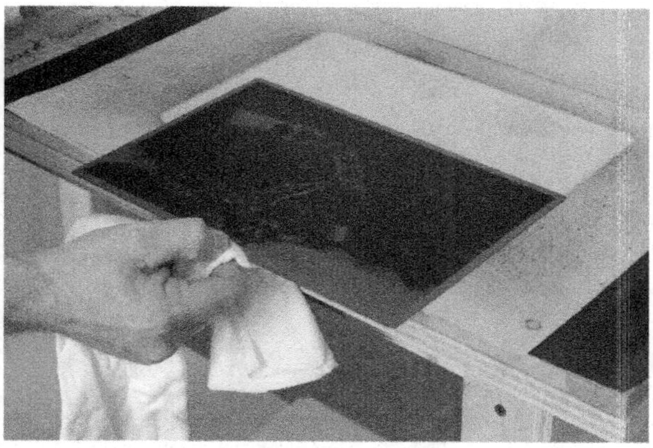

(image 2-78) Use a cloth to wipe the edges of the plate. Make sure that the edges do not have any ink that you do not intend to print.

This part of the wiping process can sometimes take as long as all of the inking/wiping steps that came before it. It may seem like a lot of work for little reward, but making sure that the edges are clear can sometimes be the difference between a fair print and an excellent print.

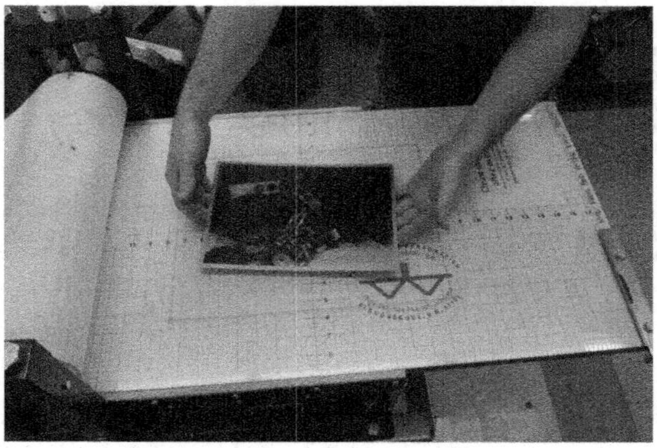

(image 2-79) Place the plate on the bed of the etching press with the image facing up.

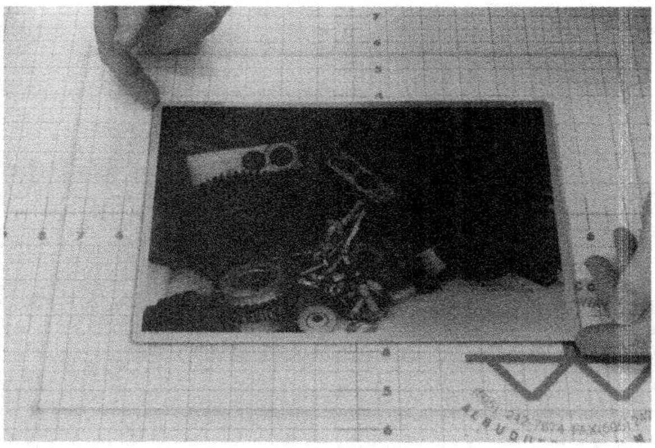

(image 2-80) Use your fingernails on the corners of the plate to make sure it is centered on the registration marks.

Check the bed of the press for any errant ink or dirt that will transfer to the printmaking paper, ruining your print.

Clean your hands before you handle paper.

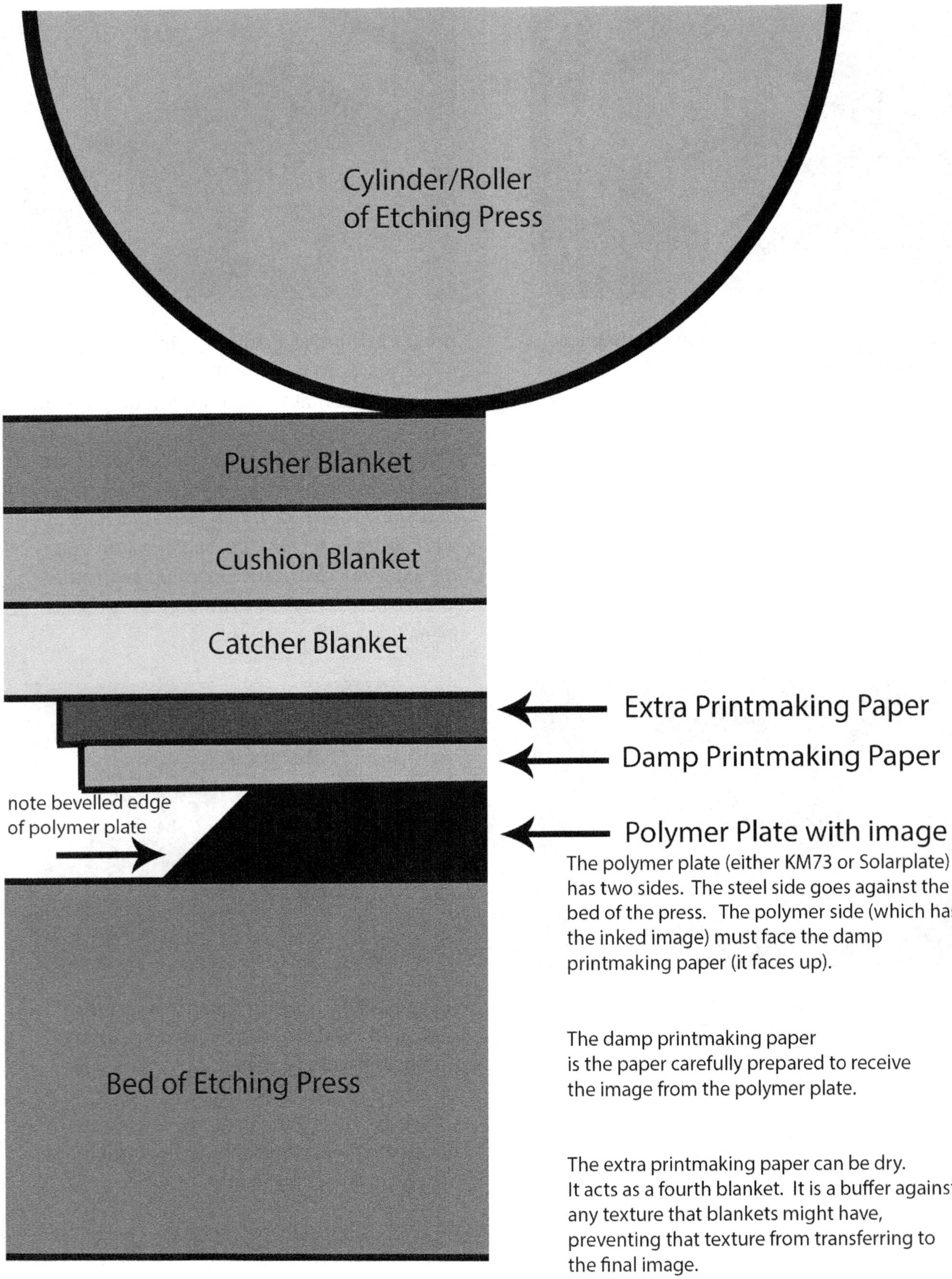

The polymer plate (either KM73 or Solarplate) has two sides. The steel side goes against the bed of the press. The polymer side (which has the inked image) must face the damp printmaking paper (it faces up).

The damp printmaking paper is the paper carefully prepared to receive the image from the polymer plate.

The extra printmaking paper can be dry. It acts as a fourth blanket. It is a buffer against any texture that blankets might have, preventing that texture from transferring to the final image.

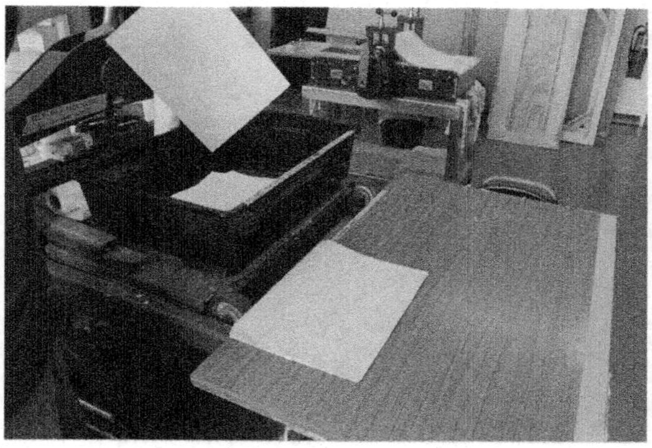

(image 2-81) With clean parts of your fingers, remove a piece of printmaking paper from the water. Holding the paper by one corner, let water run off it until the drips are more than 1 second apart.

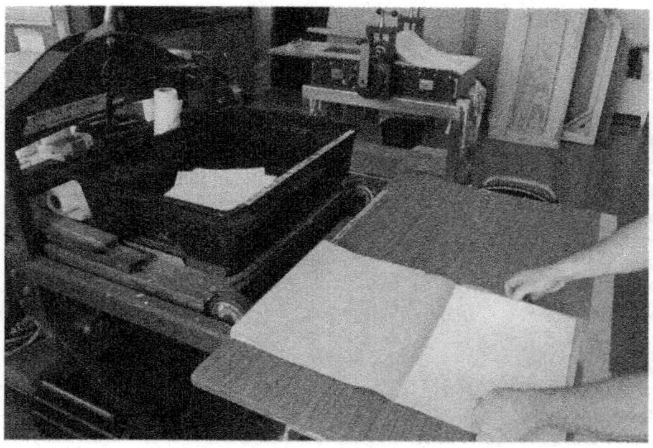

(image 2-82) Place the printmaking paper on a piece of clean blotter paper.

Newsprint is used as blotter paper in this example,only because it is inexpensive. This is not he best practice since newsprint is a wood-based paper, therefore contains acid. Ideally, 100% cotton blotter paper should be used. Realistically, newsprint is significantly less expensive, so can be used until you are making good prints.

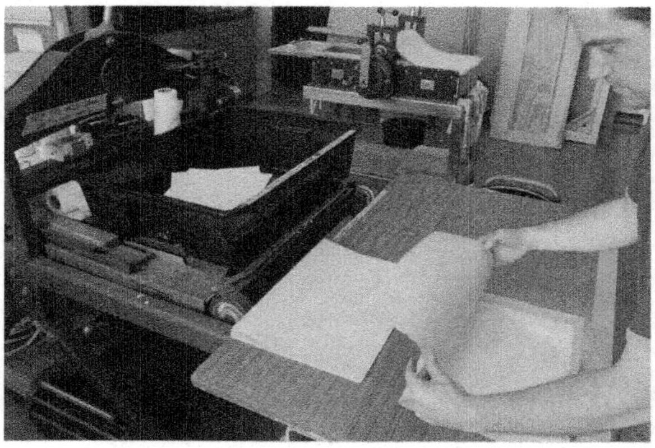

(image 2-83) Fold the blotter paper on top of the printmaking paper (or place a second sheet on top, depending on size).

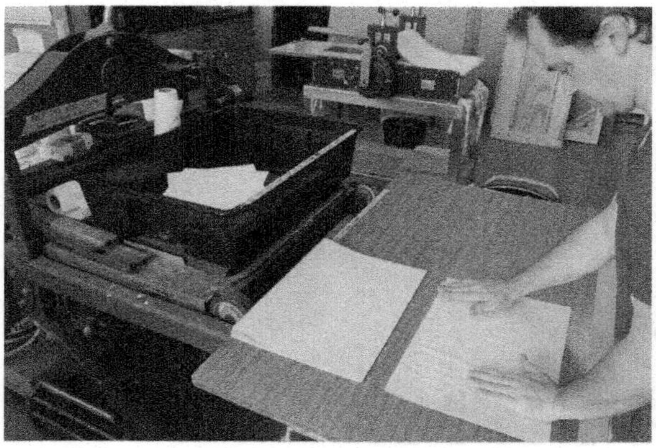

(image 2-84) Firmly press and apply pressure across the surface of the blotter paper to absorb excess water from the printmaking paper.

Repeat this step a second time, with new sheets of blotter paper, to make sure that moisture in the printmaking paper is even. You should not see any standing water. The printmaking paper will be damp and cold to the touch, but not appear wet.

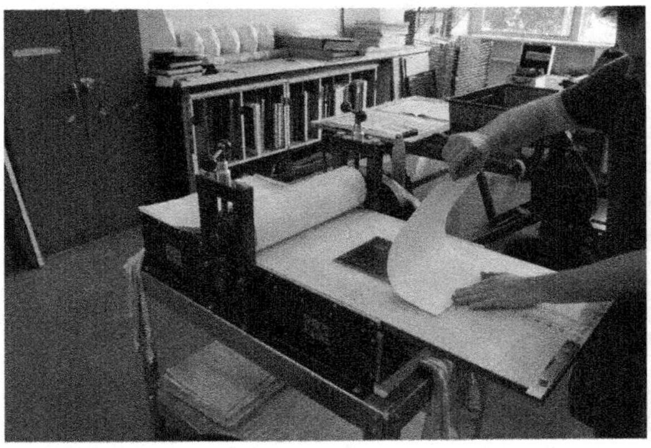

(image 2-85) Line up the printmaking paper with the registration marks on the bed of the press. Hold one side of the paper firmly.

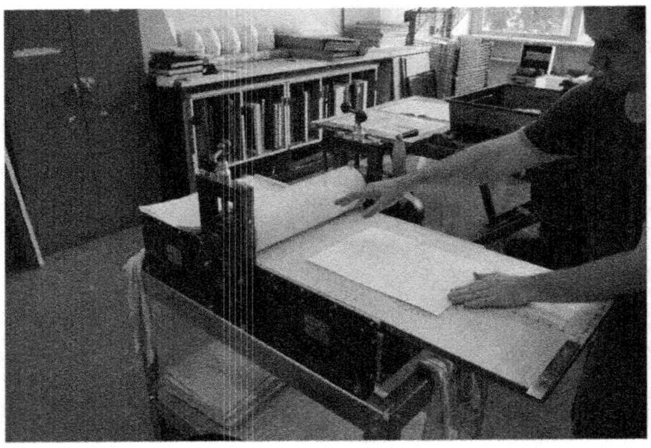

(image 2-86) Let the printmaking paper gently fall across the KM73 plate. Do not move it once it is on top of the plate or you run the risk of smearing ink.

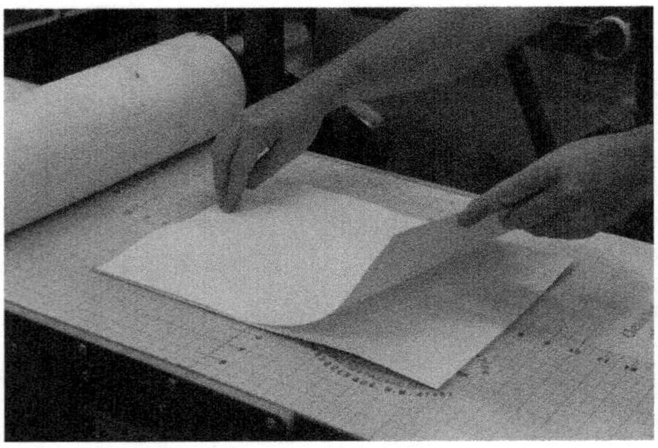

(image 2-87) Place a second sheet of printmaking paper on top of primary sheet of printmaking paper. This second piece of paper acts as a fourth blanket, adding pressure, but doing so in a manner that exactly matches the unique grain pattern of the printmaking paper used.

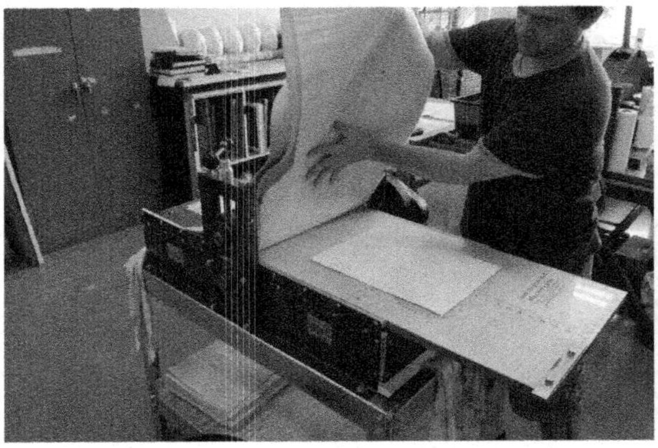

(image 2-88) Pull the three blankets on top of the paper and plate.

From top to bottom, you will have a stack of

- etching press roller
- pusher blanket
- cushion blanket
- catcher blanket
- extra piece of printmaking paper
- damp printmaking paper
- polymer plate (KM73 in this example)
- bed of the press

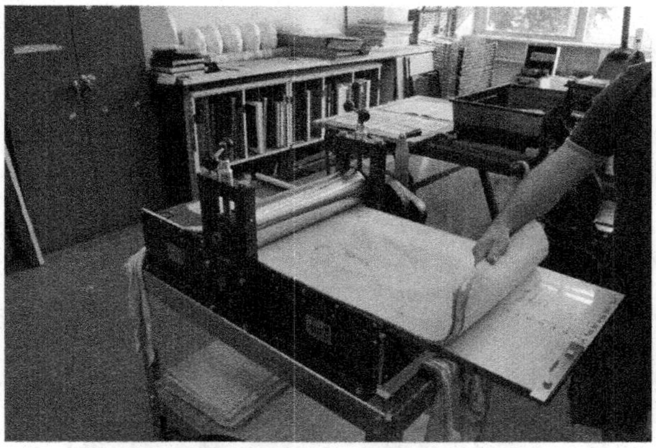

(image 2-89) Make sure the blankets are flat and lined up to feed through the etching press rollers.

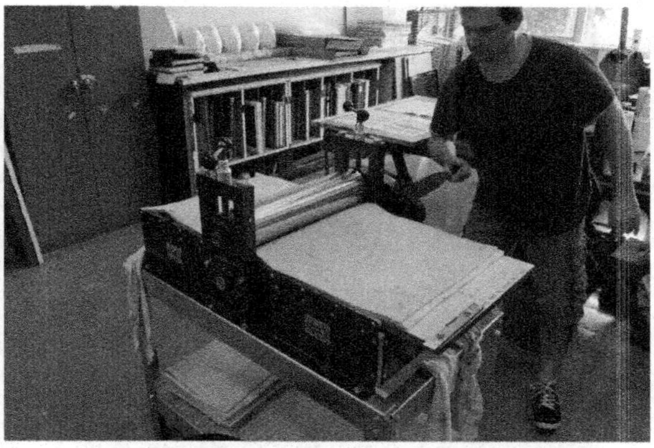

(image 2-90) Run the plate, paper, and blankets through the press at a slow steady pace.

Do not stop in the middle of the plate or you may see a strange mark in the image. Slow and steady is the key to good printing. You are part of the machine in this step.

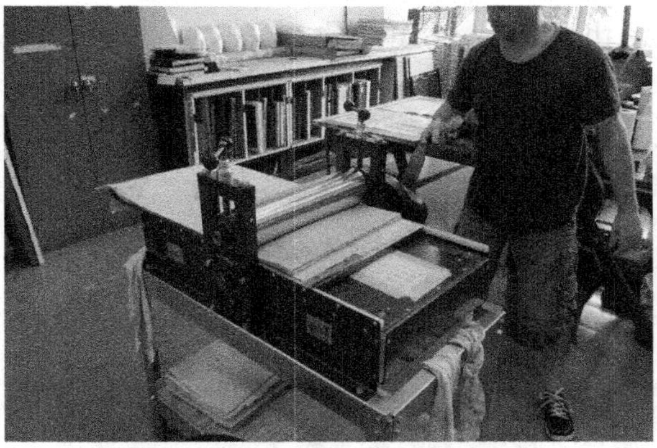

(image 2-91) You will feel the plate feed under the rollers, and feel the pressure reduce when the plate is finished passing under the rollers. Make sure that enough of the bed has passed under the rollers for you to retrieve your print. Running the bed fully from end to end is a good habit that will ensure everything is printed and that you have enough room to retrieve your print on the other side.

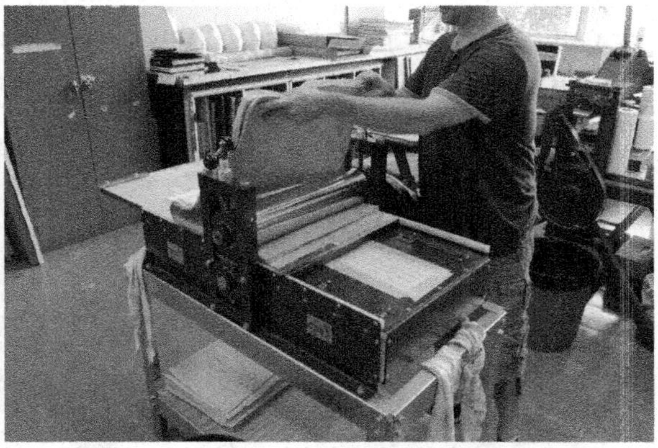

(image 2-92) Pull back the blankets and remove the extra piece of printmaking paper.

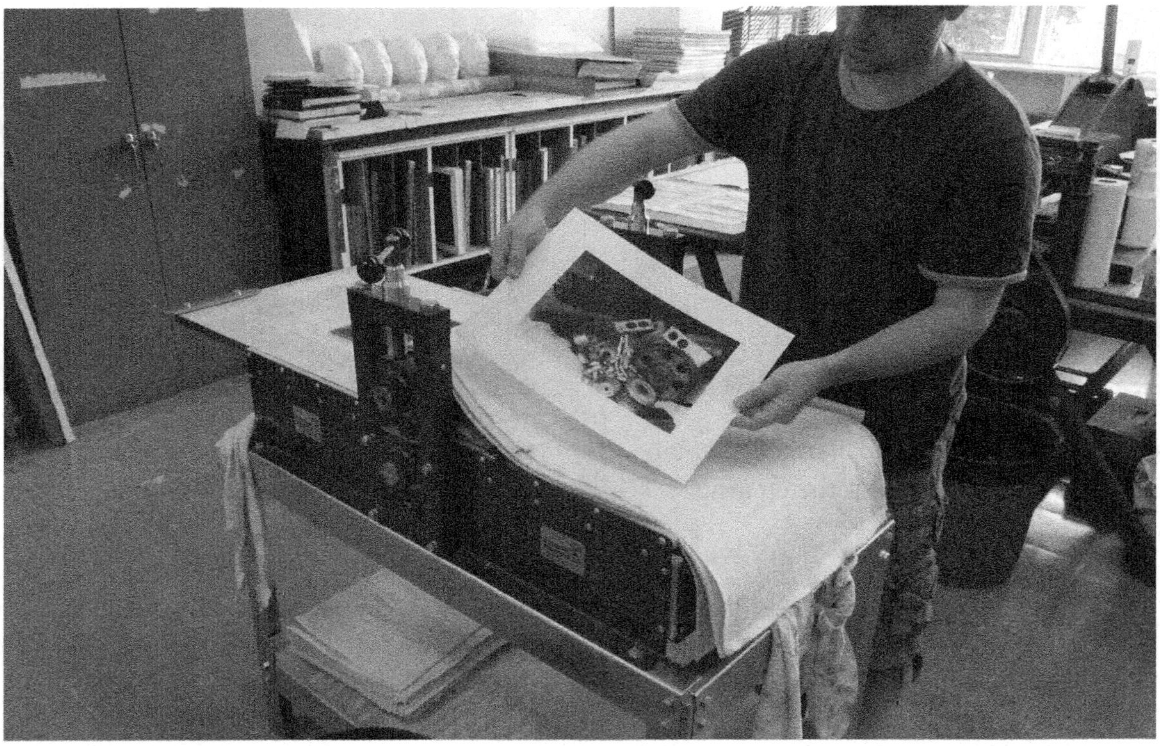

(image 2-93) Lift up one corner of the damp printmaking paper, and peel it off the plate, revealing the print.

(image 2-94) Place the print on a flat dry surface so that the paper can dry and the ink can cure. The print can be handled in 24 hours, but the ink needs at least a week to cure before you can store it (stack it) with other prints

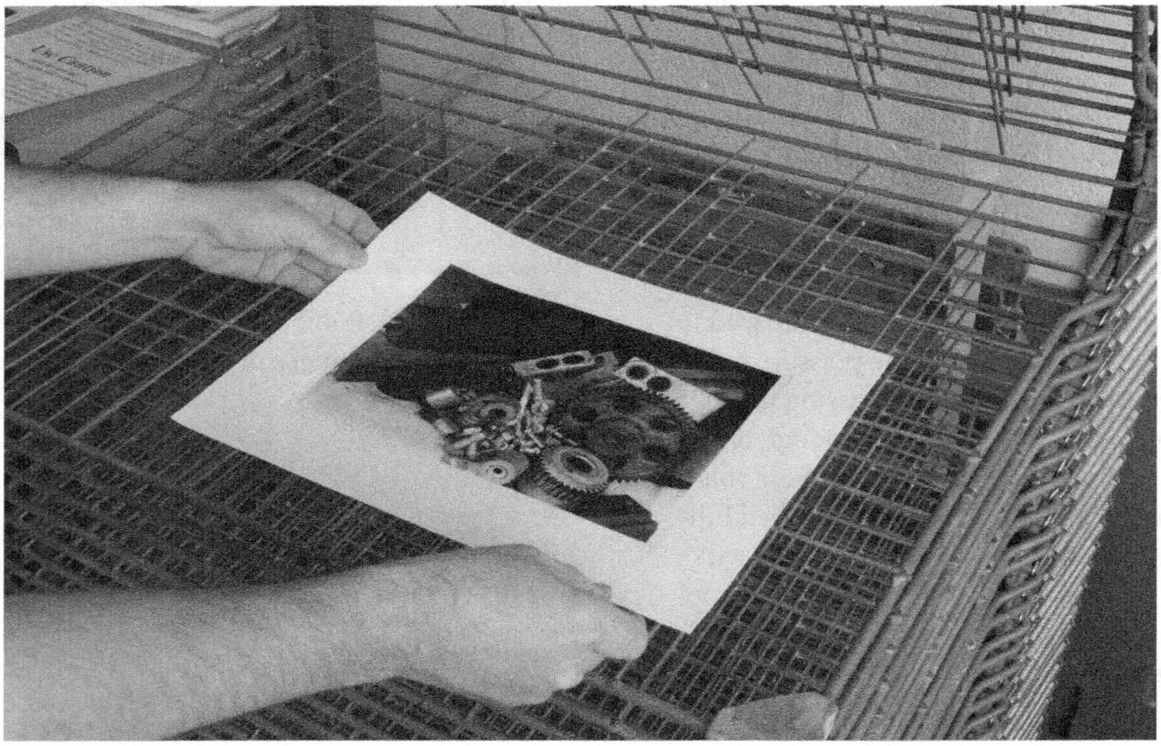

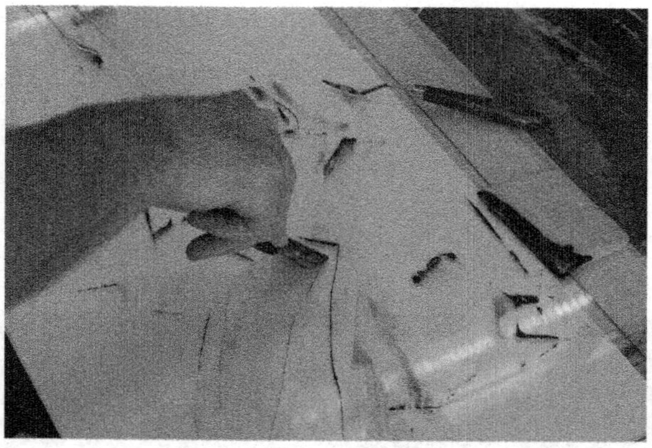

(image 2-95) After you have made many prints, use the flat scraper to remove excess ink from the glass palette. Most of the clean-up work relies on physical work like scraping and scrubbing. 98% of leftover ink can be removed with a scaper and one paper towel.

Wear gloves when cleaning up.
Open a window, or use direct ventilation depending on the requirements of solvents used.

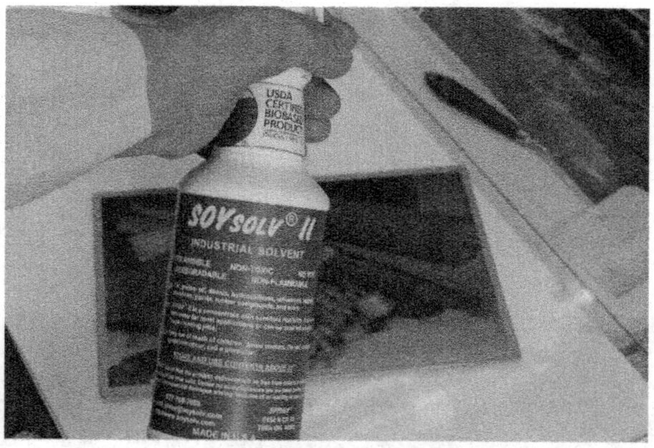

(image 2-96) Spray some SoySolv II on the KM73 plate. Let it sit for 2 minutes as it emulsifies the ink.

Other solvents work too (at your own risk). Mineral spirits (odorless or not) are petrochemicals, thus should be used as little as possible. Turpentine will irritate skin and lungs. Mineral oil, baby oil, vegetable oil work quite well since they emulsify oil-based ink, and do not give off any irritating vapors.

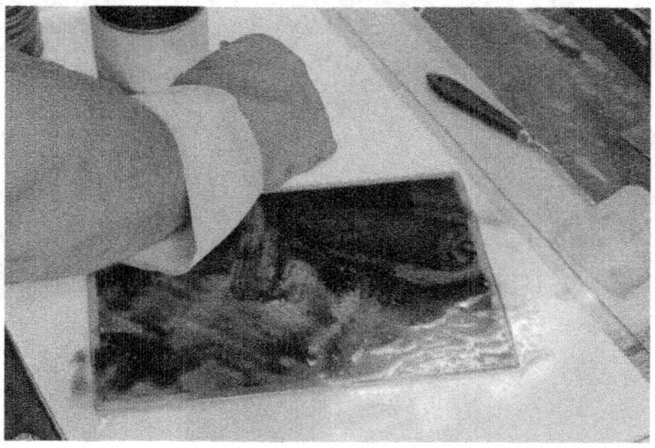

(image 2-97) Once the ink is emulsified, use a soft brush to gently scrub the plate, pulling ink from the depths of the aquatint matrix.

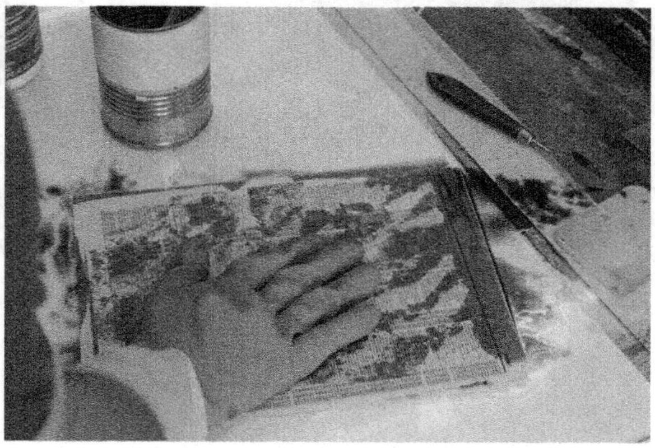

(image 2-98) Use old pieces of newsprint or phone book pages to absorb the SoySolv & Ink mess. Repeat this process until the plate is clean. It will have been stained, thus not as perfect as when it was first made, but the plate should not have any significant signs of ink left on it.

Caution: solvents and oils are subject to self combustion. Dispose of all rags and papers that contain oil or solvents properly.

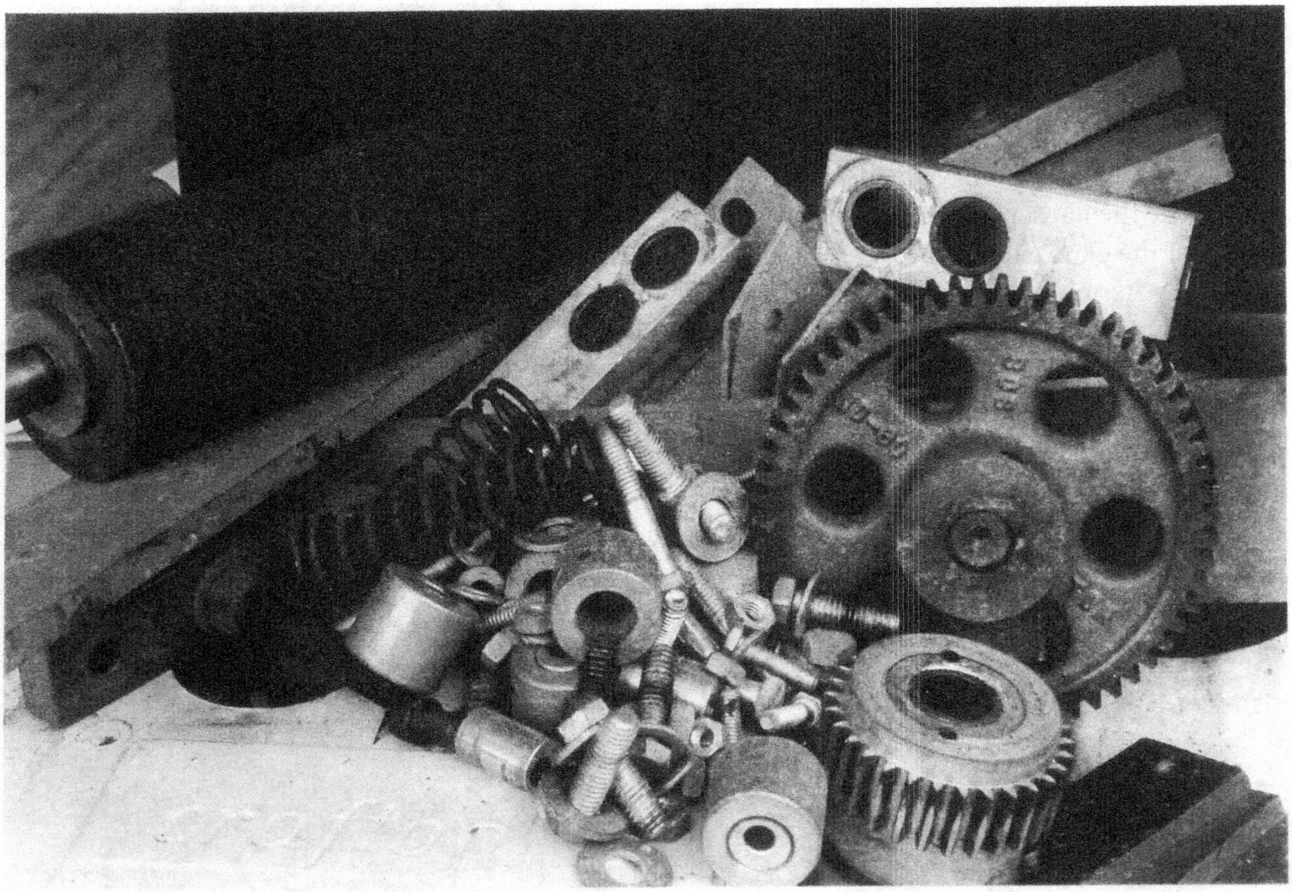

"Craftool"

photogravure

Scott Barnes

Chapter 3
Making Contact Printing Frames

Using a vacuum frame with kreen plastic is the most effective way to ensure positive contact between the image transparency and the polymer plate. A quick internet search will reveal many different options for commercially available machines. The machinery, however, can be expensive. One of the goals of this book is to reveal techniques and tools that are within reach for the casual hobbyist as well as effective enough to allow the serious artist to create high quality work. In this chapter I will show you some very simple contact printing frames that I have used with great success to create exceptionally high quality photogravures with steel-backed photopolymer plates.

The greatest challenge faced by photographers using traditional contact printing frames is maintaining even pressure between the KM73 polymer plate and the image transparency. Most contact printing frames are designed for significantly thinner material (photo paper and a negative). Toyobo's Printight KM73 photopolymer plates are between three and ten times as thick as many photo papers. Dan Weldon's Solarplate brand photopolymer plates are even thicker than the KM73 plates. Contact printing frames made for other alternative photography methods either focus the pressure in the center or along the edges of photopolymer plates. This results in poor contact away from the pressure points as well as spots created by the focused light from Newton rings in the high pressure areas.

What in the world are Newton rings? I did not know when I started learning this process, but they plagued my workflow and made spots in my photographs. I realized that the smooth glass of the contact frame, when pressed against the plastic back of the image transparency, made little circular rainbows that focused and diffussed light in random patterns across my images. For several months I had moderate success with spraying the back of each image transparency with clear matte acrylic. After dicovering that many commercial printing plates had a slip coat to address plastic to plastic light refraction, I began to coat both sides of the transparency with baby powder. This helped, but did not eliminate the effects of Newton rings completely. Recalling my time working in a conservation picture framing shop, I decided to try a piece of non-glare glass. There are two problems with glass in the picture framing world. First, it is fairly thin. Second, most of the high end glass has a UV filter. Not remembering these two details, I ended up with a frustrating week of experiments in which the exposure times were over an hour long. The experiments stopped when I accidently broke the thin glass. Finally, I went to a store that sold windows and structural glass to order the 1/4" tempered glass that I have now. It is acid etched on one side, much like the non-glare glass from a frame shop. The important difference is that it does not have a UV blocking film. The acid etched side is placed against the back of the transparency. I have continued using the baby powder on the transparency too, and have greatly reduced the effects of Newton rings.

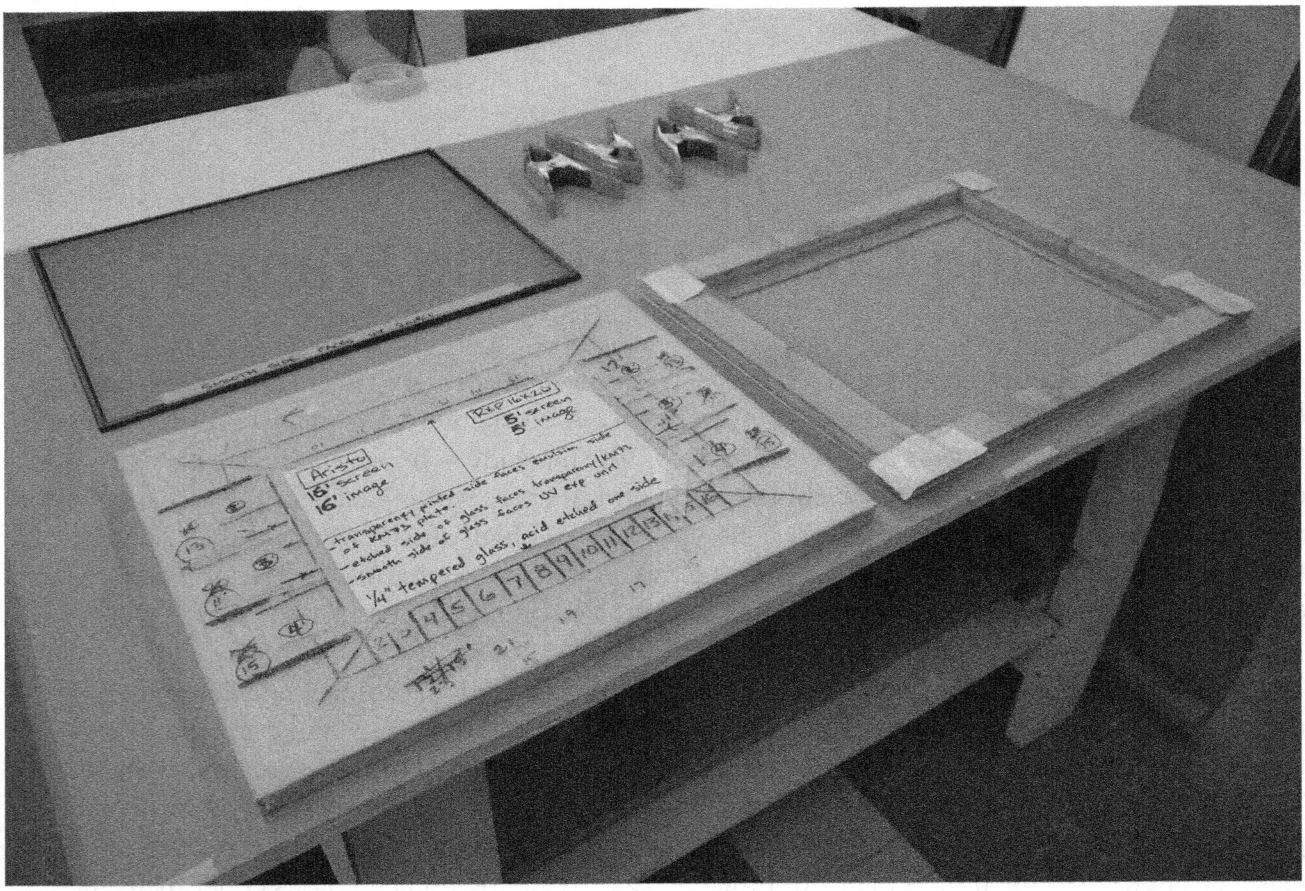

Home made contact printing frame

(image 3-01) This is my old contact printing frame. You can can see the four main pieces: the base with thin foam pad, glass, clamps, and top frame. The base and glass are probably the two most important pieces in any frame since those are the two pieces that create the pressure that keeps your photographic media together, forming even contact for exposure. The clamps and top frame are just means of applying pressure to the base and glass in the system.

The glass is the most expensive part of the contact frame. The one pictured here is 1/4" thick, tempered glass that is acid etched on one side. While thicker glass blocks some UV light (requiring longer exposure times than thinner glass) I like that it is less prone to bending when the clamps are applied. The acid etched side is placed in direct contact with the back of the transparency to reduce the incidence of newton rings.

The base is 3/4" thick hardwood ply. The hardwood stays flatter than soft species like pine. Medium density fiberboard (MDF) works well too. The foam pad on top of the base is very thin. I like thin shipping foam because it is inexpensive and I don't mind writing notes on it with a sharpie.

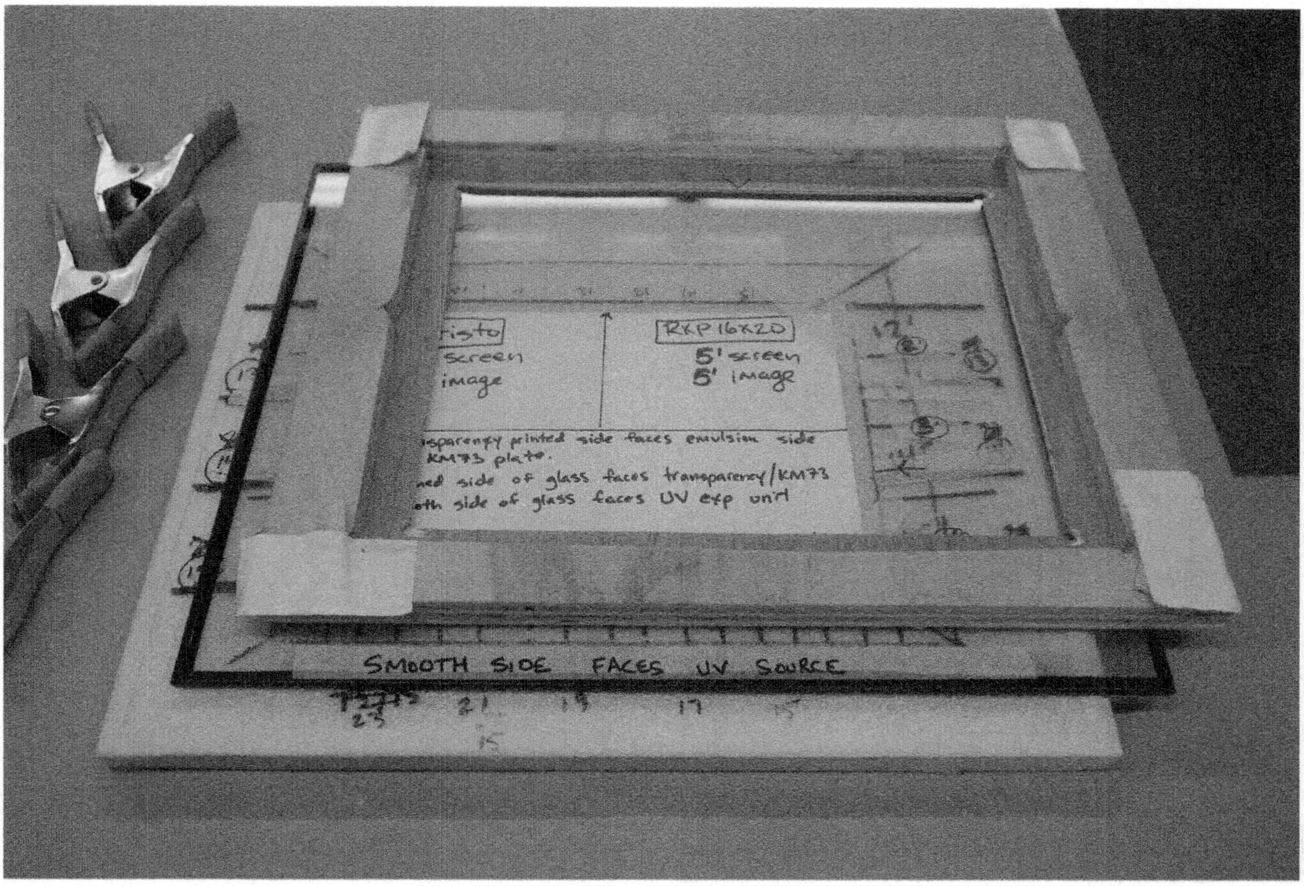

(image 3-02) This image shows the order in which the flat pieces fit together: base, glass, top frame. They are staggered in the photo to better illustrate the order. When printing, everything will be in line and clamped together.

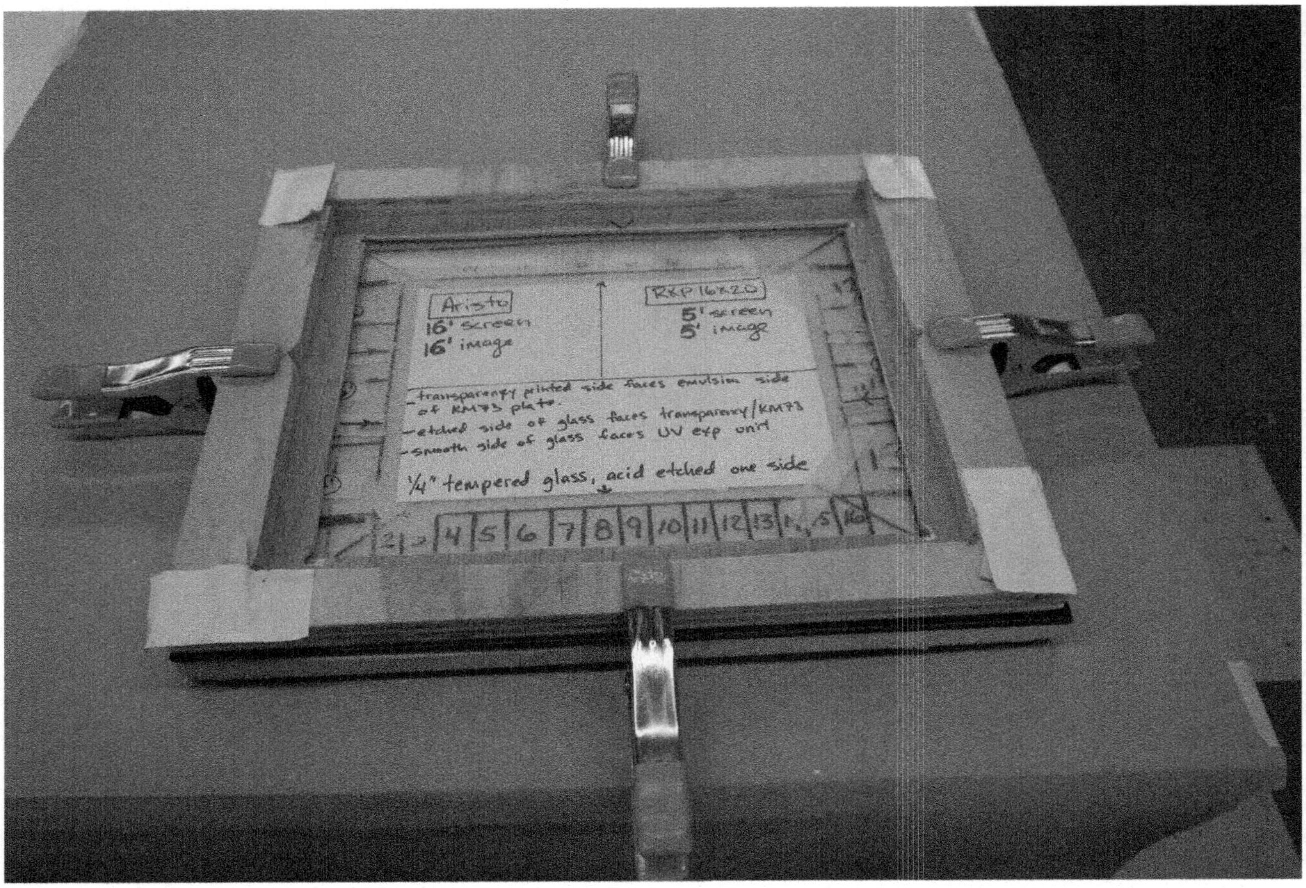

(image 3-03) This shows everything clamped together (without KM73 plate or image transparency). I only use 4 clamps with this system since the top frame helps spread the pressure more evenly. Even pressure is required for this process. To compensate for a little bit of warping in the glass and wood, I have placed two pieces of printmaking paper in the center of the system. The paper stays under the center of the polymer plate during exposure to maintain full contact over the entire surface.

The notes I have written on the paper are:
Aristo: 16' screen 16' image (indicates stochastic screen and image transparency exposure times)
RXP 16x20: 5' screen 5' image (indicate stochastic screen and image transparency exposure times)
- transparency printed side faces emulsion side of KM73 plate
- etched side of glass faces transparency/KM73
- smooth side of glass faces UV exp unit

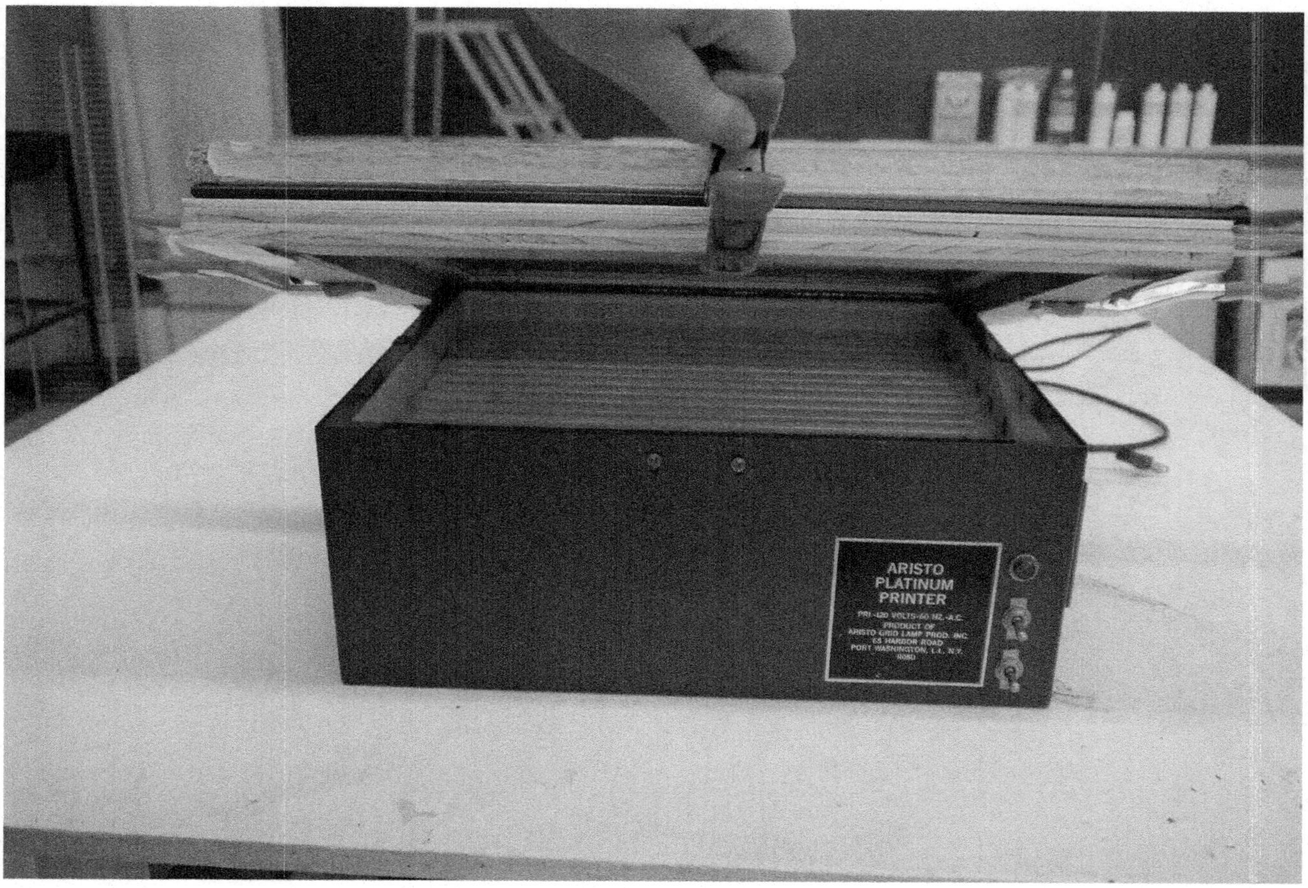

(image 3-04) This contact frame was made to fit over the Aristo Platinum Printer. I designed it for a tight fit so that very little light would escape, allowing me to stay in the dark room during exposure without exposing myself to harmful UV radiation.

This UV unit has lost much of its power recently so I had to replace it with an RXP 16x20 from Ryonet. I found someone who makes new bulbs for the Aristo Platinum Printer, but it cost as much as the small Ryonet machine. Additionally, the RXP 16x20 was lighter, easy to repair, and replacement bulbs are readily available. Exposure times were different, so it took a few experiments to get the new UV unit dialed in, but I think that time and initial cost will end up being more practial and less expensive in the long run.

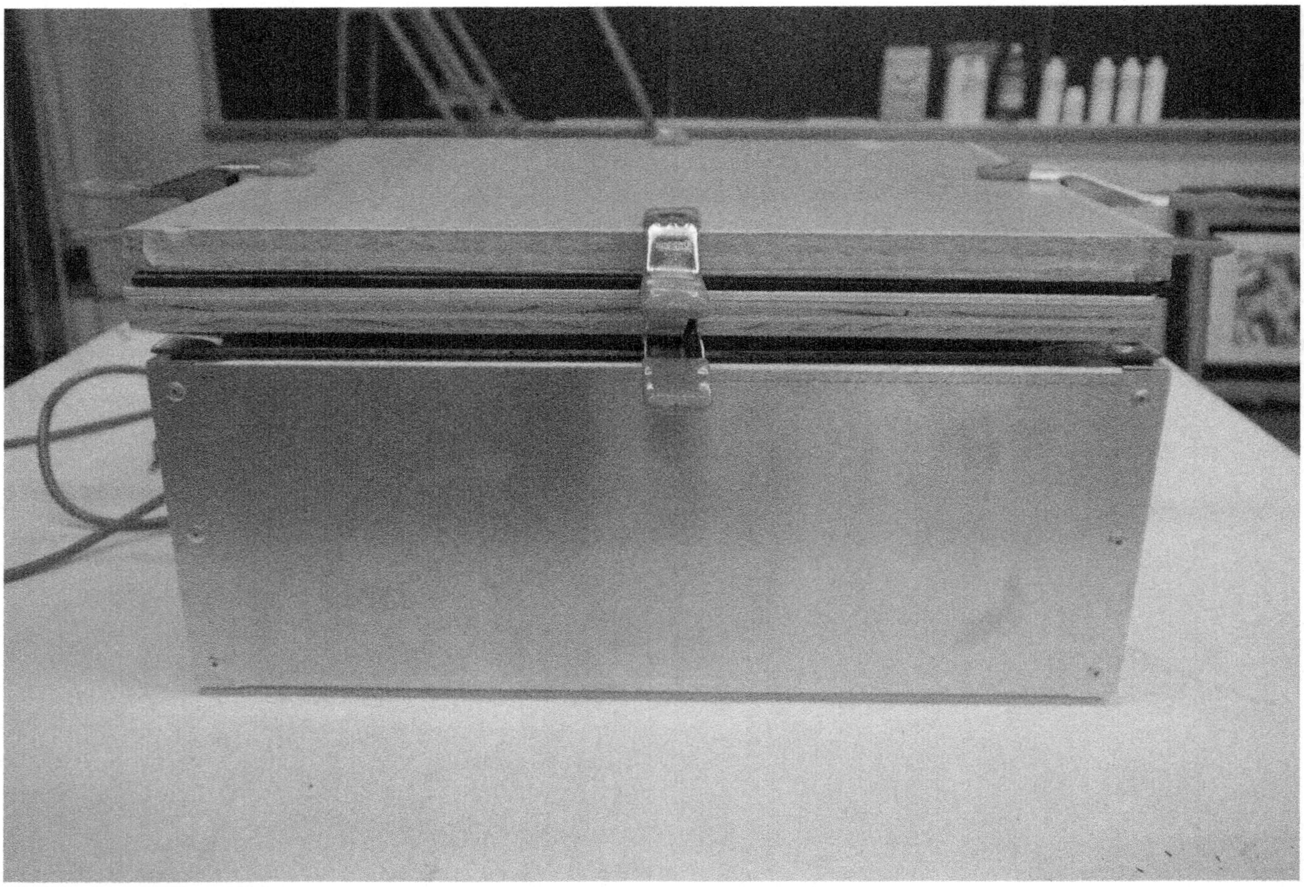

(image 3-05) The Ryonet RXP 16x20 is larger than the Aristo Platinum Printer. You can see in this images that, while the frame rests nicely on top of the new UV unit, it does not fit over the lip. (Further illustrated by image 3-06) This means that UV light will escape during exposure. To minimize my exposure to this type of light I cover the entire system with a thick black bag before starting the timer, and I leave the dark room immediately after starting the timer. At some point I may make a new wood frame to fit around the Ryonet RXP 16x20 that fits as nicely as the frame I made for the Aristo Platinum Printer.

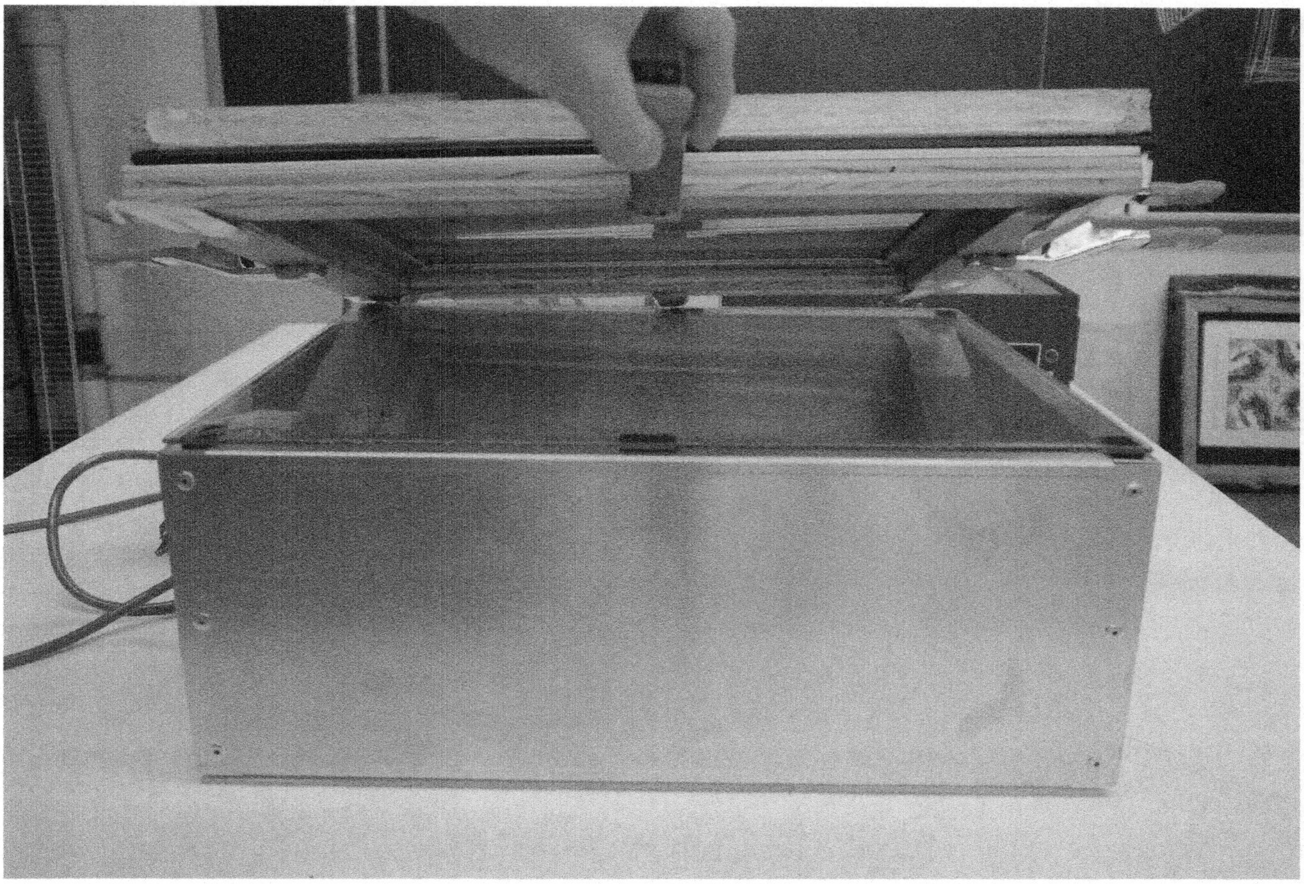

(image 3-06)

Note: *The cost for the setup you see in this image cost about $304.*

16" x 20" tempered glass (acid etched one side) 1/4" thick = $85
Ryonet RXP 16x20 UV exposure unit = $200
Two pieces of 16" x 20" hardwood plywood, 3/4" thick = $15
4 clamps (2" opening) = $4

*I think this is the least expensive setup that provides high quality contact printing. Shop around and see what you can find. According to their website, Toyobo KM73 plates are sensitive to UV light that ranges from 300 - 400 nm but are formulated to work best at 360 nm. **

*(*source: http://www.toyobo-global.com/seihin/xk/pdf/print.pdf)*

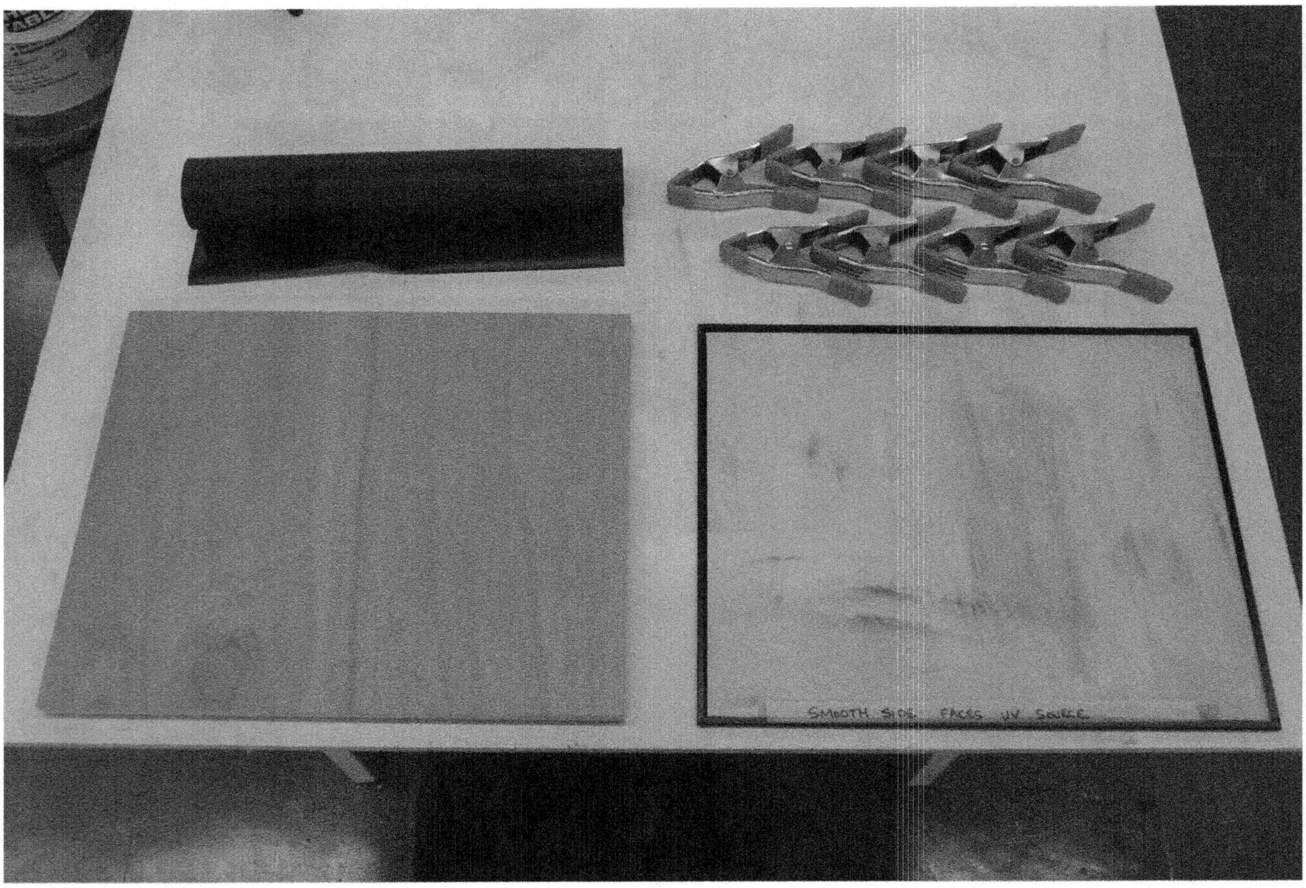

Building a New Contact Frame (4 simple variations)

Version 1:

(image 3-07) This picture shows a very simple contact frame
- one 3/4" piece of luan plywood cut to 16" x 20"
- a piece of 1/4" tempered glass, acid etched on one side that measures 16" x 20"
- 8 steel spring clamps (2")
- a roll of thin foam shelf liner

Use scissors to cut the shelf liner to fit on top of the 16" x 20" piece of plywood. Place the glass on top and apply the clamps (2 per side) to make the contact frame.

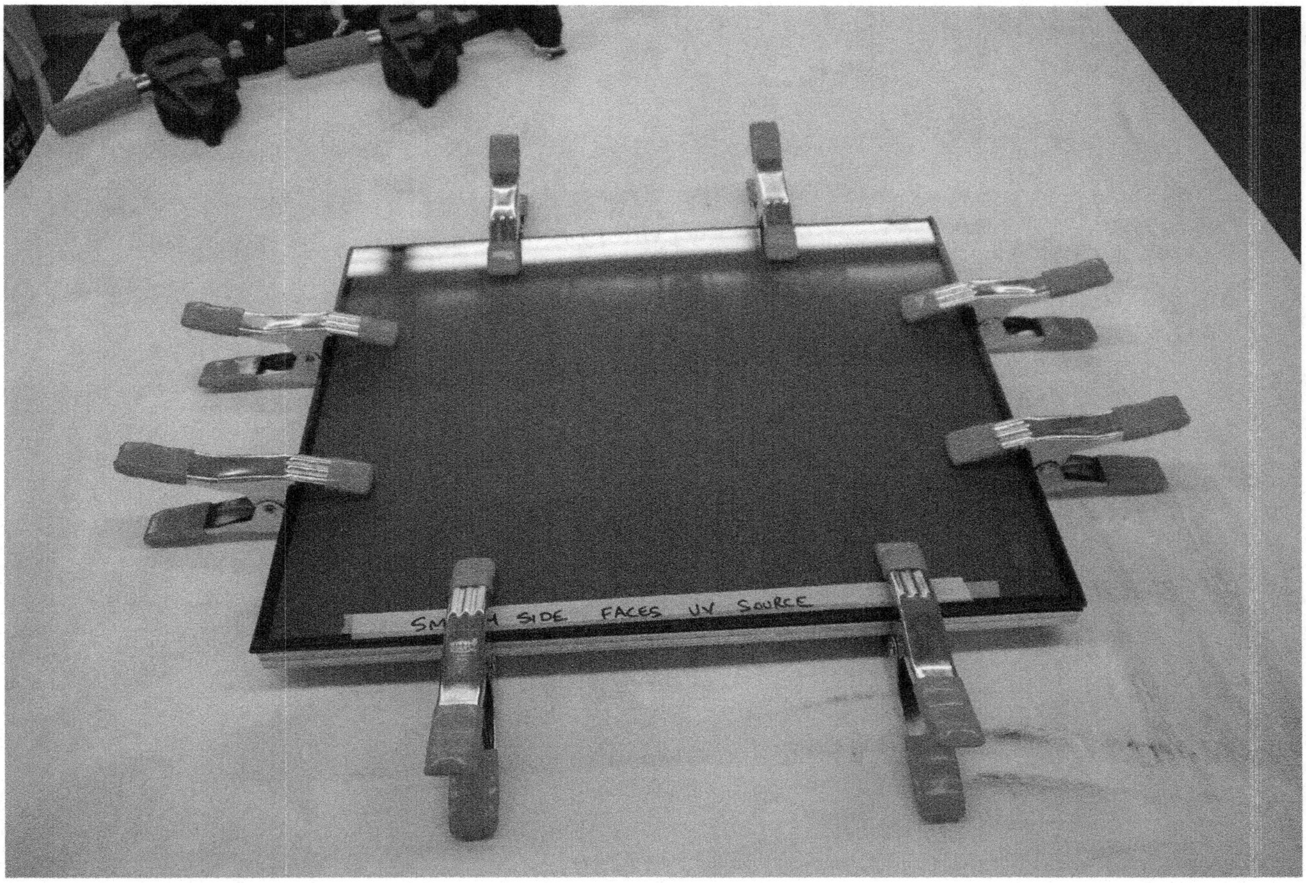

(image 3-08) As mentioned earlier, the glass will bend a little bit.. While thicker glass can minimize the distortion, it will still bend. This is why this frame uses foam shelf liner. The foam will compress under the KM73 polymer plate, allowing for more even contact.

Pay attention to the warp of the wood that you use for the base (in this case the 3/4" piece of luan cut to 16" x 20"). It should be as flat as possible, but keep in mind that all wood is biased so you can find some warp in every piece. If you favor the side where the center is a bit higher than the ends, this can act in your favor by matching the curve that the glass will have under clamping pressure.

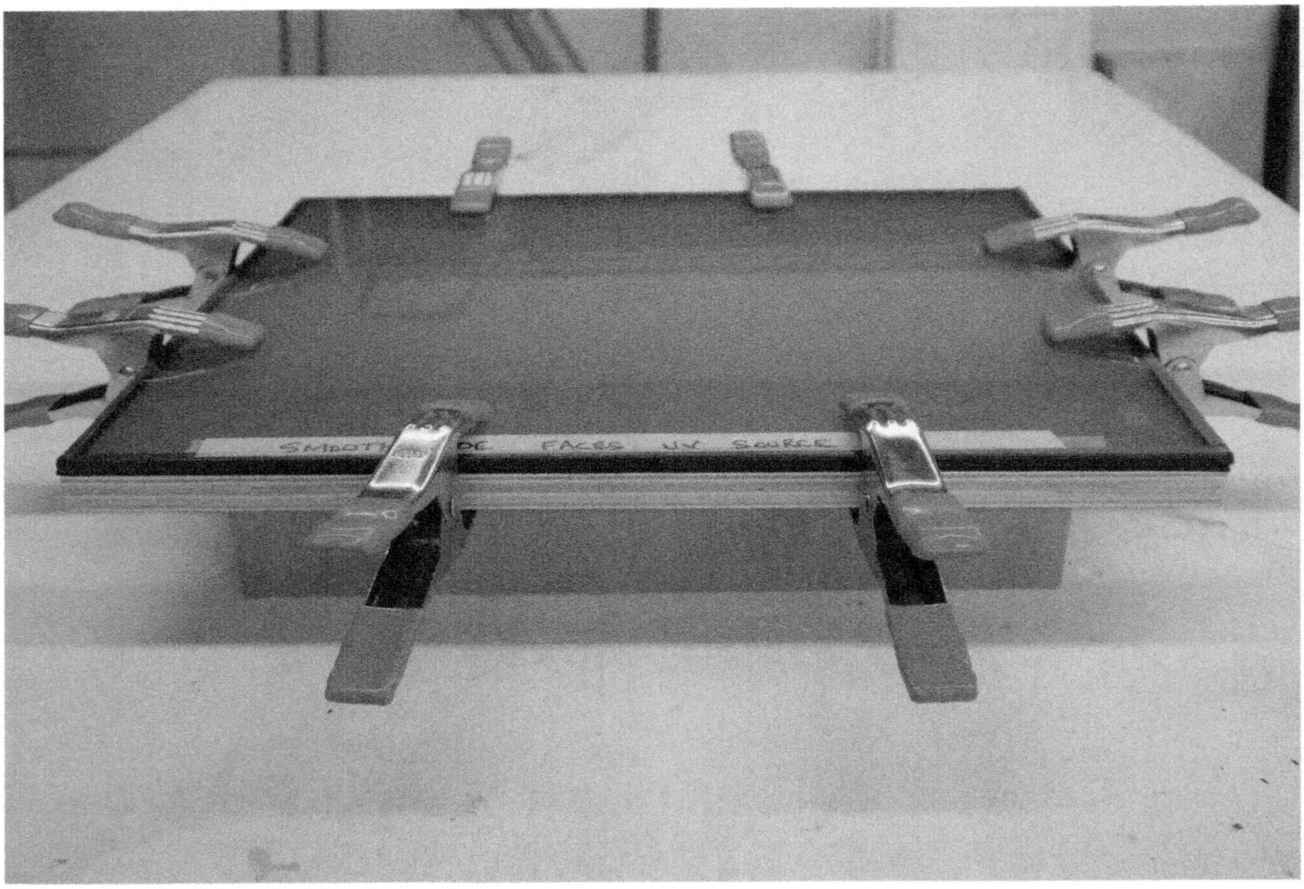

Version 2:

(image 3-09) Here is a variation of the previous simple contact frame in which 3" stringers were added to reinforce the bottom of the 3/4" piece of luan plywood, helping to keep it straight. The added bonus to these 3" stringers is that they lift the base off the table enough so that clamping is easier.

Contact printing frames are designed for paper/film printing,. Consider the forces acting on contact frames. Since the KM73 photopolymer plates are thicker than paper (and are also backed with steel) they resist conforming to the frame as easily as paper would.

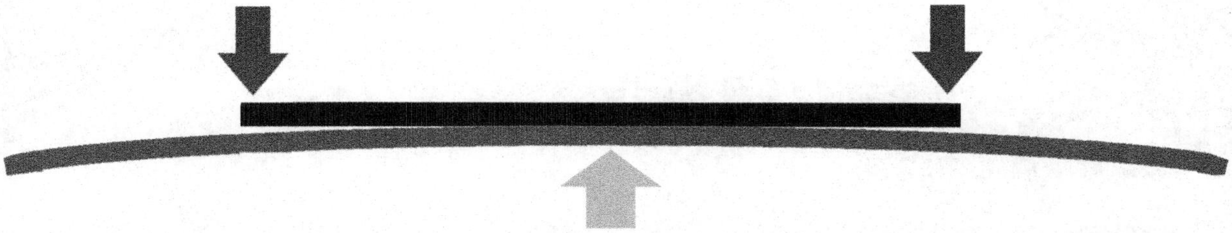

(image 3-10) Above is an illustration of pressures found in a traditional spring-back contact printing frame that is used for most paper printing. For the process in this book, most spring-back frames don't provide enough pressure for good contact. They are fine for paper, but not for metal backed polymer plates.

The pressure is applied to the center of the backing by the springs (bottom layer in illustration), with resistance along the edges of the glass. There is some deflection to match the center pressure (which is probably why it works ok for paper printing), but the introcuction of a material as thick as the KM73 plates makes for uneven pressure, leading to many light leaks between the transparency image and the polymer plate.

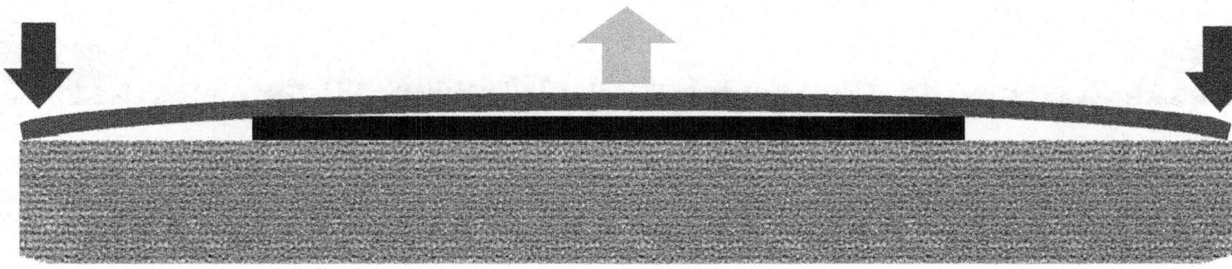

(image 3-11) The next illustration shows the forces involved with a system that uses clamps around the outer edges. The top layer represents the glass. The middle represents the KM73 plate. The bottom layer represents the 3/4" plywood back. Achieving high pressure is not a problem. Add or subtract clamps around the edge to increase or decrease the pressure. The challenge lies in the way the glass will bend. Thicker glass will minimize the bending, but it will still bend. You must either shim out the edges that surround the KM73 plate, so that the glass can meet a level surface, or you need to provide some kind of padding to allow the plate to lie in some sort of recess.

There will still be some deflection, and you will have to make some minor adjustments. Two pieces of printmaking paper (smaller than the KM73 plate) are what I have used with great success. Other suggestions are made in this chapter.

I must reitterate that nothing works better than Kreene plastic and a vaccum frame. The plastic is pulled around the KM73 plate by the vacuum frame, forming even pressure across the entire surface, preventing any light leaks. If you continue making photogravures with these polymer plates, you are encouraged to look into this option. It is expensive, and in my opinion, many more important steps need to be learned before spending the money on that kind of heavy equipment.

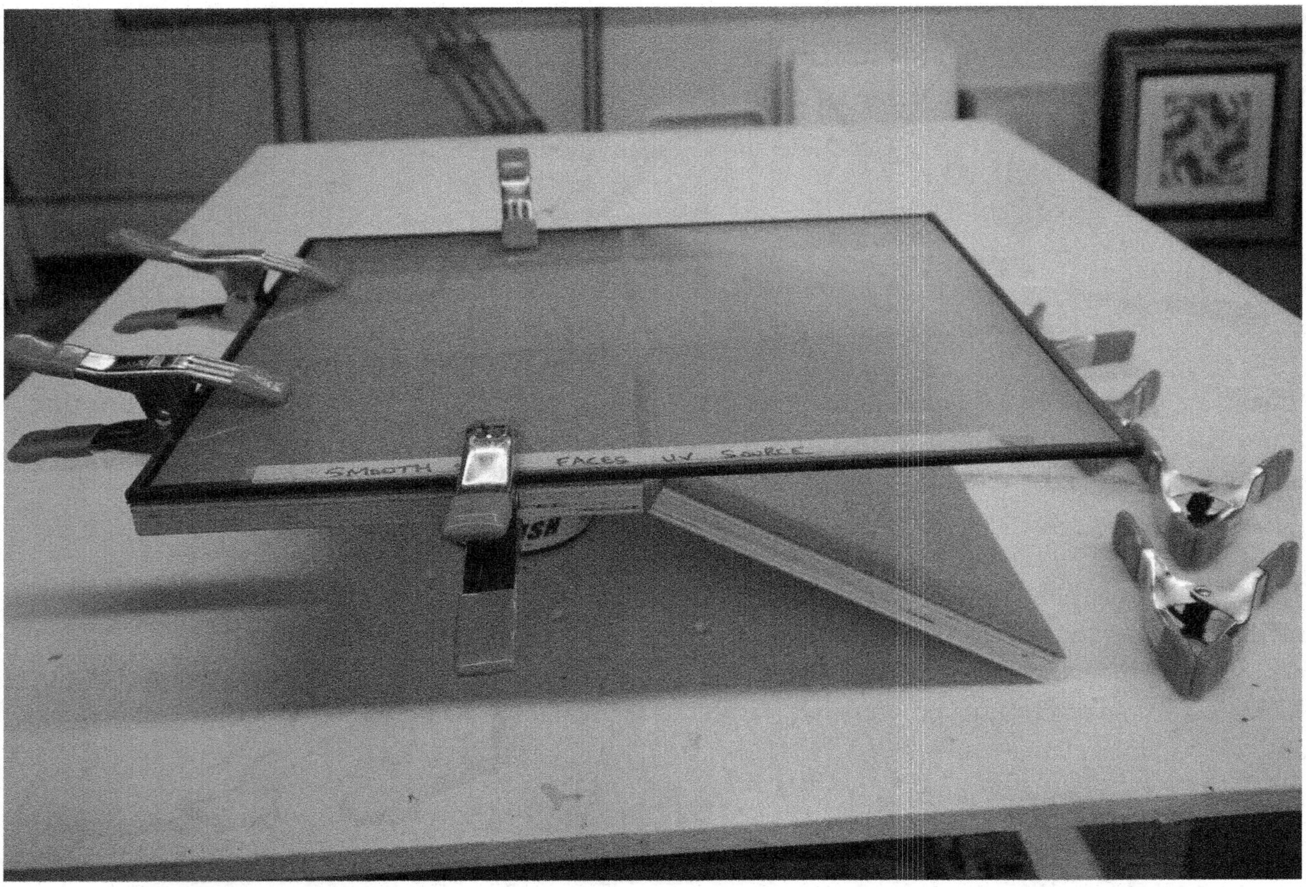

Version 3:

(image 3-12) This is a split-back variation of the simple contact frame. This is a multi-use frame for different contact printing techniques. The challenge to a multi-use frame is that the padding on the 3/4" luan plywood cannot be as thick as it may need to be for the KM73 polymer plates. Paper printing techniques would bend too much with thick padding, making good overall contact difficult. In this version, I have used thin cork shelf lining instead of the foam shelf lining. Cork still has some flexibility to it, but is rigid enough for contact printing with paper.

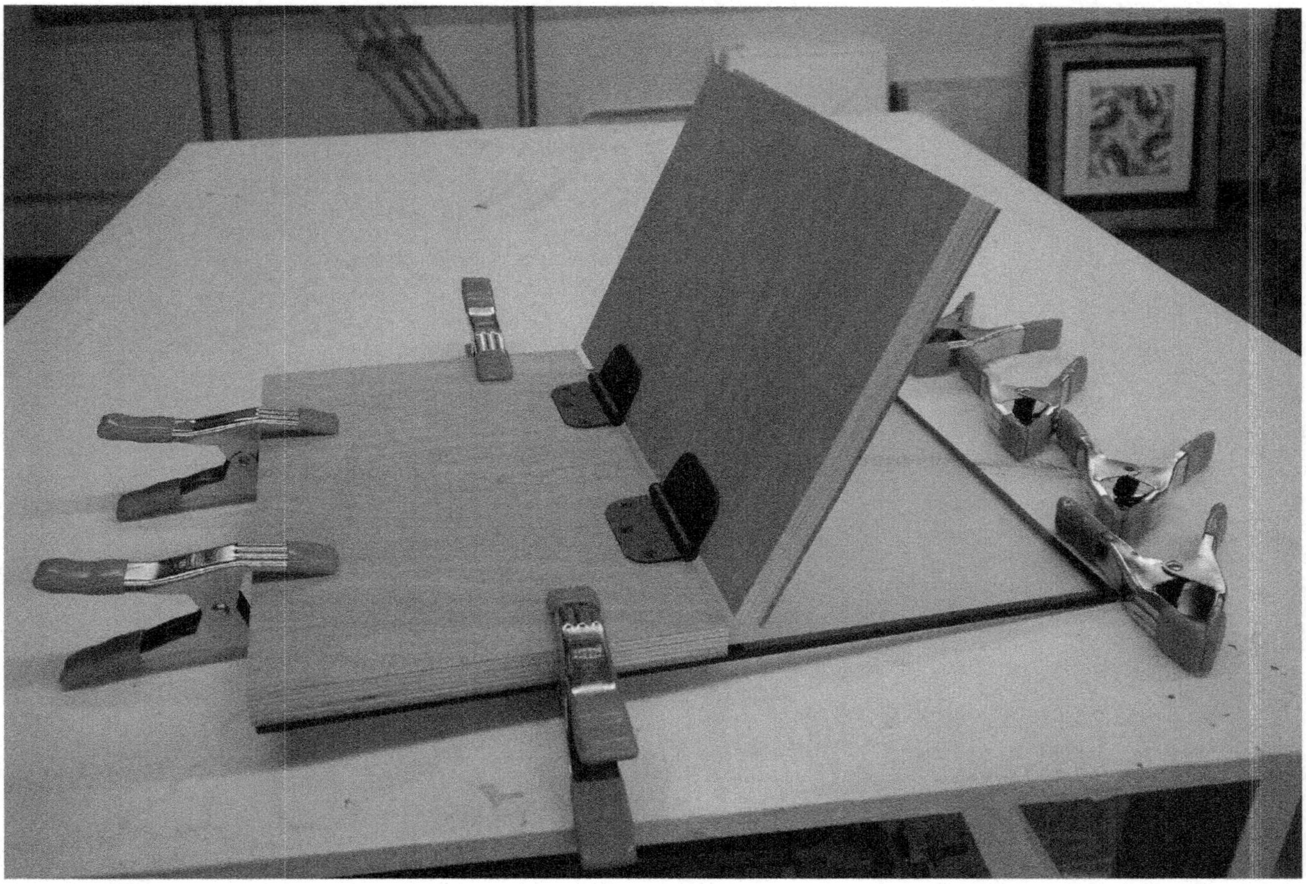

(image 3-13) There are only two differences between the first version of this simple frame and this split-back version. The first difference is the use of cork instead of foam for the backing. The second difference is that the 3/4" piece of luan plywood is cut into two pieces and joined together with hinges so that print-out processes can be checked for exposure. A split-back frame like this is not needed if you only plan to make photopolymer plates. This option is for those who want to make a contact printing frame that can be used for multiple photographic processes.

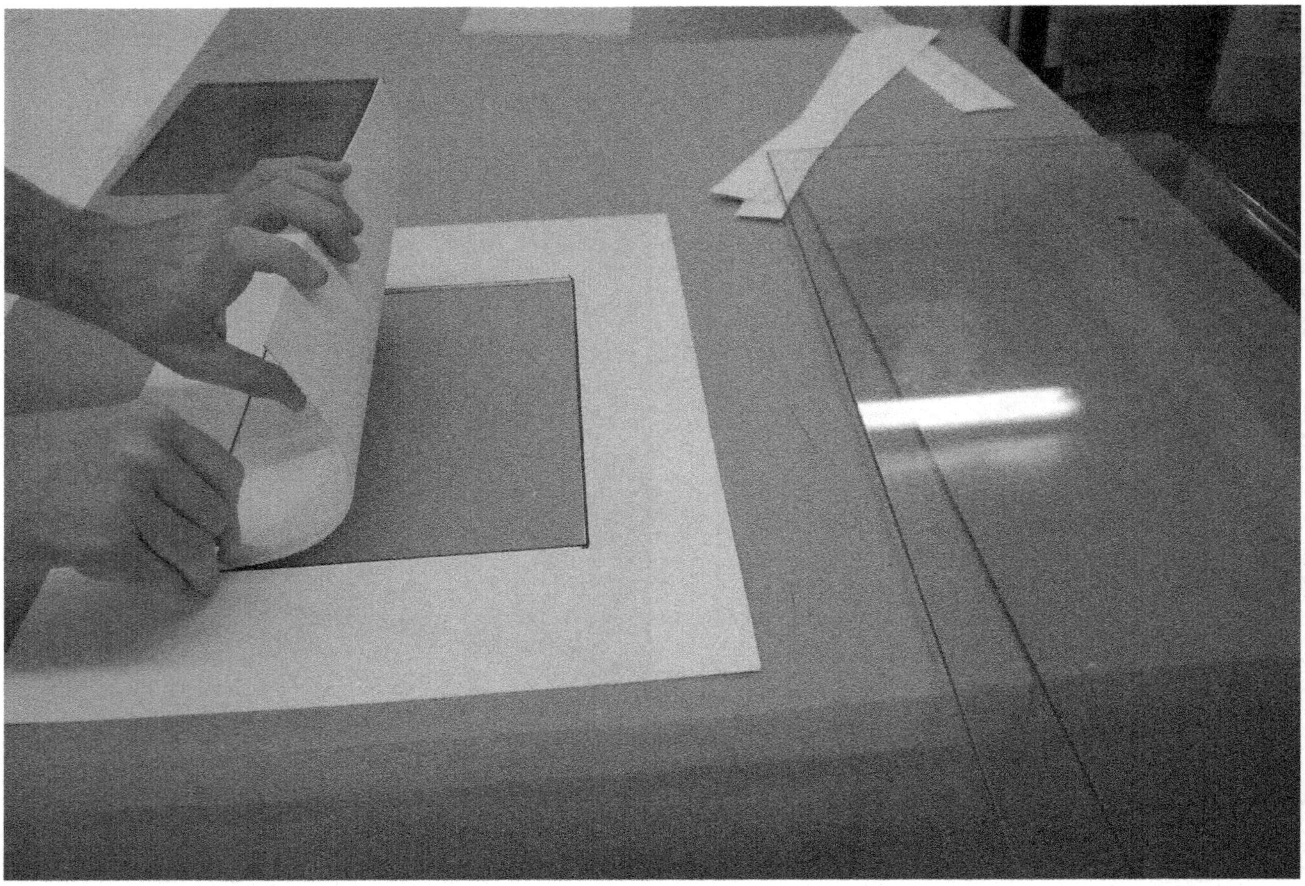

Version 4:

(image 3-14) This image shows me cutting 2 pieces of Rising Stonehenge 90 lbs (250 gsm) printmaking paper so that an A4 size plate will fit in the center. The 2 pieces of paper are just barely thinner than the KM72 polymer plate. 3 pieces were a bit thicker, and may be appropriate once the transparency is added to the top of the polymer plate. These pieces of paper act as shims that provide even distribution of pressure around the surface, allowing for good contact across the entire image area. The polymer plate sits in the cutout in the center of the paper stack.

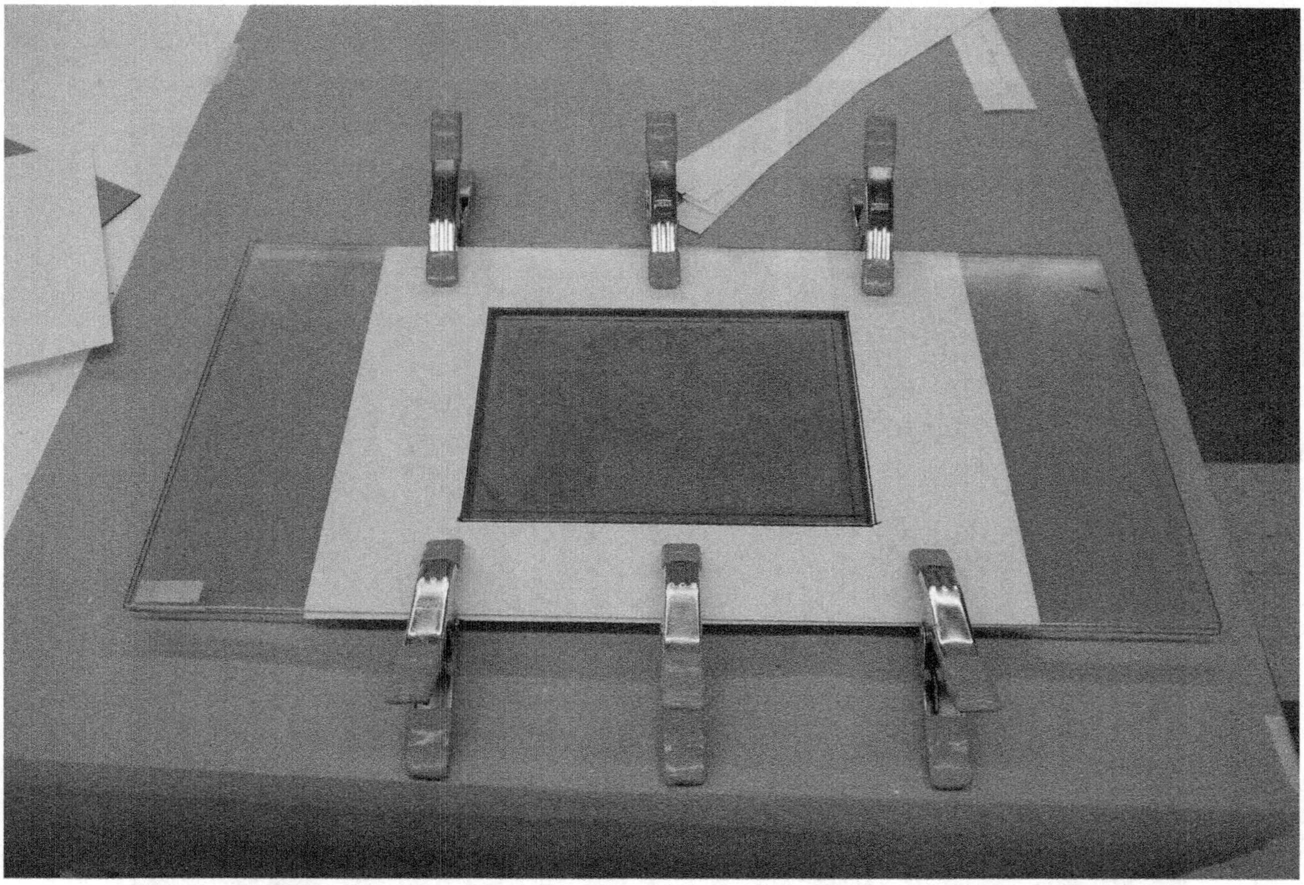

(image 3-15) I have only tested this inexpensive variation one time, but it seems to work well. You do not have to cut any wood. You just need to buy two pieces of clear tempered glass shelves from IKEA, and cut some pieces of printmaking paper to make a template for the KM73 polymer plate. This contact frame cost about $22 to make. The pressure seems to be ok, but I think that this principle would work even better with one piece of glass on top of the 3/4" luan plywood backing. Cut printmaking paper is a very simple way to achieve even pressure. I imagine making different templates to fit different sized plates.

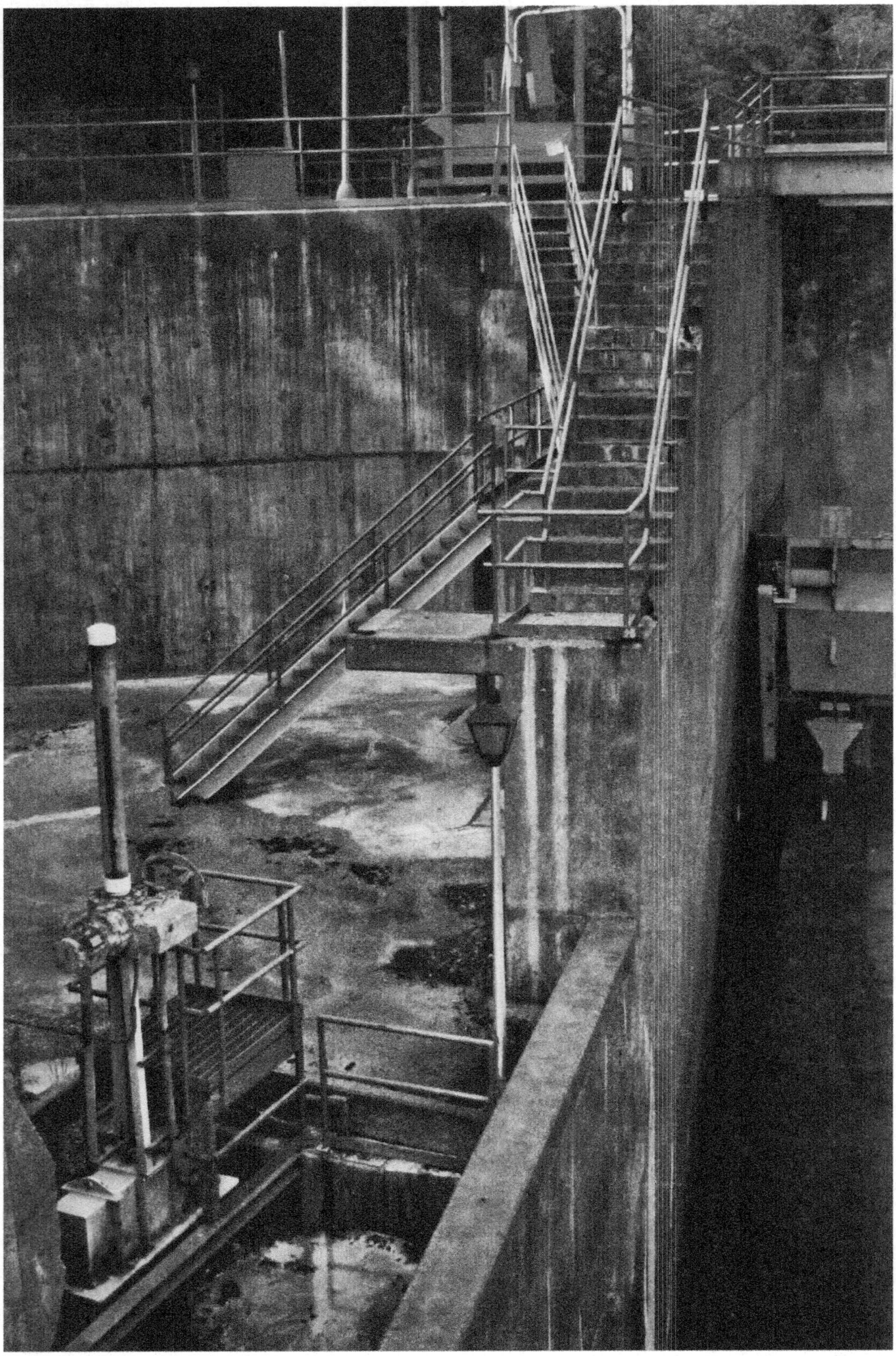

“Scalis”

photogravure

Scott Barnes

Chapter 4
Image Capture

In the context of this book, image capture is very easy because I support two very basic ideas:

1. ***Turn off as many presets as possible*** so that the capture device is providing you with raw data (or as close as possible).

   Digital Cameras: Shoot in RAW if possible. Do not use digital filters. Get as close as possible to capturing an image that is not manipulated by the capture device.

   Scanners: Turn off all auto adjustments, level compensations, presets, etc. The scan will look a bit flat, but the data is preserved so you can better manipulate it later in with digital editing software like Adobe Photoshop.

2. ***Capture, scan, and edit in 16 bit mode*** (or as high as your device will allow).

   Digital Cameras: Many digital cameras allow for 14 bit capture, some new ones higher. 8 bit works fine, but if you can find a higher setting, then I suggest you use it.

   Scanners: These devices are usually in line with image editing software, so you can use 16 bit.

Images captured on film will have to be scanned so they can be processed and turned into positive inkjet transparencies. Turn off all automatic adjustments and presets. The scan will look flat, but it will contain a lot of information that you can adjust later. Make sure the bit rate is higher than 8 bits if possible. And, the resolution of the initial scan should be twice as large as your desired output. *(Example: You are scanning a 4" x 5" film negative, and you want to make an image for an 8" x 10" plate. The resolution of the 8" x 10" plate should be 360 dpi. 360 x 2 = 720 To achieve an 8" x 10" image at 720 dpi, you need to scan that 4" x 5" negative at 1440 dpi.)*

These same ideas apply to scanning test prints used to make adjustment curves (chapter 8). Turn off all presets in the scanner. If you use a camera, capture an image that is as large as possible, preferably in RAW.

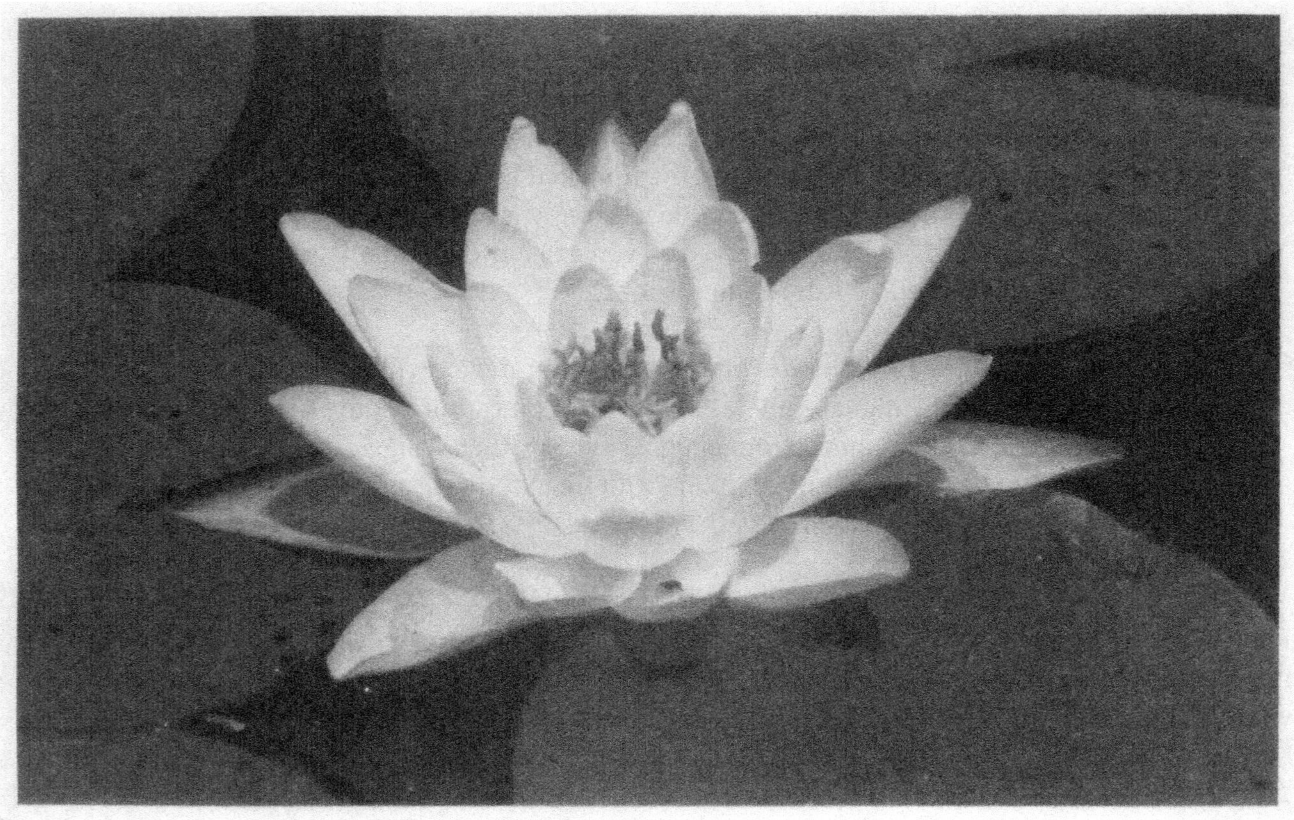

“White Water Lilly”

photogravure

Scott Barnes

Chapter 5
Base Exposure Time

The base exposure time is the minimum time needed to achieve 100% black. The time is different for each person's workflow because of several variables that affect the intensity of ultraviolet radiation.

Strength (and type) of UV radiation

Different exposure units emit diffent levels of ultraviolet light. They will also emit different wavelengths of ultraviolet light. Most commercially available exposure units are calibrated to emit between 340 - 370 nm, but you should check the bulb type to make sure.

Distance from UV source

The farther away the polymer plate is from the ultraviolet source, the less UV radiation it will receive in any given time. The plate will need more exposure time the farther away it is from the UV source.

UV absorbing layers

Glass and plastic block varying amounts of ultraviolet light. Thicker glass or plastic will block more ultraviolet light than thinner glass or plastic. The image transparency is made of plastic, and will block some ultraviolet light before it has any ink printed on it. The glass in the contact frame will block some ultraviolet light. Some UV exposure units have glass that protect the bulbs. That glass will also block some ultraviolet light. (***caution:*** *while these layers block small amounts of UV light that will make a difference in your pictures, they do not block enough to make the work environment safe for your eyes. Protect your eyes by making sure your system does not have any places where light can escape, and by wearing UV filtering safety glasses!)*

Photogravure is an intaglio printmaking process. Traditional copper photogravure uses an aquatint pattern (made with rosin) to create a very fine dot matrix in which the artist controls the depth of each dot. The deeper the dot, the more ink it will hold. More ink means deeper tone. Less ink means lighter tone. KM73 polymer plates are fine enough to hold a similar dot matrix. However, the way the "aquatint" is created is different. Instead of using a traditional aquatint process, polymer plates must be exposed to a film that has a random dot pattern (preferably using a stochastic screening process that appears random to the human eye). This "stochastic screen" creates the "aquatint" on the polymer plate. The terms "stochastic screen" and "aquatint screen" are used interchangebly in many printmaking circles.

Each artist must experiment to discover how long to expose the KM73 plate, with the stochastic screen, to make a good enough aquatint pattern to print 100% black. Once the base exposure time (minimum time) is found, a simple calculation can be made to find the optimum exposure time.

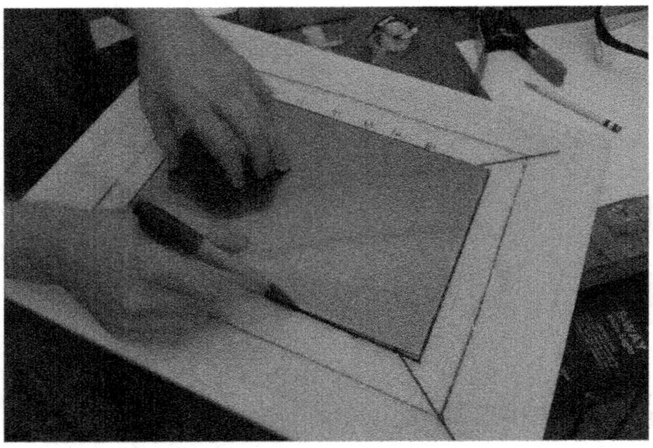

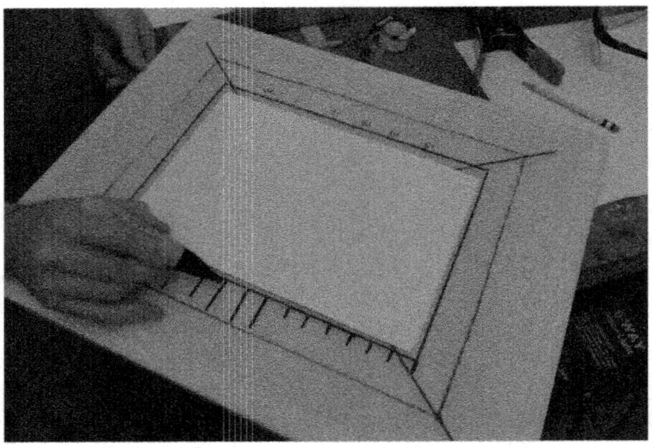

(image 5-01) With the safe light turned on in the darkroom, take out one of the KM73 plates and place it on the contact frame. Trace a line around the plate. (If the frame you made is has a black backing, you can use tape to trace the outline of the KM73 plate.)

(image 5-02) Make marks at regular intervals outside the traced rectangle of the plate. These will help guide you as you expose different parts of the plate for different amounts of time to UV light.

Depending on the exposure unit you have, times can vary from just over 1 minute to 16 mintues long. If you do not know the intensity of your system, you may want to make many marks, allowing you to make many exposures.

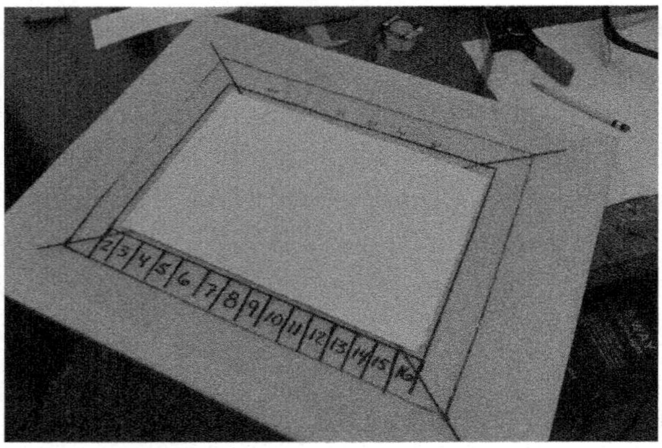

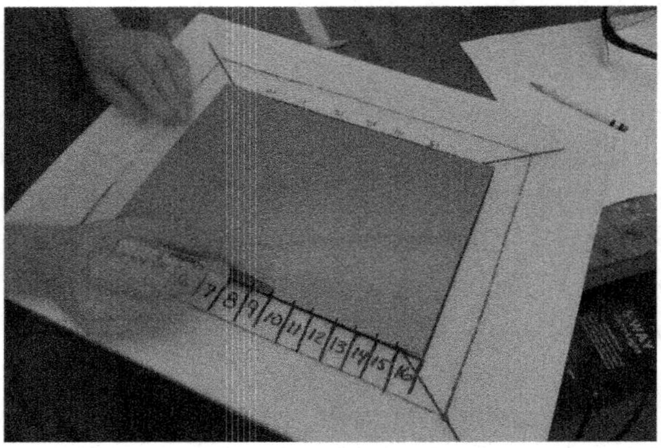

(image 5-03) Write the times on the contact frame. Do not rely on memory to record the exposure time.

(image 5-04) Place the KM73 plate back on the contact frame and transfer the lines from the contact frame to the plate.

The marker will wash off the plate during processing, but the ink will have blocked enough UV light to leave visible marks. You can also scratch the plate instead of using a marker. The plate needs to be marked so that the times can be found later.

The experiment shown in this chapter exposed this plate from 2 minutes to 16 minutes, in 1 minute intervals.

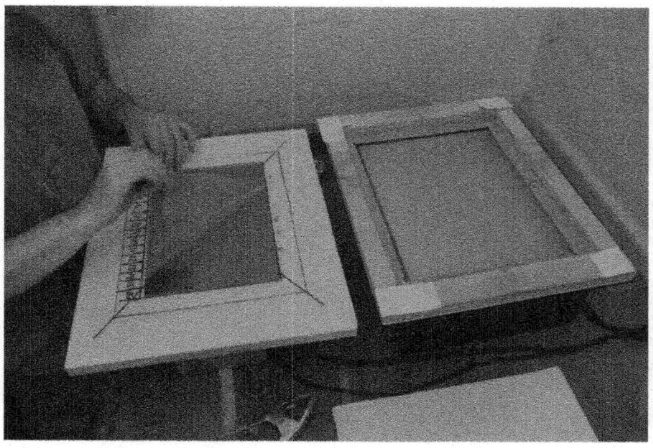

(image 5-05) Remove the protective UV film from the top of the plate.

(image 5-06) Make sure that the marks on the contact frame and the marks on the plate are lined up.

Being slow and methodical during this entire process will save you a lot of headache in the future. The goal is to get very useful information that is going to be the basis of future calculations. Make sure that the plate does not move during this experiment.

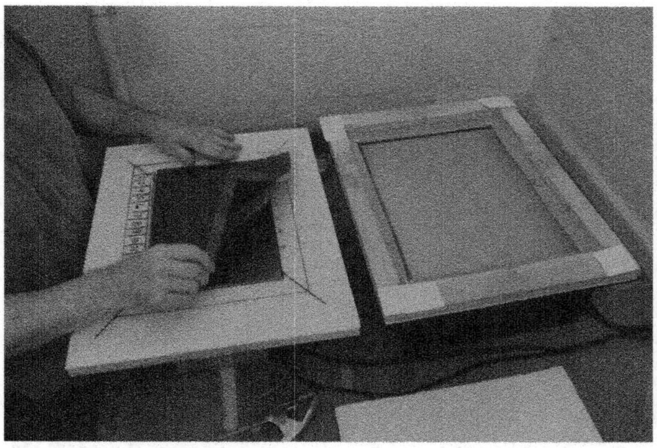

(image 5-07) Place the stochastic screen ("aquatint screen") on top of the plate.

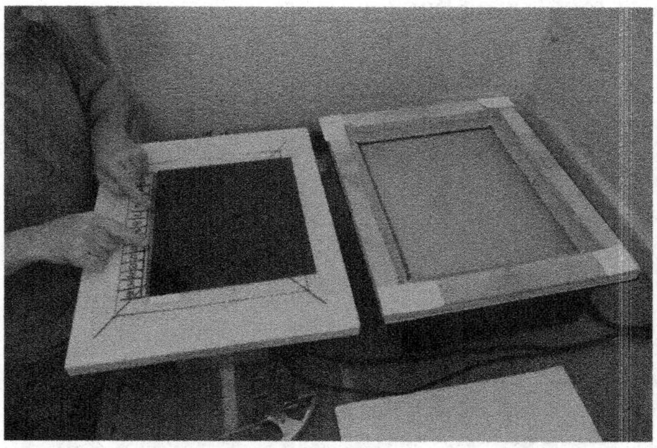

(image 5-08) Leave a small part of the plate uncovered by the stochastic screen.

The printed side of the screen must face the emulsion side of the plate. The KM73 plates have steel backings with greenish polymer emulsion on the front. The printed side of the stochastic screen has a matte appearance to it. The other side will appear glossy.

Leaving a small part of the plate uncovered will give it full exposure to UV light, curing it. Any writing on that part will be readable. This is the part where you will have made marks by scratching (or with some kind of marker) that will allow you to track the different exposure times.

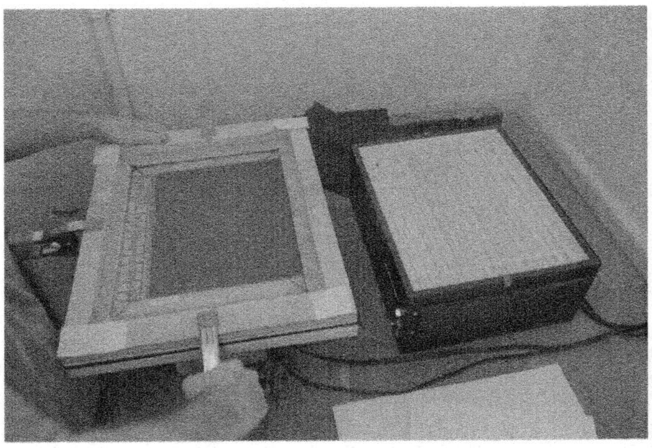

(image 5-09) Clamp the glass to the top of the contact frame to hold everything in place.

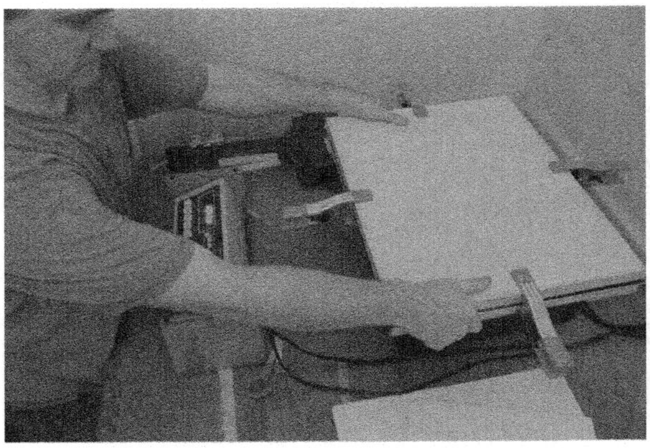

(image 5-10) Place the contact frame over the exposure unit.

The acid etched side of the glass (matte) must go against the stochastic screen.

Here is the order for the stack you have created:
UV exposure unit, (ultraviolet light shines through the glass, through the screen, onto the plate)
contact frame glass,
stochastic screen,
KM73 plate,
contact frame back

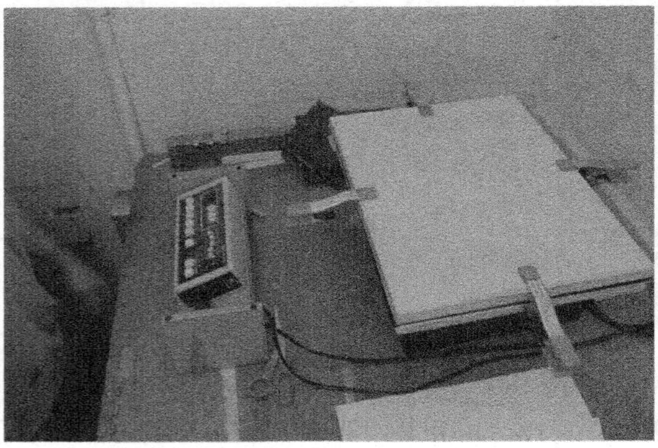

(image 5-11) Expose the plate for 2 minutes.

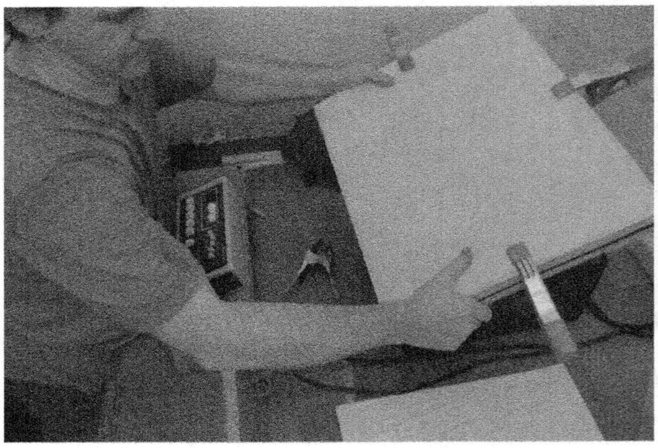

(image 5-12) Remove the contact frame from the UV exposure unit.

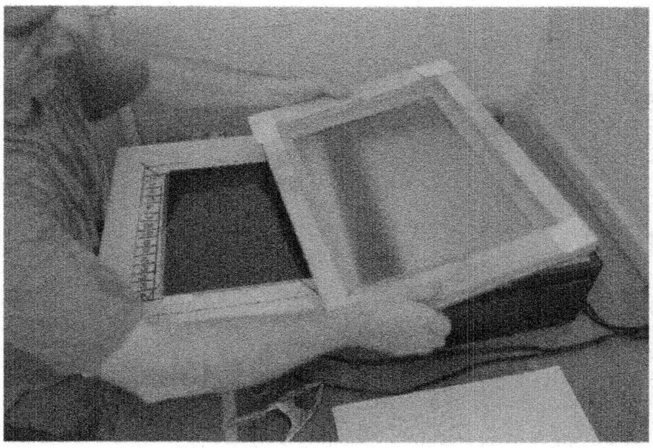

(image 5-13) Carefully unclamp and remove the glass. Do not allow the screen or the plate to move in this process.

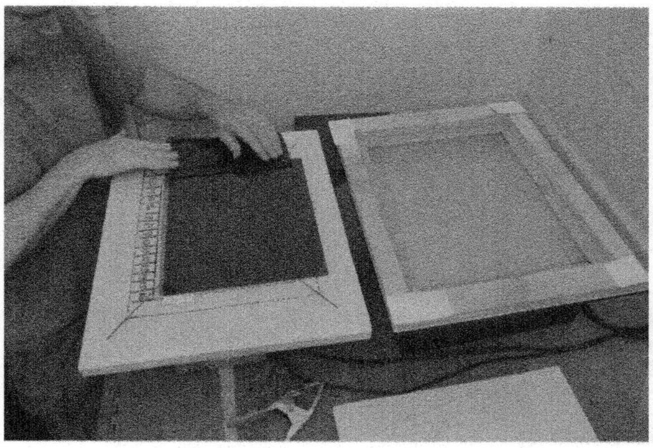

(image 5-14) Using the light-blocking bag that the plates are shipped in, cover a strip of the plate that was marked with a 2'.

The light-blocking bag goes on top of the stochastic screen. If it went between the screen and the plate, it would create gaps through which light could leak.

Make sure that the edge of the light-blocking bag lines up with the mark that was made on the plate and contact frame. This is how you are tracking the exposure times.

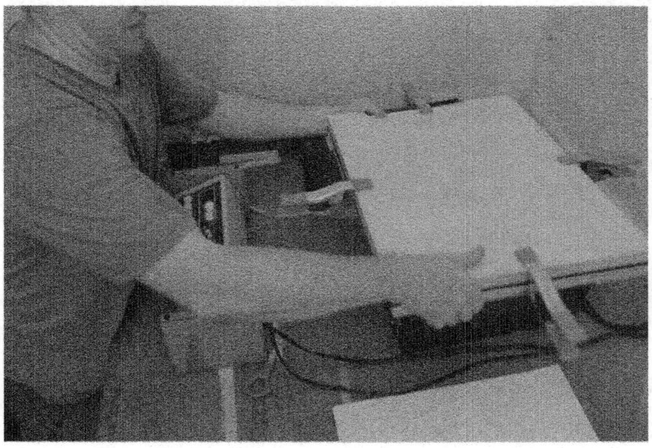

(image 5-15) Clamp the glass on top of the bag (screen, and plate). Place the entire contact frame on top of the UV exposure unit, and expose it for 1 minute.

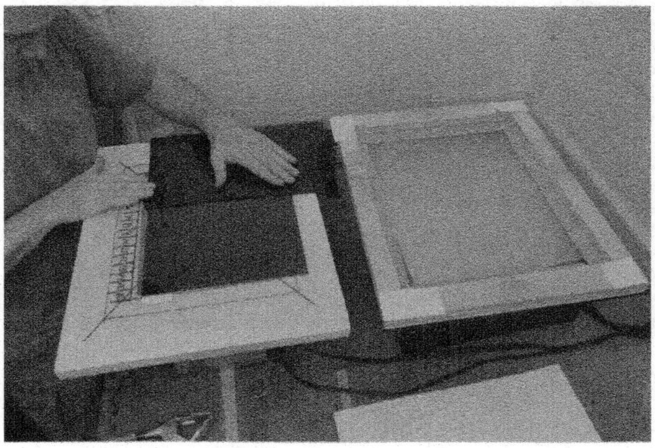

(image 5-16) After the 1 minute exposure, move the light-blocking bag over by one mark. Replace and clamp the glass. Expose for 1 more minute.

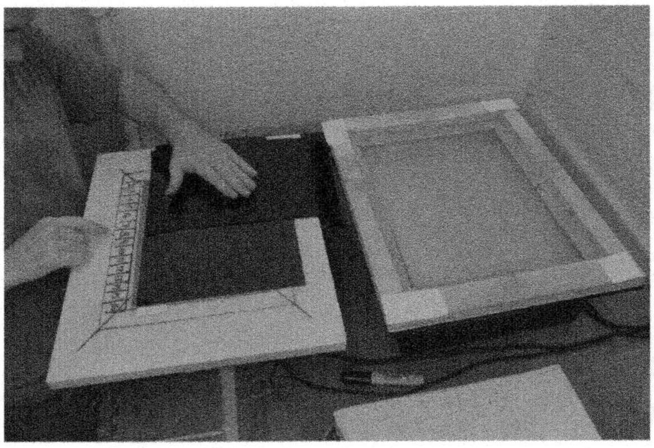

(image 5-17) After the 1 minute exposure, move the light-blocking bag over by one mark. Replace and clamp the glass. Expose for 1 more minute.

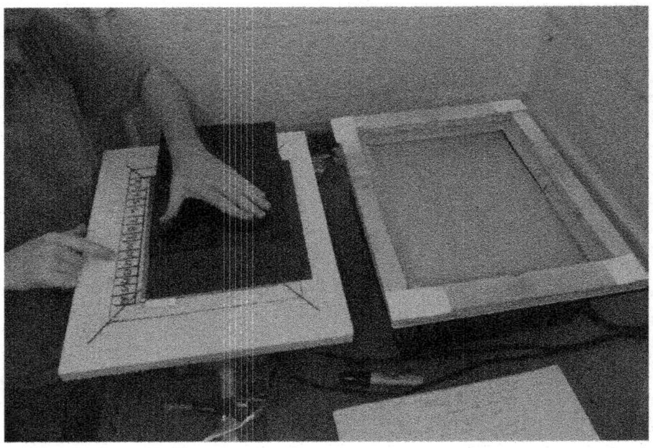

(image 5-18) After the 1 minute exposure, move the light-blocking bag over by one mark. Replace and clamp the glass. Expose for 1 more minute.

This exposure process is additive. The initial exposure of 2 minutes plus any additional time that the section of the plate is left uncovered. 2 minutes, +1= 3minutes, +1= 4 minutes, +1= 5 minutes, +1= 6minutes, +1= 7minutes, +1= 8minutes, +1= 9minutes, +1= 10minutes, +1= 11minutes, +1= 12minutes, +1= 13minutes, +1= 14minutes, +1= 15minutes, +1= 16minutes. If you have some data that gives you an idea of how long your exposure needs to be, you may choose a smaller time range for your experiements, and work with shorter intervals, to achieve finer results.

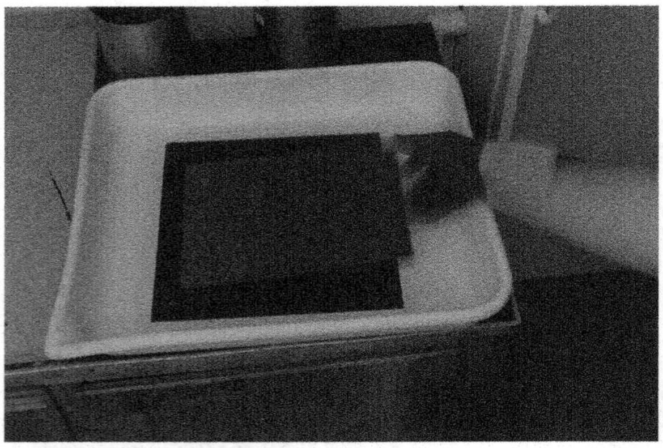

(image 5-19) After making all of the exposures, place the plate in water and let it sit for 1 minute.

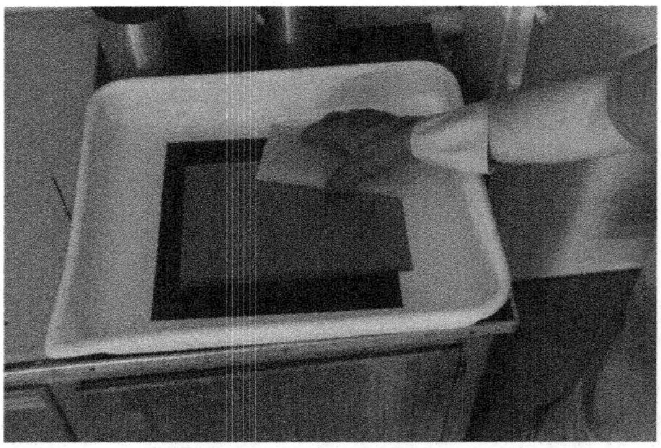

(image 5-20) Gently move the soft brush across the surface of the plate to remove unexposed polymer for 1 minute.

This entire washout process only takes 2 minutes: 1 minute soaking, 1 minute gently brushing. The brushing process is not a scrubbing process. The brush should move back and forth across the plate in a varying pattern with no more weight on it than the weight of your resting and relaxed hand. (see chapter 1)

Caution: *wear gloves for this part of the process. These commercial plates were not designed for handling with bare hands.*

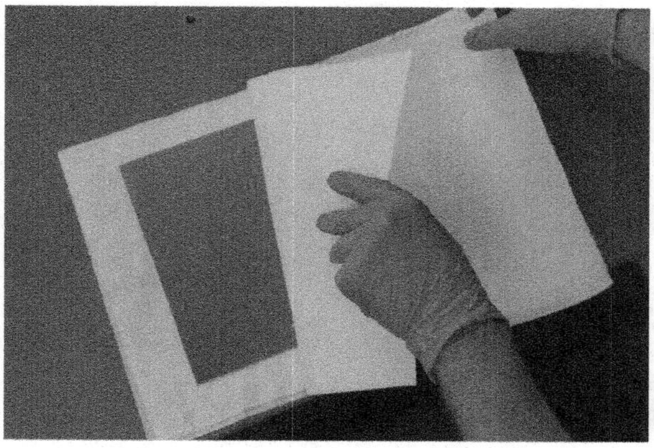

(image 5-21) Immediately after washout, bring the plate over to a flat surface and dry it with paper towels.

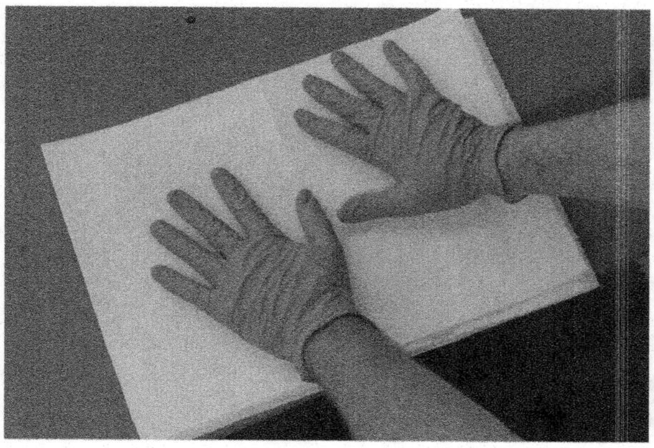

(image 5-22) Gently pat the paper towels to quickly absorb most of the water.

Wet polymer plates are still not 100% cured, and are vulnerable to over-handling. Remove the water quickly and gently. Do not scrub the plate or you will ruin the dot matrix that has been created by the stochastic screen.

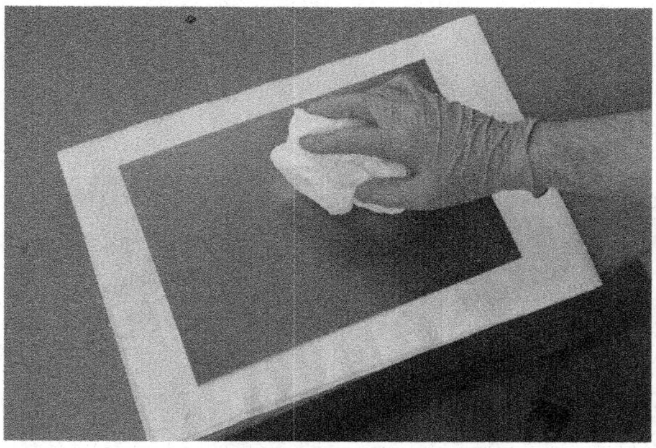

(image 5-23) Crunch the paper towels into a ball, quickly and carefully blot the rest of the water from the plate.

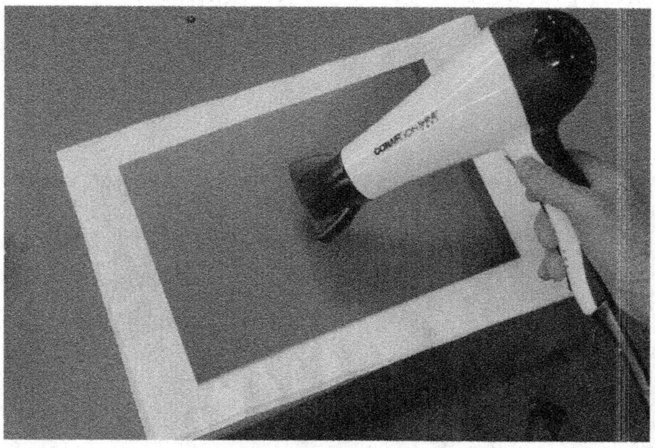

(image 5-24) Run a hairdrier across the plate for 5 - 9 minutes. This will heat cure the polymer on the plate.

This part of the process is tricky. Applying too much pressure with the paper towels will leave an impression on the polymer plate. Any water that is nzot removed from the plate quickly will leave marks as well. Set up paper towels before beginning the exposure process so that they are ready to go as soon as the plate comes out of the washout tray.

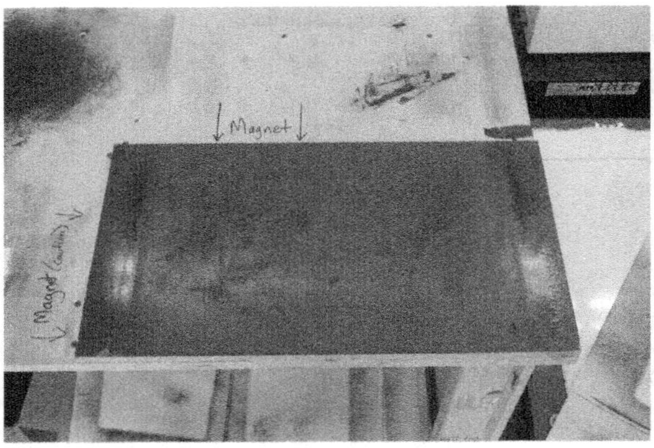

(image 5-25) Prepare the magnetic work surface for printing.

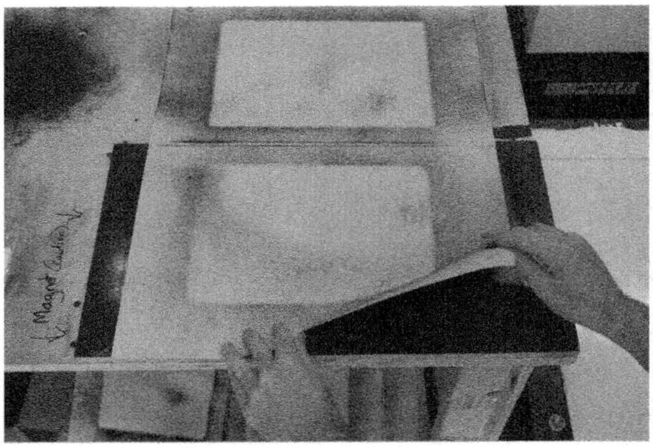

(image 5-26) Placing a piece of newsprint over the magnetic surface will help keep the work area clean, and allow you to pick up the steel-backed polymer plate easily.

The polymer plate must still be post-exposed (after being fully heat-cured) before printing. The post-exposure time is at least as long as the base exposure time. Since this experiment is about finding the yet-to-be-known base exposure time, then it is better to err on the side of caution. Let the heat-cured plate sit in a sunny window for an hour. After that exposure to sunlight, post-expose the plate for the same amount of time as the longest exposure time in the experiment (in this example: 16 minutes) More is explained in chapter 1.

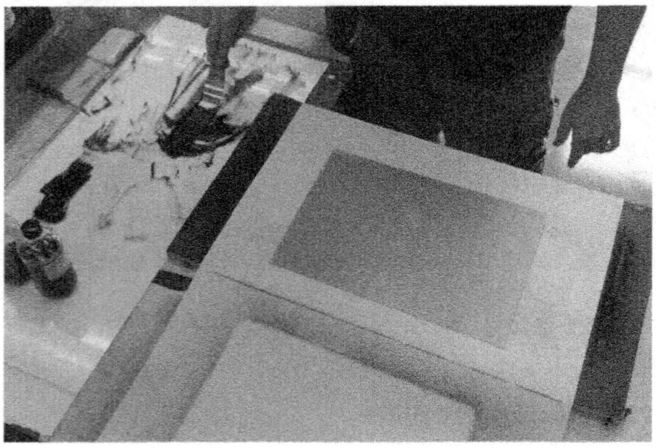

(image 5-27) Prepare ink for printing.

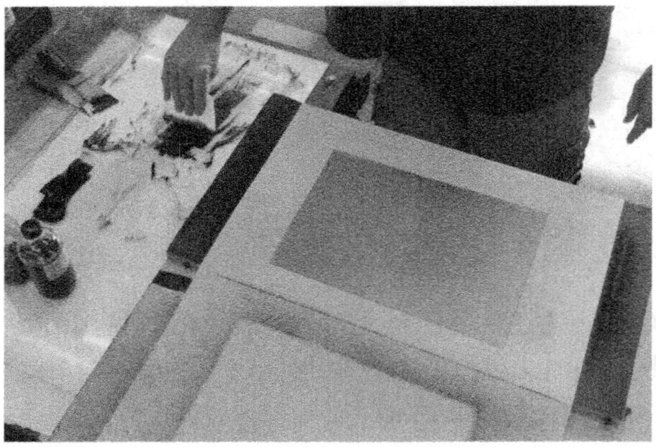

(image 5-28) Use a soft plastic scraper to pick up the prepared ink.

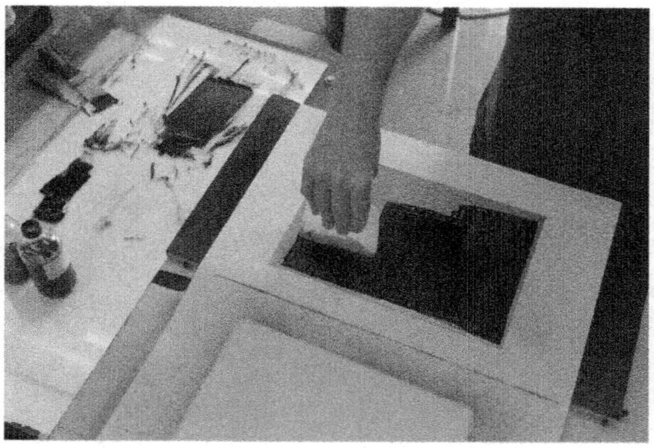

(image 5-29) Spread ink on the plate.

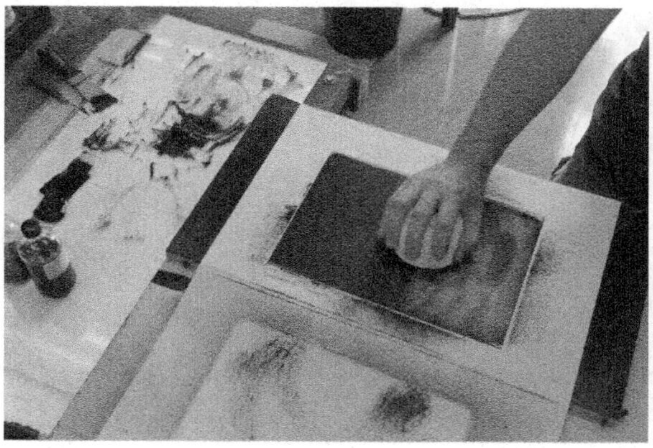

(image 5-30) Wipe plate with tarlatan.

Note: *Some steps are skipped, with the assumption that you have read other chapters about preparing ink, inking and wiping a plate, and printing. These selected steps have been left in this chapter so that you can see the overall workflow involved with finding the base exposure time.*
chapter 1 Main Workflow: (includes all missing steps for inking and printing)
chapter 9 Preparing Paper
chapter 11 Preparing Ink
chapter 12 Folding Tarlatan
chapter 13 Inking tips

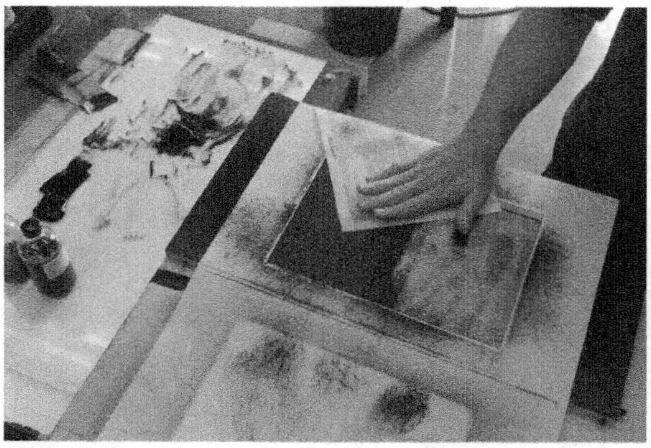

(image 5-31) Final wipe with pieces of phone book or tissue paper.

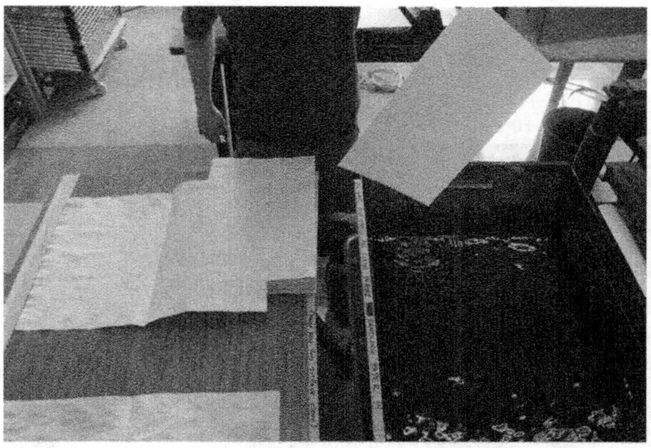

(image 5-32) Get a piece of paper.

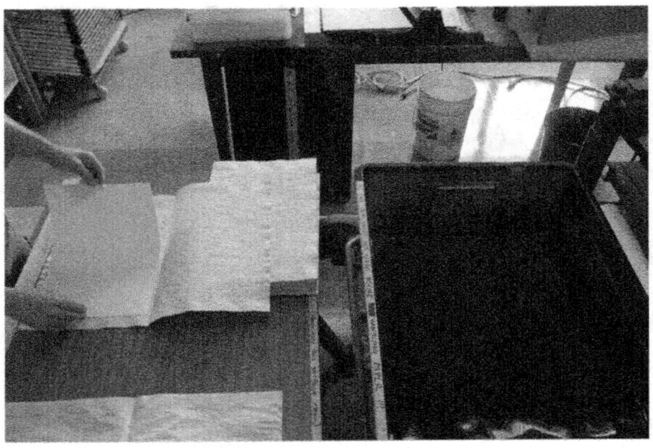

(image 5-33) Place paper on blotter.

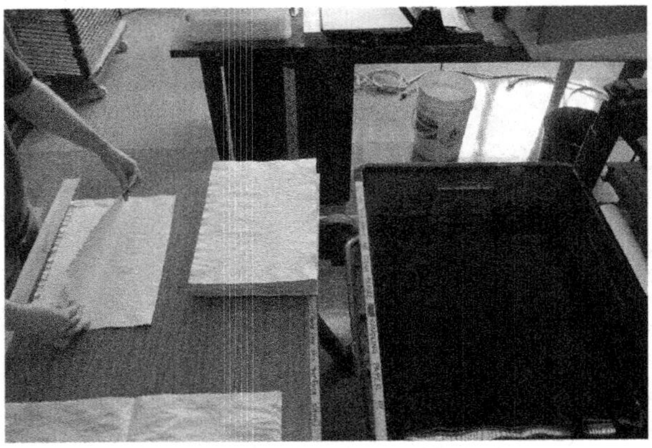

(image 5-34) Blot the paper once.

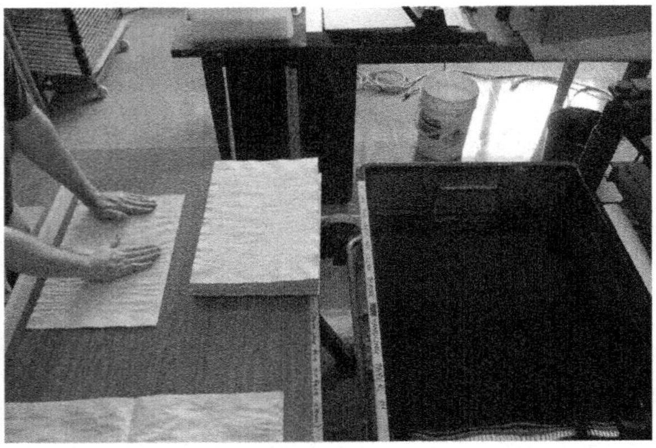

(image 5-35) Blot the paper again.

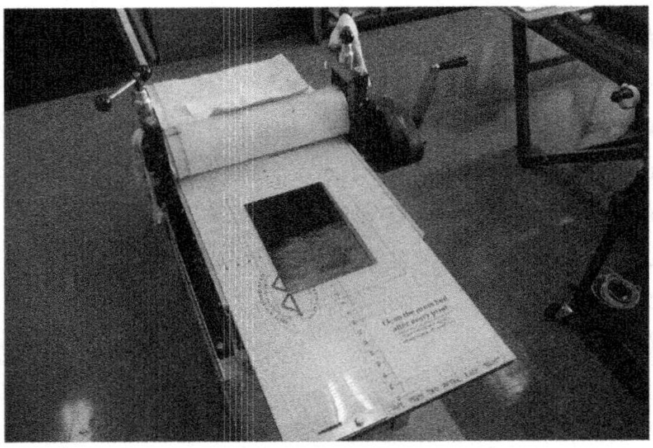

(image 5-36) Center the inked plate on the bed of the press.

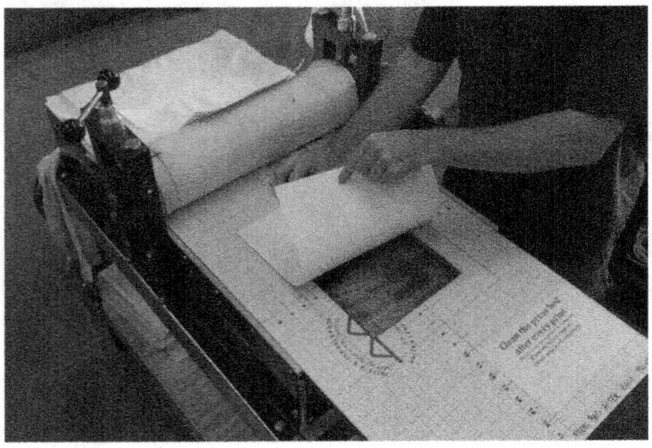

(image 5-37) Place the piece of blotted print-making paper over the inked plate.

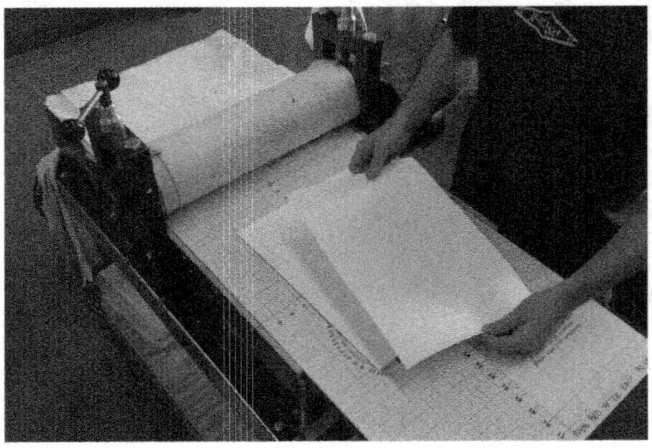

(image 5-38) Place a second piece of print-making paper (dry) over the blotted print-making paper.

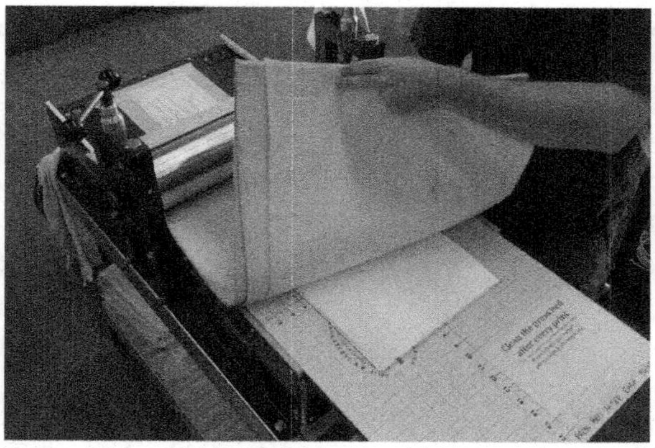

(image 5-39) Pull the wool blankets over the paper and plates. Run everything through the press to make a print.

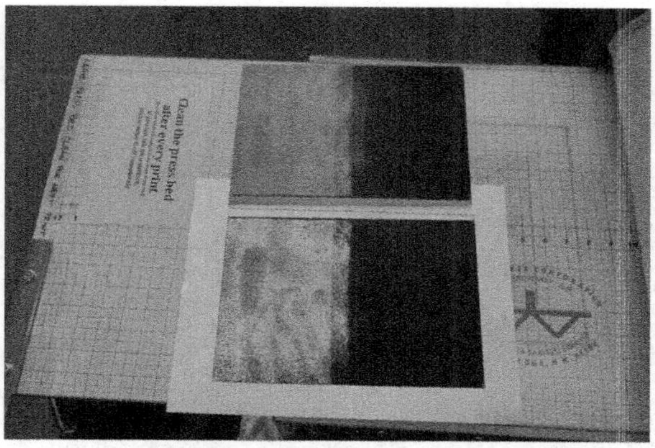

(image 5-40) Compare the print with the plate. Look for the first strip that prints 100% black. Note the exposure time for that strip.

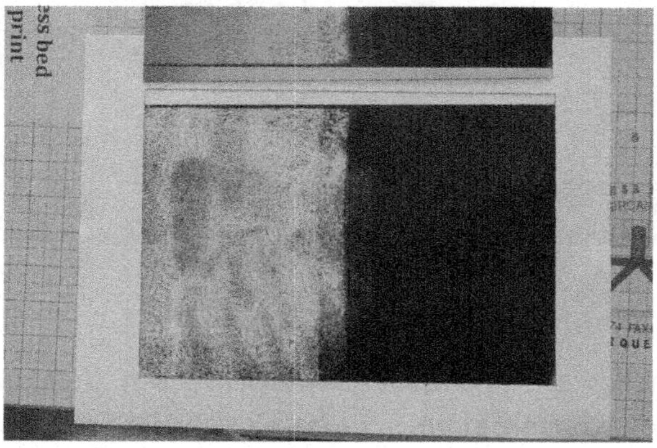

(image 5-41) Paper towel pattern will show up in the print because of the underexposed areas in the polymer plate. Do not worry about this pattern in this test plate.

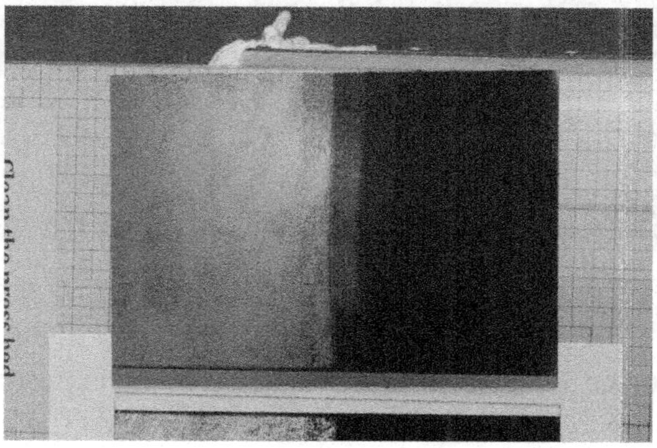

(image 5-42) Do not clean the plate right away. It contains valuable information that is easier to read when it has ink in it after printing.

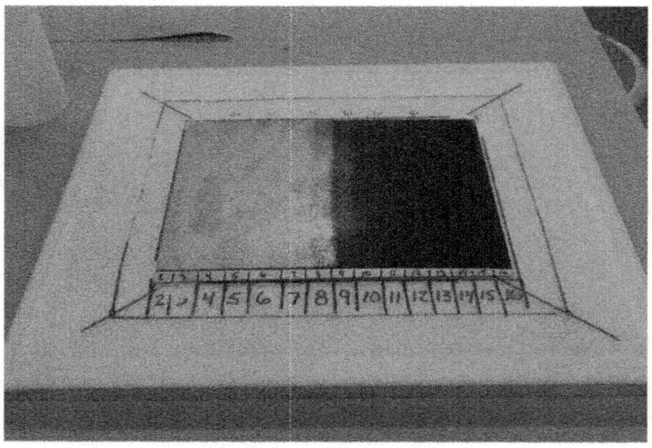

(image 5-43) Place the inked plate on to the contact frame and match the numbers.

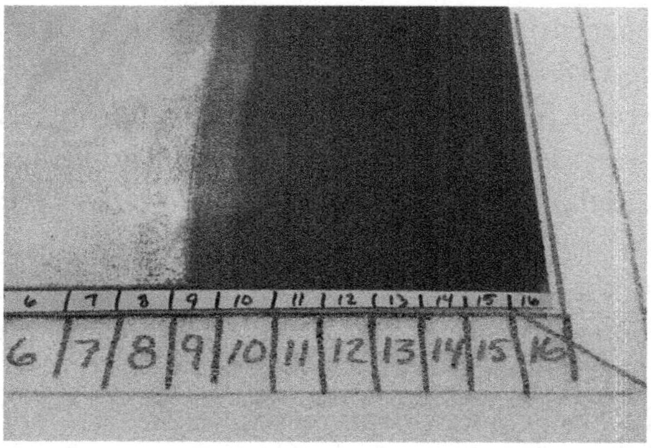

(image 5-44) In the print, 10 minutes seems to be the time needed. Looking at this plate, however, seems to indicate that there is some more density in longer times.

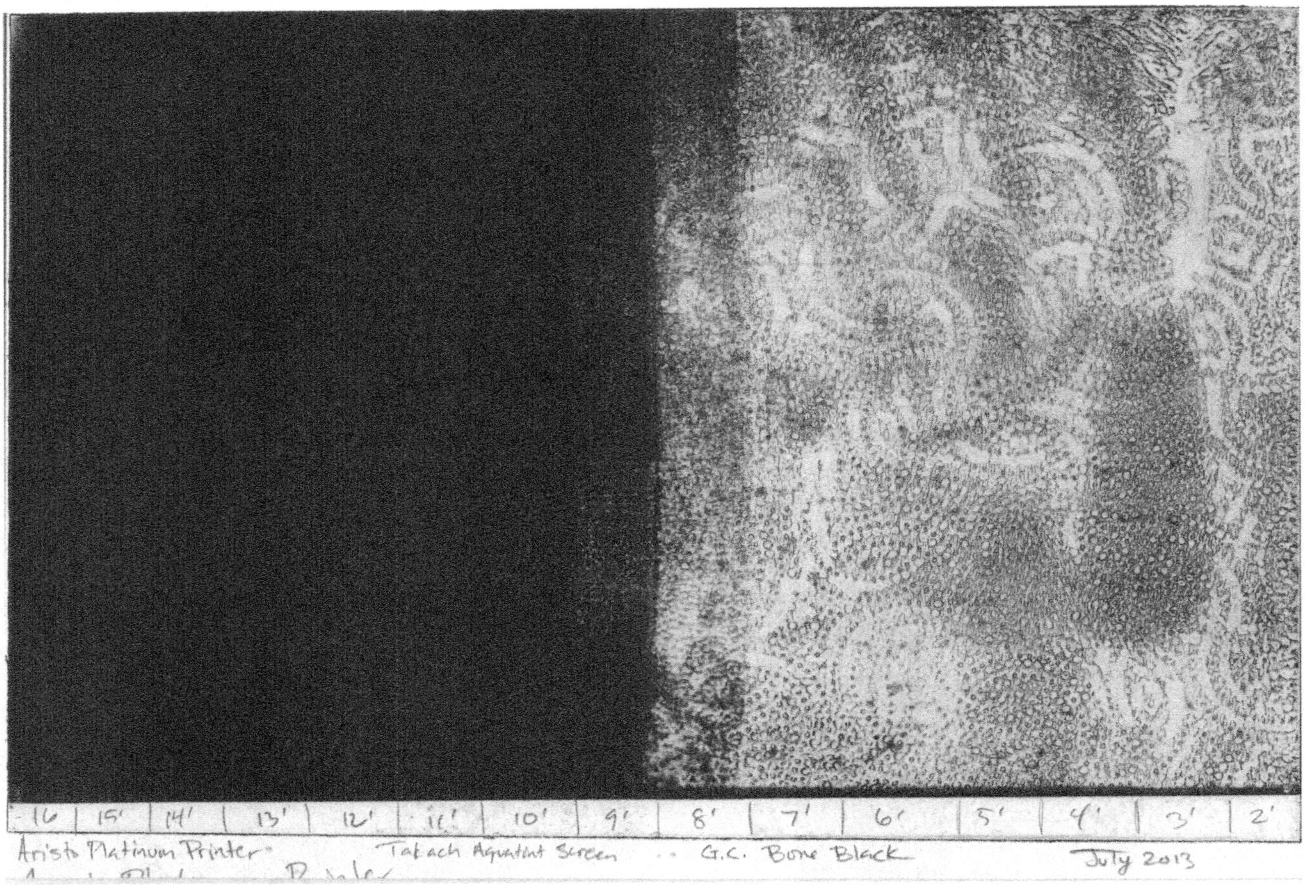

(image 5-45) 10 minutes is the shortest exposure that acheives 100% black in this print. But, there is more to it than just reaching 100% black. The minimum exposure time is the base exposure time, but it is not the optimum exposure time. Looking at the plate, which still has ink in it (image 5-44), indicates that the 10 minute strip has a rough aquatint pattern. Longer exposure times still print 100% black, but the plate shows a finer aquatint pattern. A finer aquatint pattern will yield better tonal range in later steps.

Under such high printing pressure, ink blurs and blends a bit. This blending compensates for some imprefections in the aquatint pattern on the plate. But, it only compensates for 100-90% black. The imperfections start to show at 80% and lighter. After experimenting with a few different exposure units, having run this base exposure time experiment several times, I have developed a formula that provides an optimum exposure time. The optimum exposure time is one that produces an aquatint pattern that most accurately matches the pattern of the stochastic screen.

minimum exposure time x 1.6 = optimum exposure time

I use the optimum exposure time as the time for both the stochastic screen exposure and the image exposure. For the experiment in this chapter the minimum exposure time (a.k.a. base exposure time) is 10 minutes. To find the optimum exposure time, multiply 10 minutes by 1.6 to get 16 minutes. I'd use 16 minutes for the stochastic screen exposure, and 16 minutes for the image exposure.

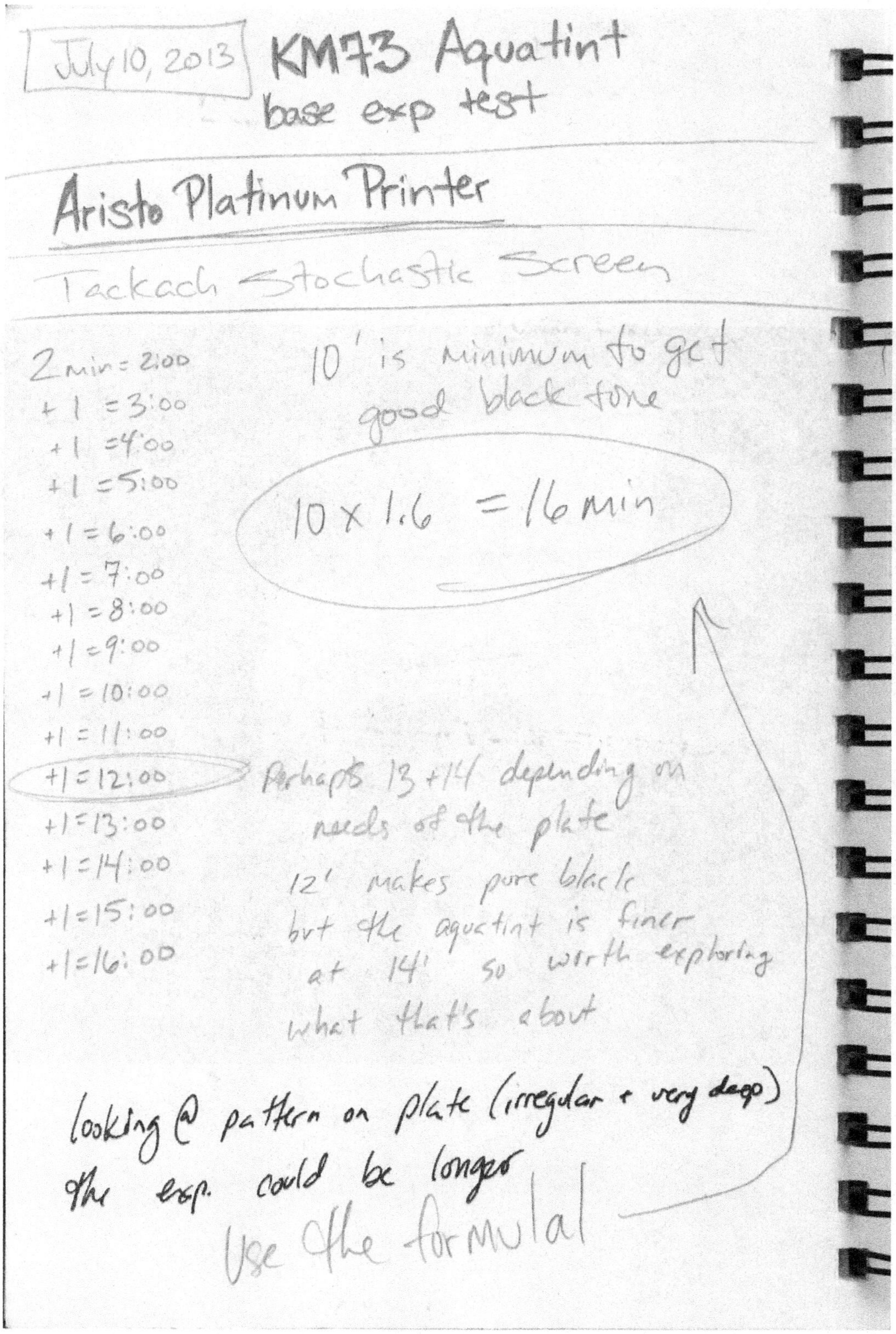

(image 5-46) Here are the notes from the experiment run in this chapter.

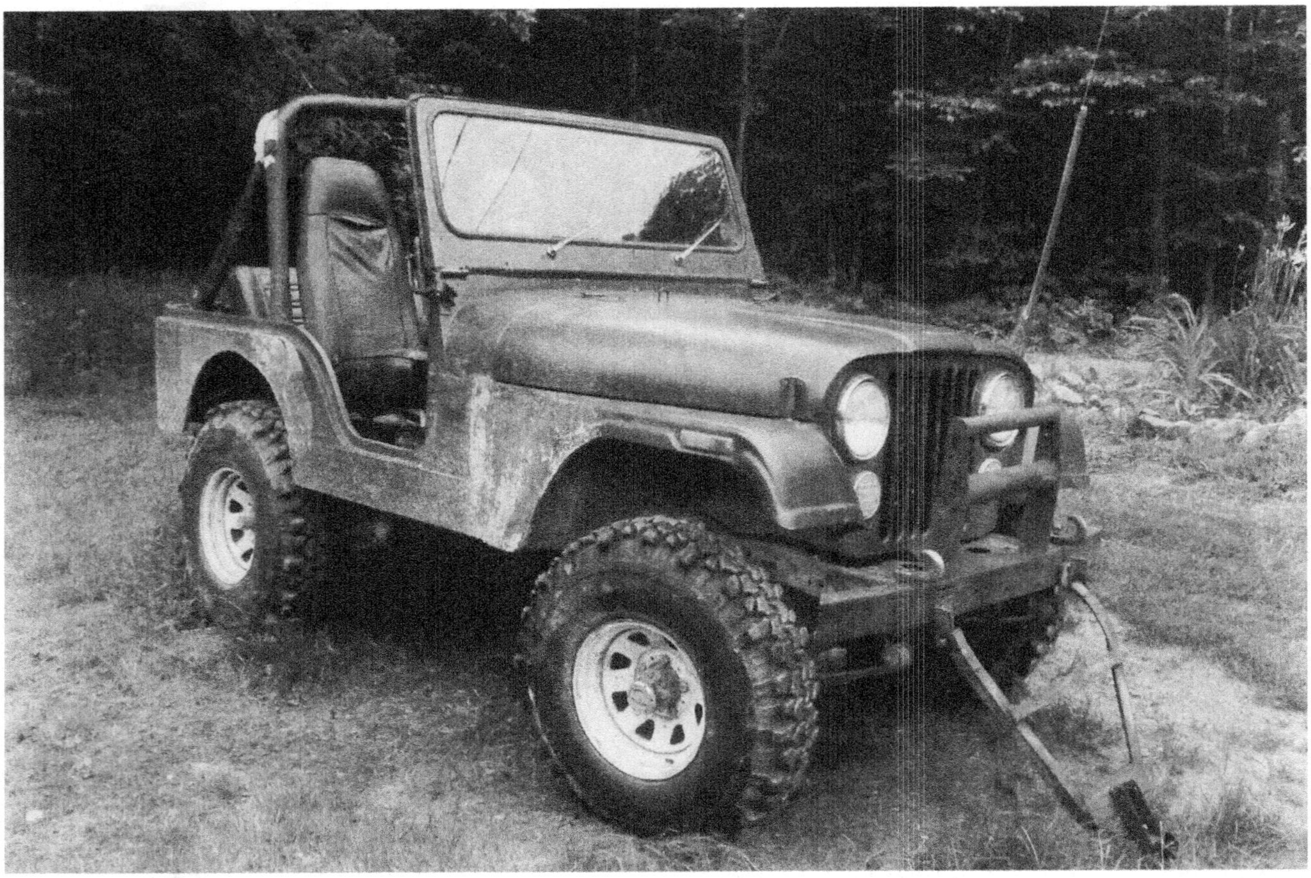

"Jeep"

photogravure

Scott Barnes

Chapter 6
Inkjet Printer Settings

The quality of plate that is produced relies heavily on the quality of image transparency that is made. Film positives will make beautiful plates. This book assumes that most people do not have access to the equipment needed to make film positives. Using inkjet printers is increasingly the norm with both alternative photographic printing processes and the commercial printing industry. Regardless of who's method you choose to use, maintaining consistent settings is the only way to ensure repeatable results.

The inkjet printer settings that I use have already been revealed in chapter 2. Posting the settings as a separate chapter is intended to make them easier to find when needed. The over riding principle is to turn off as many automatic adjustments as possible, and make sure that Adobe Photoshop (or whichever software you use) controls the image, and not the printer. Here are the settings I use for the Epson Stylus Pro Photo 3800 inkjet printer, through Adobe Photoshop 5 on a PC.

File --> Print --> Print Settings

--> Media Type: Premium Glossy Photo Paper
--> Color: Color
--> Print Quality --> Quality Options: Speed 5 (quality)
Print Quality: 2880 x 1440 dpi
Microweave: On
High Speed: Off
Edge Smoothing: Off
Finest Detail: Off

--> Paper Config --> Color Density: 0
Dry Time: +3 (or longer)
Paper Feed Adjust: 0
Paper Thickness: 3
Platen Gap: Auto

--> Mode: Custom --> No Color Adjustment

--> Paper Settings --> Source --> Sheet
Size --> (just choose the correct size)

--> Print Preview: On

The settings on the previous page can be saved as a preset. I have it saved as "Digital Negatives", and only have to find this preset instead of having to reset each time I print.

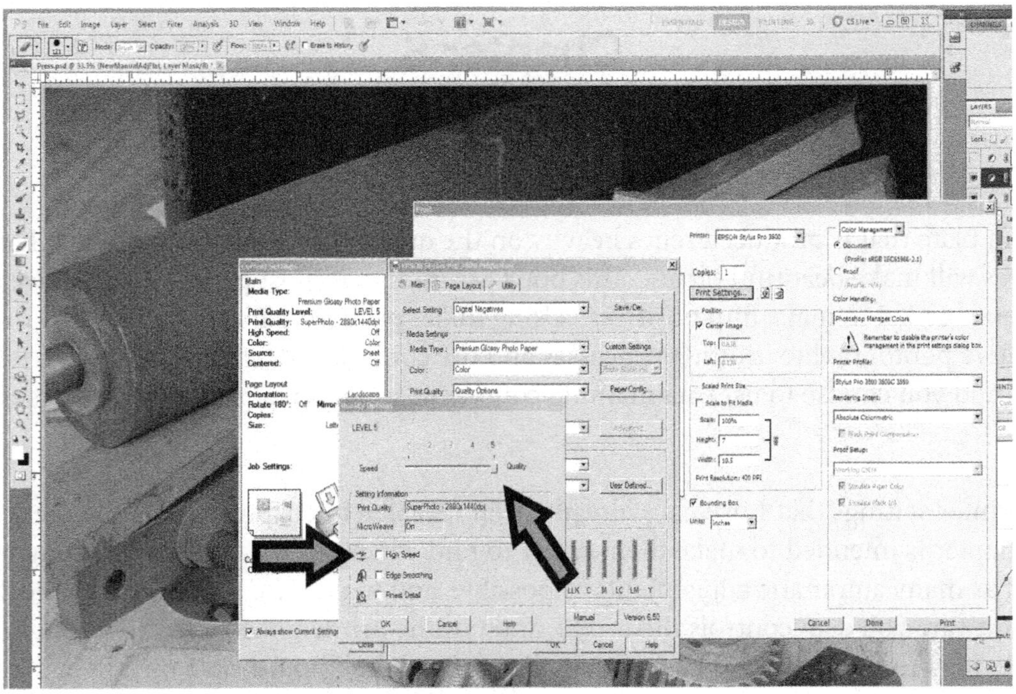

(image 6-01) This is the menu found through the path
File --> **Print** --> **Print Settings** --> **Print Quality** --> **Quality Options**

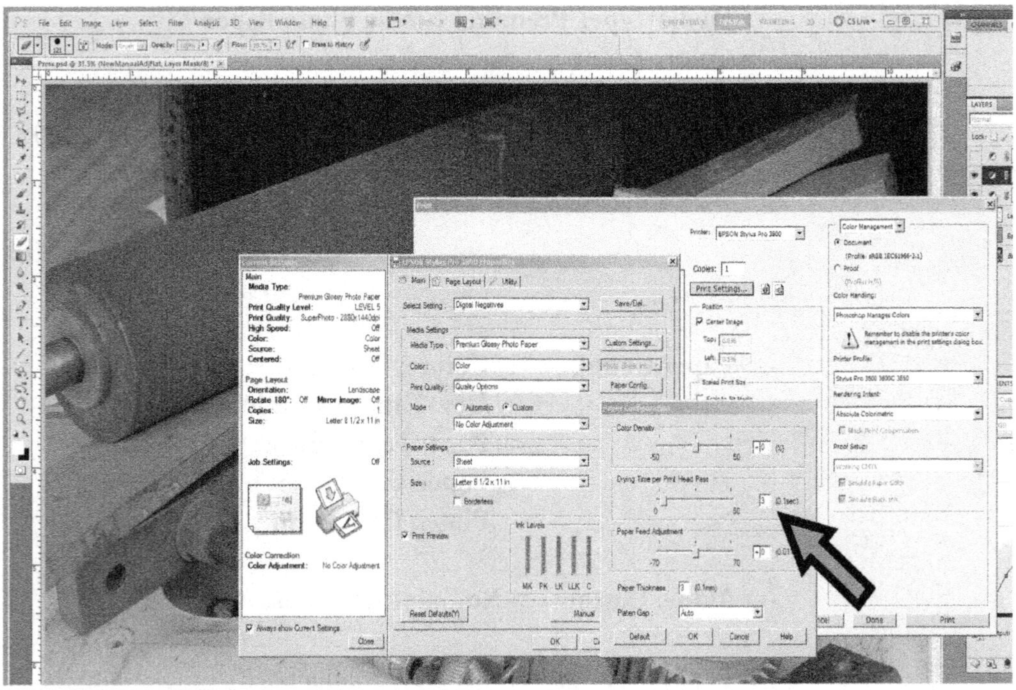

(image 6-02) This is the menu found through the path
File --> **Print** --> **Print Settings** --> **Paper Config...**

There are a few settings that cannot be saved, and must be checked before every image is printed.

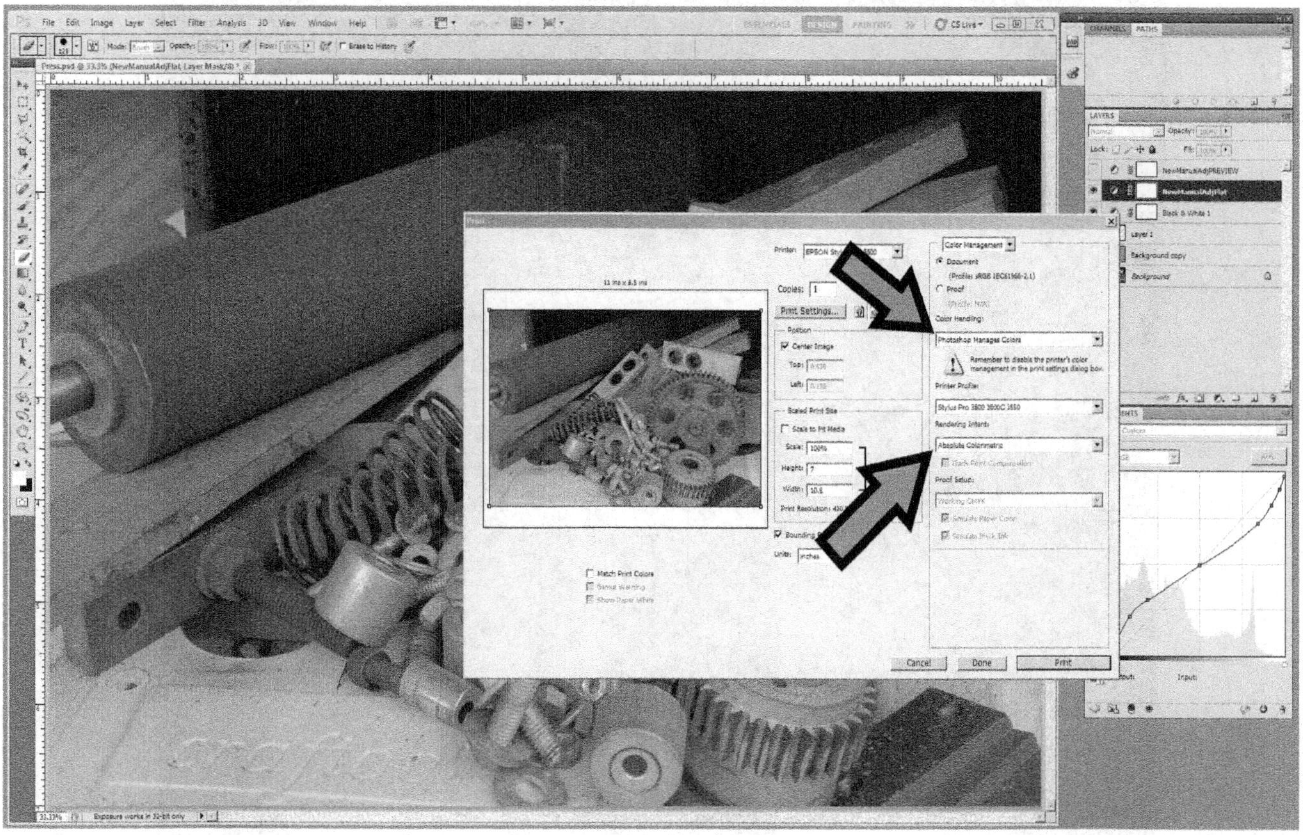

(image 6-03) This is the initial menu that shows up through File --> Print.
The settings in the center of the print window can be named and saved (as mentioned in the previous two pages). The settings on the right of the print window (where the arrows are) has to be checked with every print job. I use the following setting for this color management window:

Document radio button is **on.** This tells the printer that you want to print with the same color profile as that is embedded in the document.
(notice that the profile of the image file shows up beneath this option)

Proof radio button is **off**.

Color Handling: **Photoshop Manage Colors**

Printer Profiles: **Stylus Pro 3800 3800C 3850** (this is my printer, be sure to choose your printer)

Rendering Intent: **Absolute Colorimetric**
Black Point Compensation: Off
Proof Setup: should be faded, meaning that it is not on or available

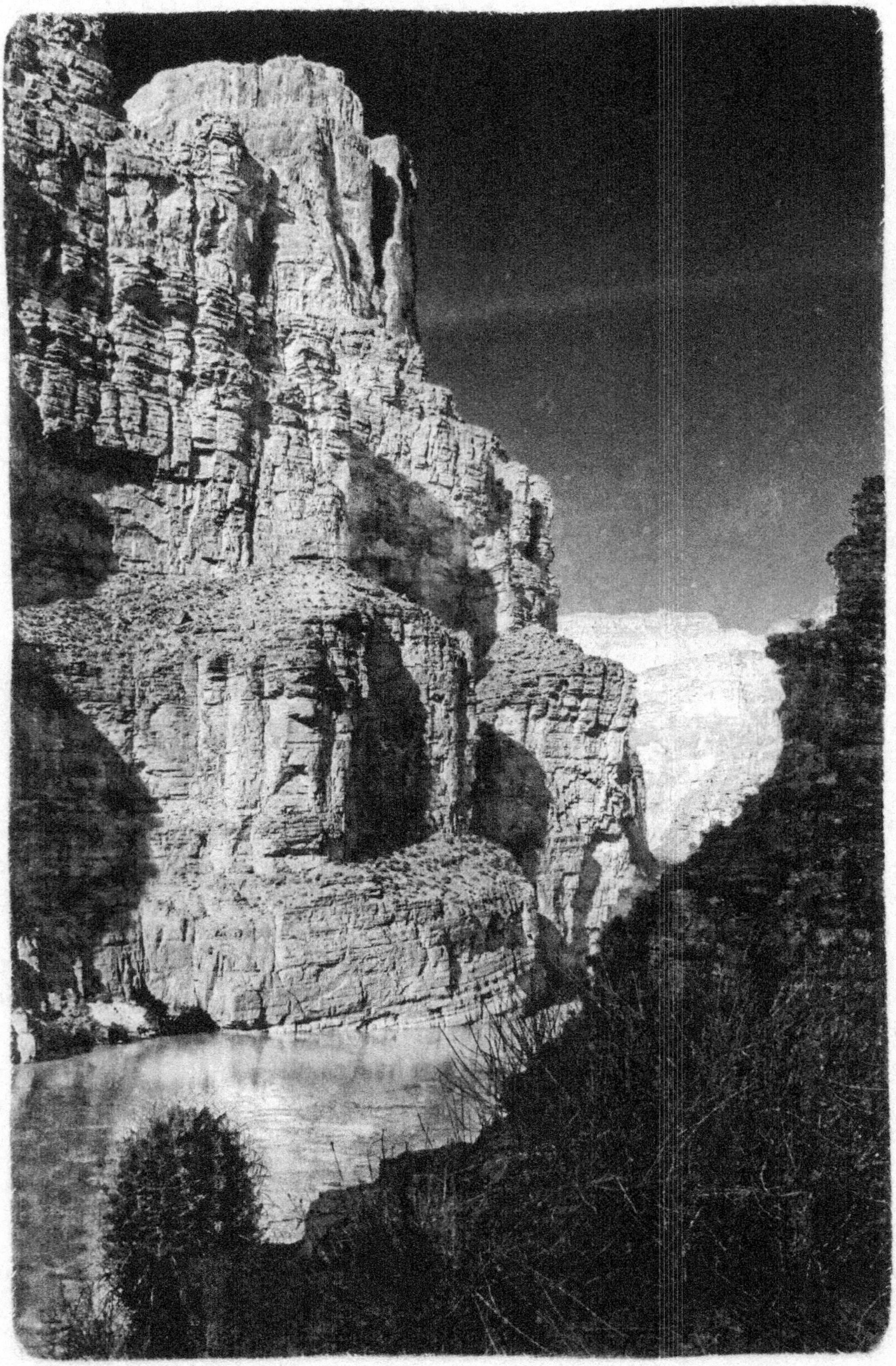

"Cactus East"

photogravure

Scott Barnes

Chapter 7
Image Exposure Time

The work flow shown in this book involves a double exposure technique for burning an image to the KM73 plate. Both the **Base Exposure Time** ("screen") and the **Image Exposure Time** ("image") must be found. Frequently, the times are the same. But, going through the extra steps of finding a separate Image Exposure Time will make sure that both times are correct and the highest quality plate is made.

Over the years, I have figured out the Image Exposure Time in three ways:

1. **Parity Option:** Assume that the time needed for image exposure is the same as time needed for the initial aquatint exposure. This frequently works, but it does not provide much data for troubleshooting.

2. **Basic Option:** Find the Base Exposure Time needed to make a good aquatint matrix. Use that time to make a good aquatint on a new plate, then make variable exposures of an image to that same plate.

3. **Advanced Option:** Find the Base Exposure Time needed to make a good aquatint matrix. Use that time to build an experiment in which both the exposure to the stochastic screen and the exposure to the image transpareny is varied. This seems complicated, but it is just a more controlled version of the previous experimcent.

Some notes on nomenclature:

"Base Exposure Time" is used to mean the same thing as **"screen time"**, which is just shorthand for **"aquatint screen time"** and **"stochastic screen time"** or simply **"screen".**

"Image Exposure Time" is the same things as **"image time"** or **"transparency time"**, or simply **"image".**

It seems confusing, but I am using these interchangeably to expose you to the varied nomenclature found in help forums, social media, and the writings of other artists.

Parity option:

The parity option is not shown in this chapter, because this chapter would not be needed for that option.

Basic Option:

The first part of this chapter demonstrates the basic option, using my home made contact frame and an old Aristo Platinum Printer. Here is how the experiment was set up.

Base Exposure Time of :
13 minutes
Image Exposure Times of:
1 minute less than the Base Exposure Time (13 - 1 = 12 minutes)
The same time as the Base Exposure Time (13 minutes)
1 minute more than the Base Exposure Time (13 + 1 = 14 minutes)
2 minutes more than the Base Exposure Time (13 + 2 = 15 minutes)

The notes I wrote on the back of the plate are:
Screen: 13'
Image: 12', 13', 14', 15'
Fixxons transparency
Aristo Platinum Printer
Epson 3800

Advanced Option:

The second part of this chapter reveals the advanced option that varies the initial Base Exposure Time ("screen" time), as well as the Image Exposure Time. It uses a transparency that has a series of step wedges that will create a useful exposure grid on the KM73 plate.

First, the plate is exposed to the stochastic screen for three different potential screen times, then five different potential image times.
(screen) Base Exposure Times of: 12 minutes, 13 minutes, 14 minutes
(image) Image Exposure Times of: 11 minutes, 12 minutes, 13 minutes, 14 minutes, 15 minutes

The notes I wrote on the back of the plate are:
Screen: 12' 13' 14'
Image: 11' 12' 13' 14' 15'
Fixxons transparency
Aristo Platinum Printer
Epson 3800

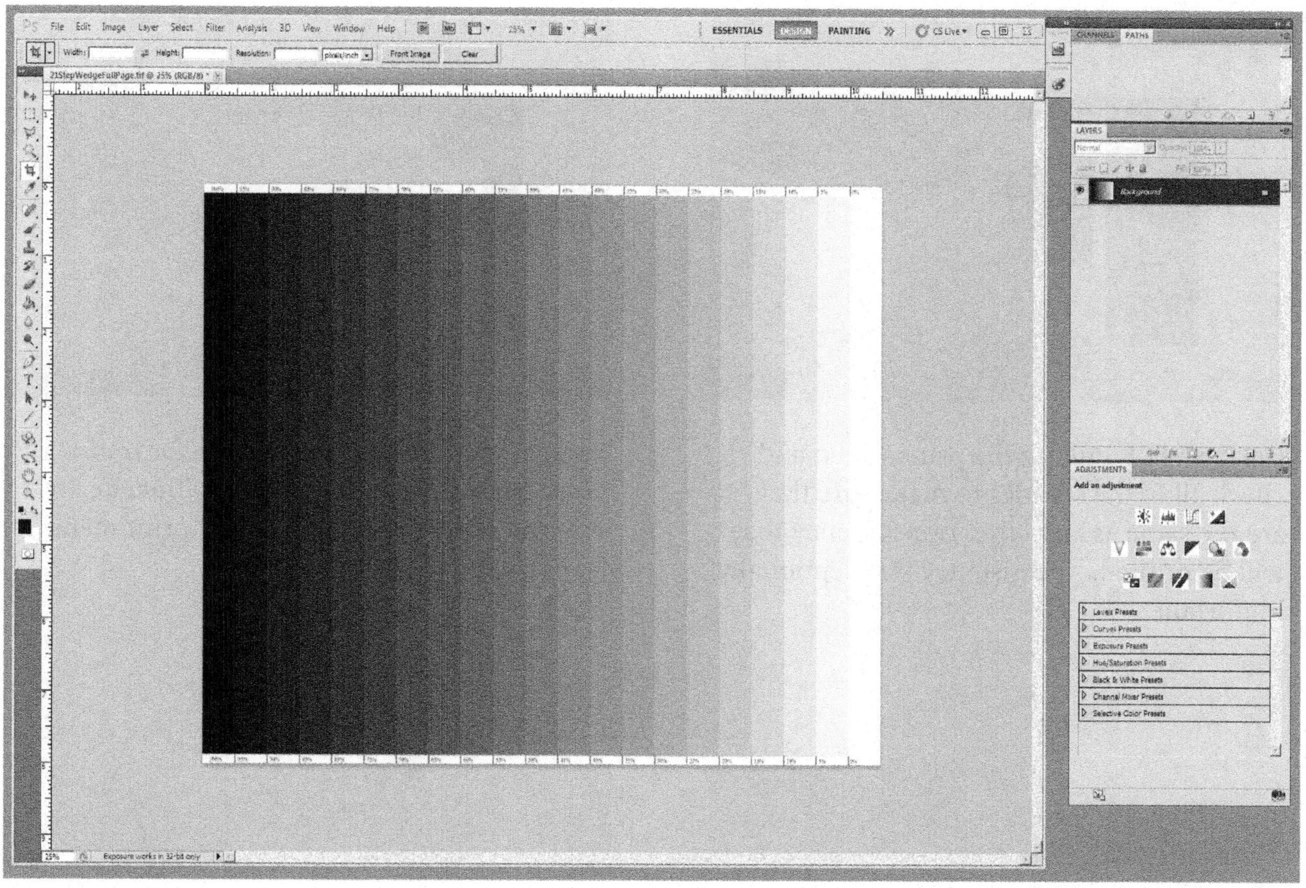

Basic Option

(image 7-01) Choose an image with enough tonal range to provide useful feedback. A digital step wedge will provide the most reliable information. Print that image with the same settings used for all other images (chapters 1 & 6).

The image in this example fits on an 8.5" x 11" piece of transparency. It will cover most of an A4 size KM73 polymer plate.

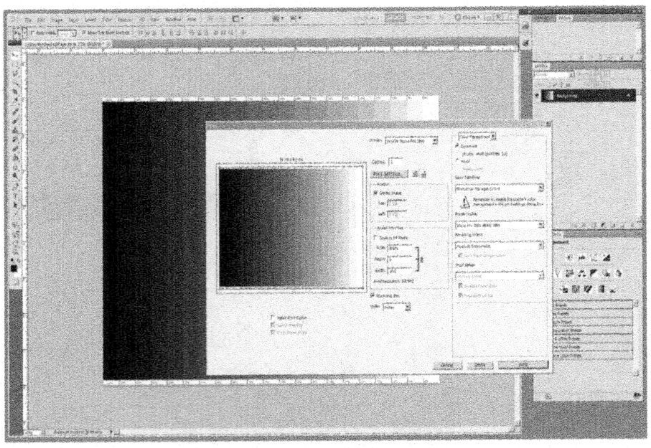

(image 7-02) Pull up the print screen and check all of the settings to make sure they are the same as any other transparency that will be printed. Consistency is exceptionally important.

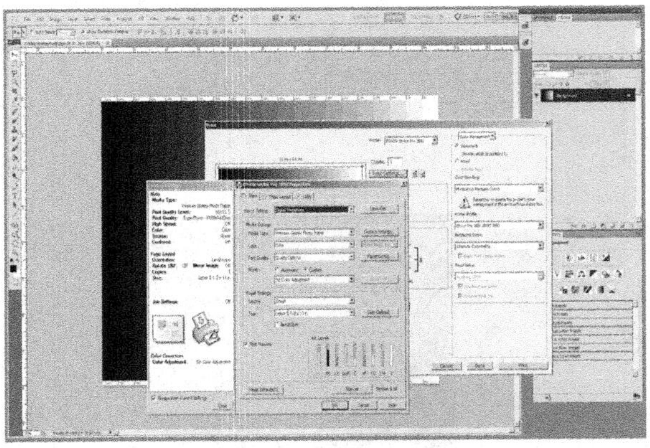

(image 7-03) If the print settings for transparencies are saved (and named) then be sure the setting is selected in the print menu. (see chapter 1 & 6)

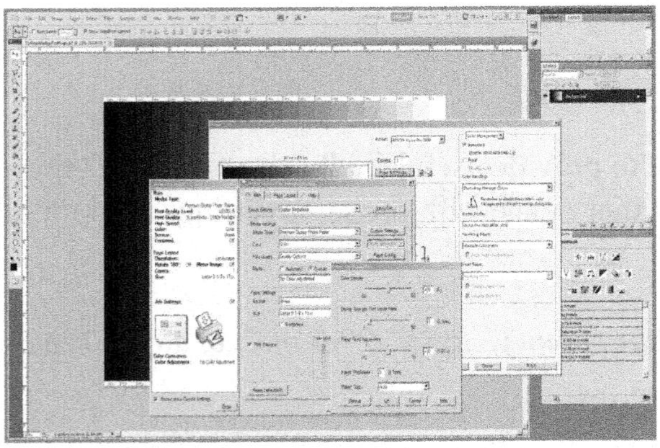

(image 7-04) Be sure the Drying Time per Print Head Pass is increased. It will slow the printing process down, and allow the ink to start to set on the transparency before it runs under the feed mechanism of the printer. The little wheels of the feed mechanism can pick up wet ink, creating a straight pattern that can be seen in the final transparency.

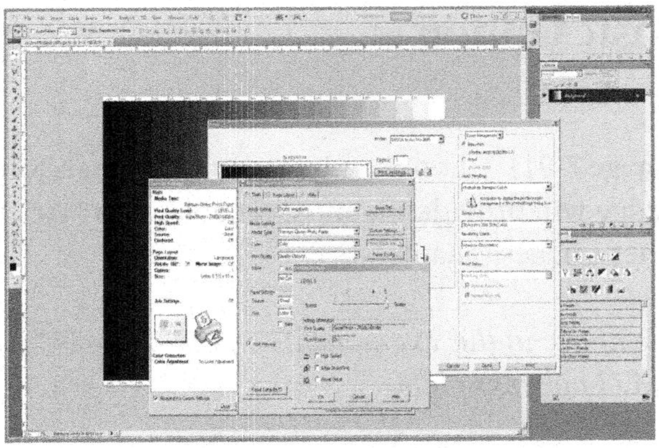

(image 7-05) Turn off high speed, and increase the quality as high as it will go.

Print the transparency and let is fully dry before using it to expose a plate. 24 hours of drying time is ideal, but the process can be sped up with a print drier or hair drier.

Put transparency image on top of polymer plate and mark a few zones for different exposures.

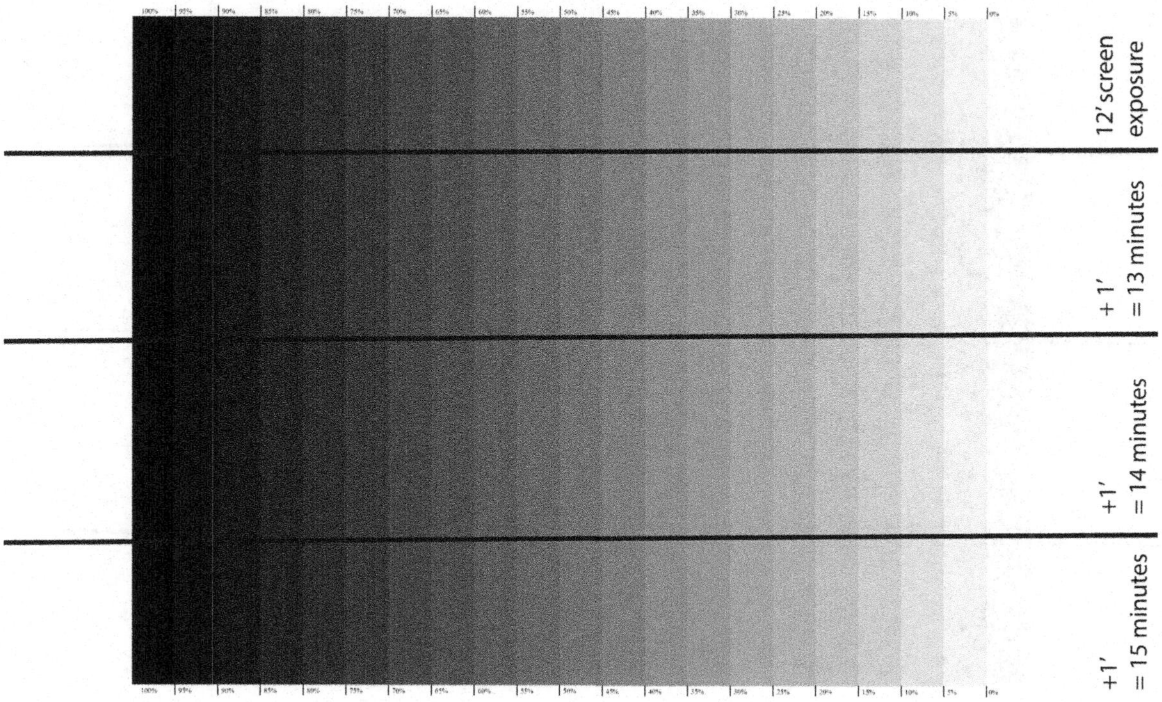

21 step grayscale tablet printed on transparency film with inkjet printer

(image 7-06) Place a polymer plate on the contact frame. Place the transparency on top. Make marks that will not the different exposure times for the experiment.

(image 7-07) Remove the transparency and replace it with the stochastic screen. Expose the stochastic screen for the Base Exposure Time.

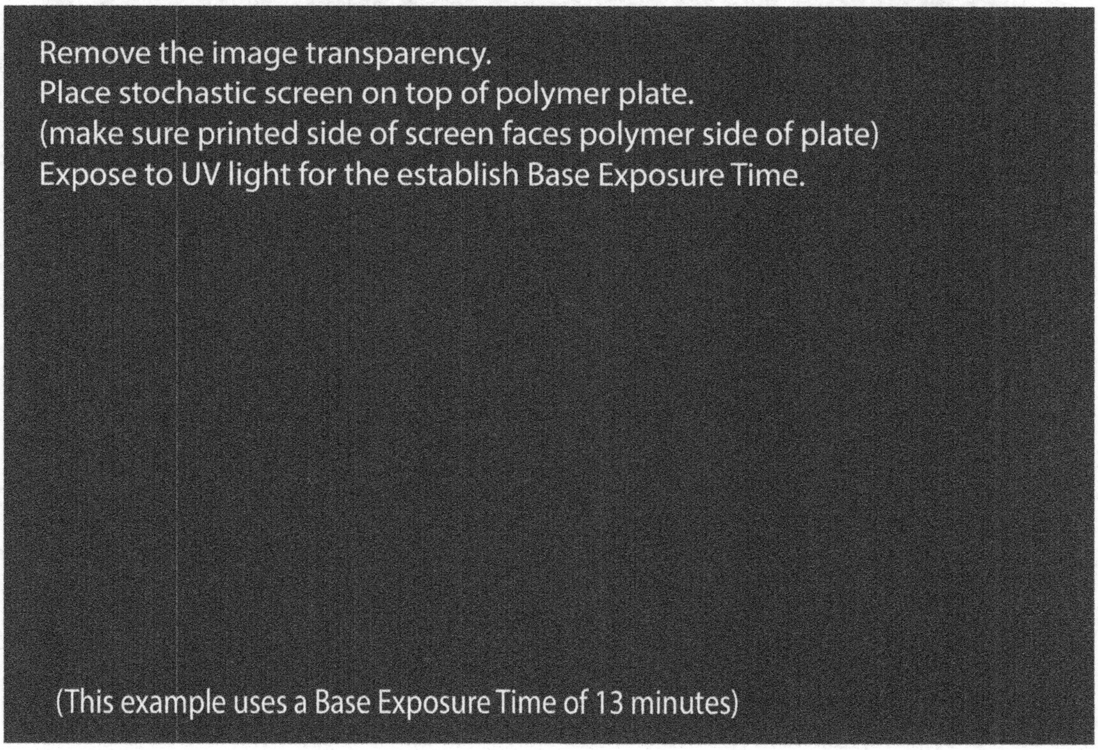

Place the image transparency on top of the polymer plate and make first image exposure to entire plate

21 step grayscale tablet printed on transparency film with inkjet printer

(image 7-08) Remove the stochastic screen and replace it with the image transparency. Line up the transparency with any registration marks you had made on the contact frame. Tape a corner of the transparency so that it does not move. Make the first exposure. **(image 7-09)** Cover the first section of the transparency, and make an additional exposure of 1 minute to the parts that are still not covered by the light-blocking plastic.

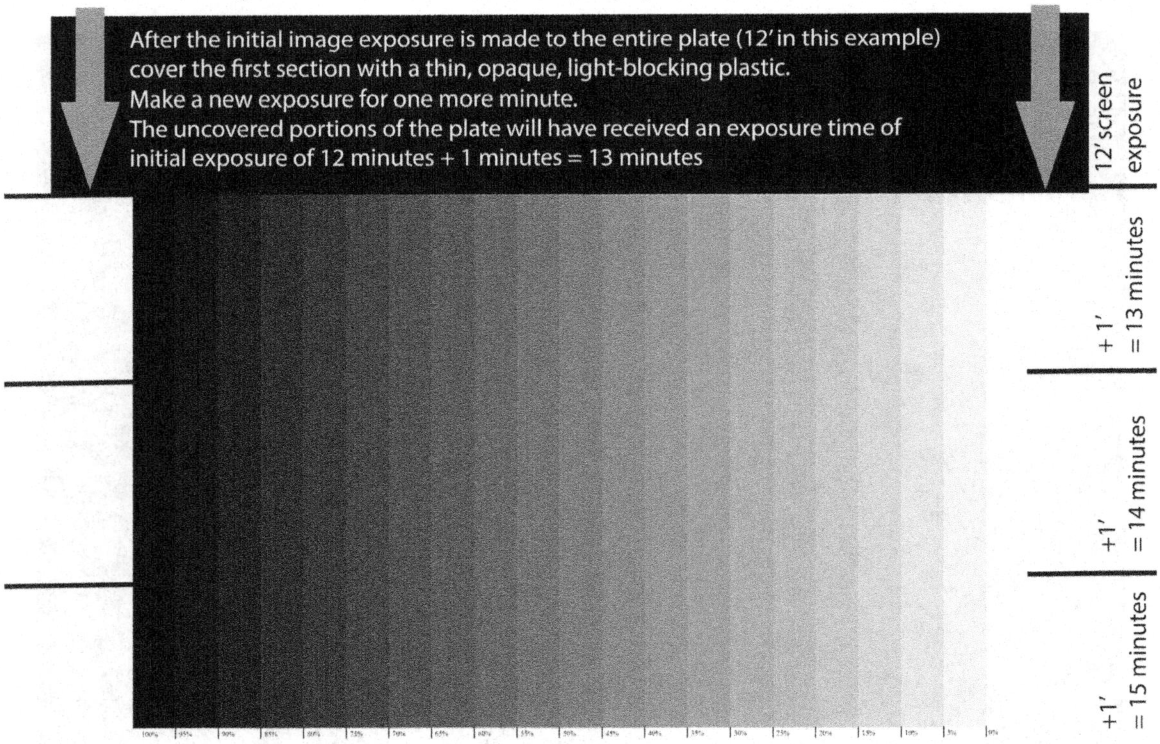

21 step grayscale tablet printed on transparency film with inkjet printer

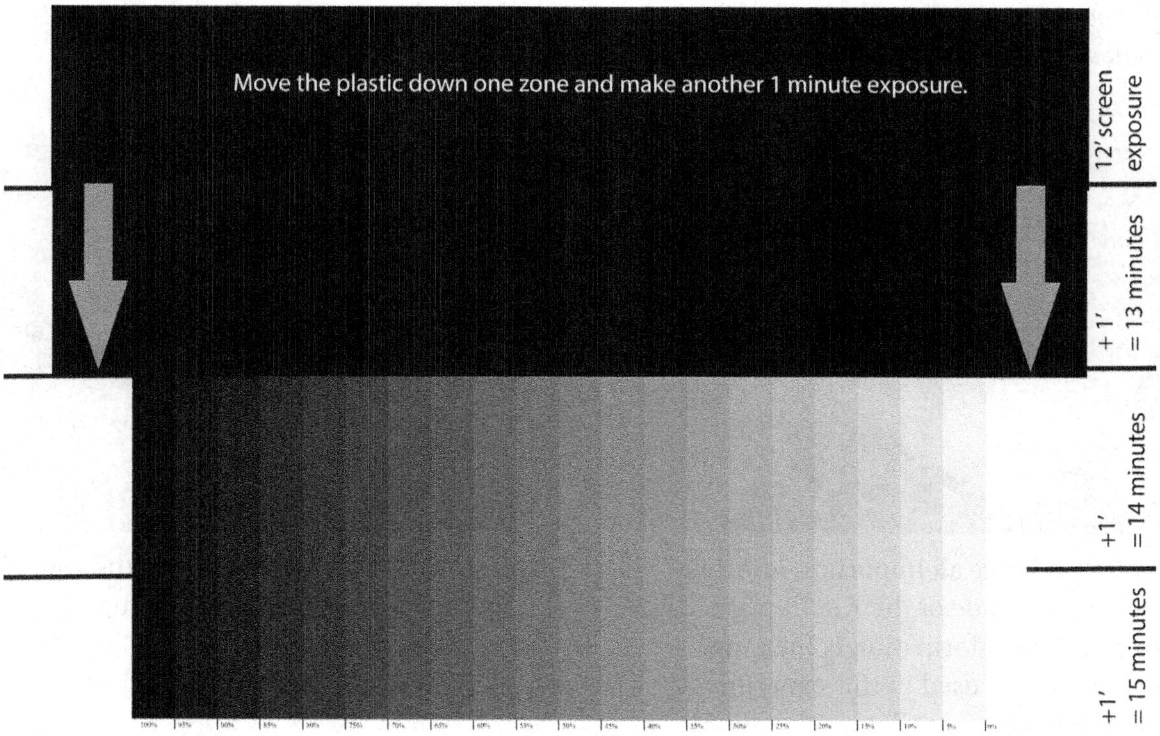

21 step grayscale tablet printed on transparency film with inkjet printer

(image 7-10) Move the light-blocking plastic down one more space, and expose again for 1 minute.

(image 7-11) Repeat this process until all parts have been exposed.

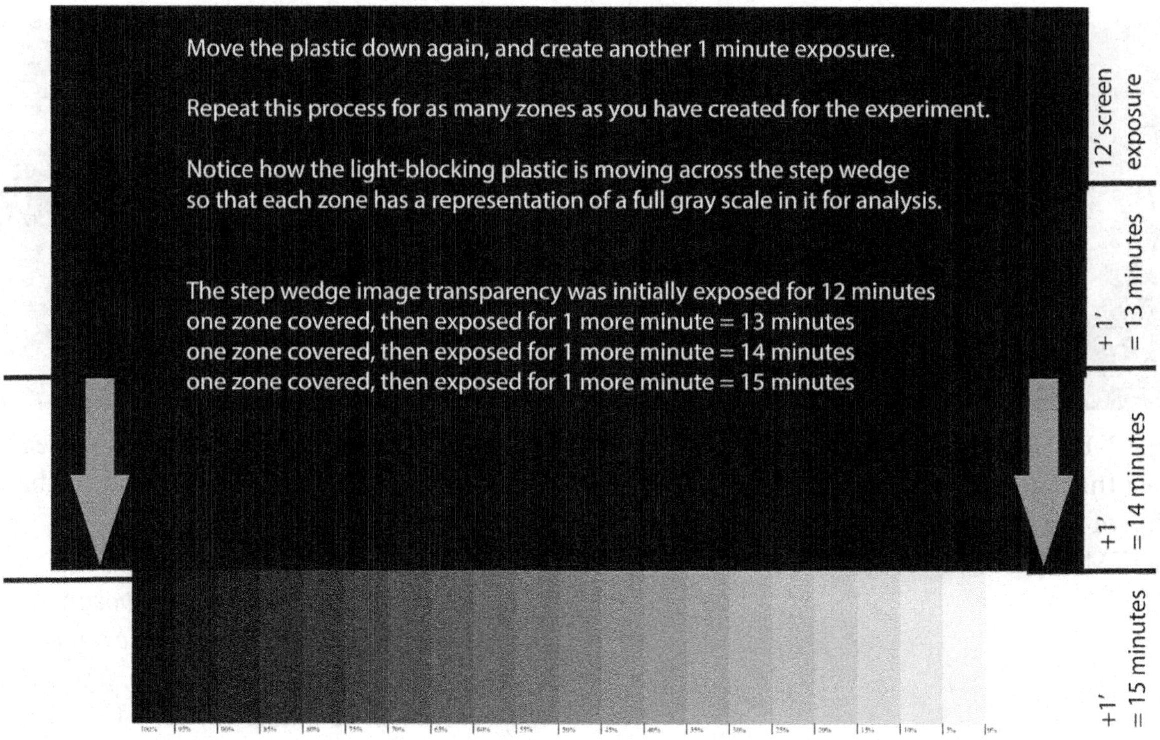

21 step grayscale tablet printed on transparency film with inkjet printer

The previous images showed graphical representation of this ***basic option*** *experiment. The next images will show real photos of the experiment being performed.*

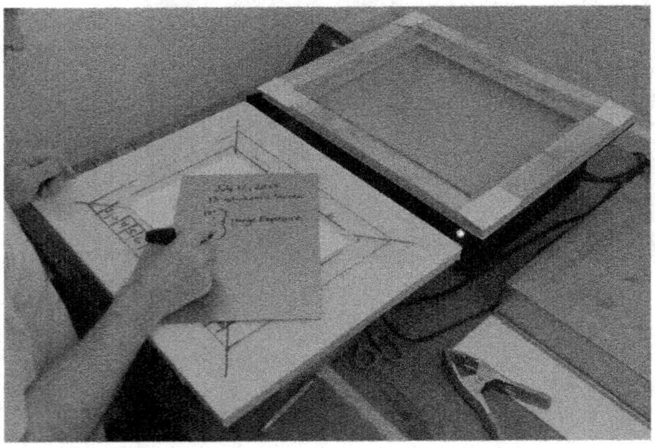

(image 7-12) Write all important information on the steel side of the KM73 plate. The most important information is the range of exposure times used in this experiment: both the Base Exposure Time (chapter 5) and the Image Exposure Times.

Other important information includes, date, brand of transparency film, inkjet printer setting, UV exposure unit type.

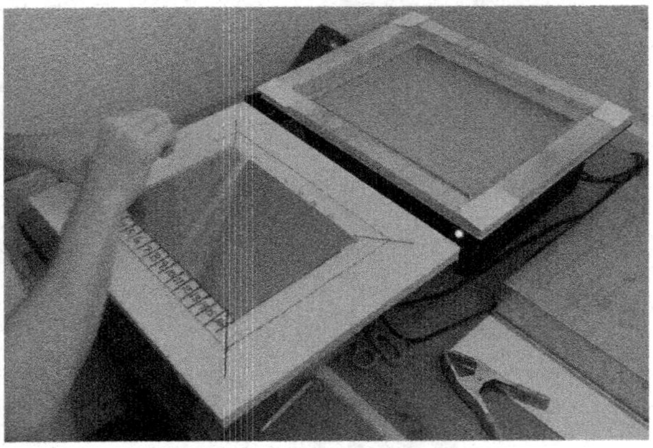

(image 7-13) Place the plate on the contact frame so the polymer side faces up. Peel off the protective film.

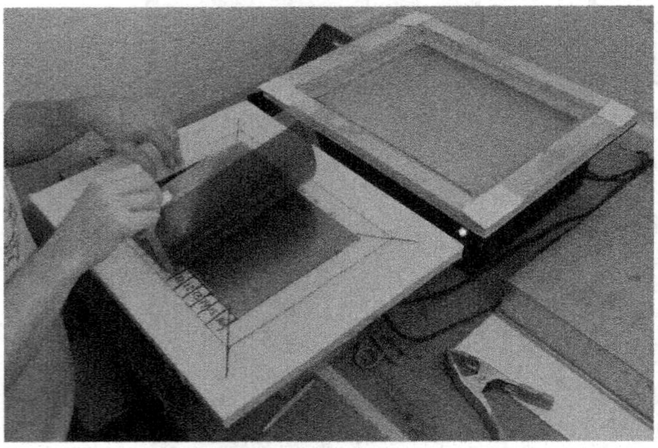

(image 7-14) Place the stochastic screen against the plate, making sure that the printed side of the screen faces the polymer side of the KM73 plate.

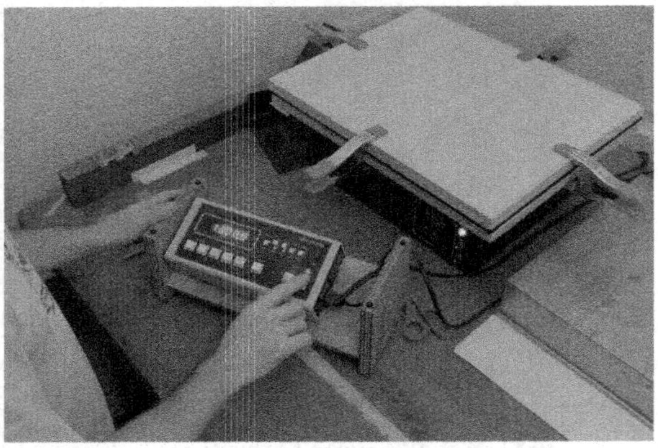

(image 7-15) Expose the stochastic screen for the Base Exposure Time found in chapter 5.

This example will have a base exposure time of 13 minutes, using the stochastic screen ("aquatint"). After that exposure, four image exposures will be made: 12, 13, 14, 15 minutes.

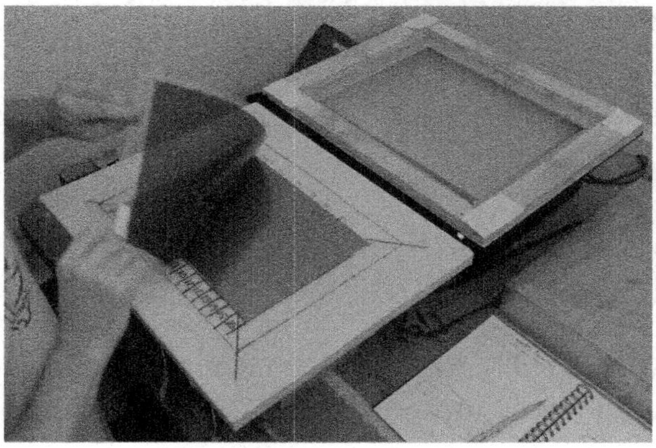

(image 7-16) After exposure, remove the stochastic screen and put it in a safe place.

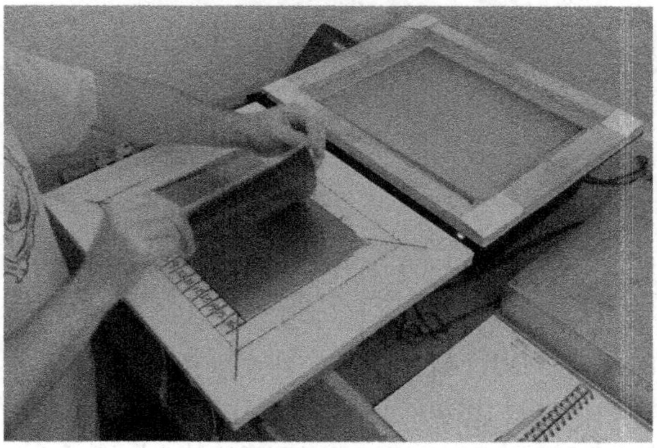

(image 7-17) Put the image transparency on top of the KM73 plate, making sure that the printed side of the transparency faces the polymer side of the plate.

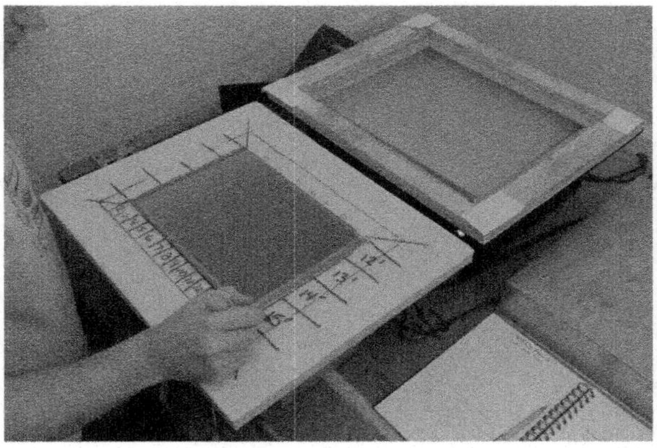

(image 7-18) Mark off four even spaces that indicate the planned image exposure times. Make marks on both the bed of the contact frame and on the KM73 plate itself. This redundancy of information can help if information is not successfully transferred to the plate or final print.

In this example, marks were made to delineate 12, 13, 14, and 15 minutes.

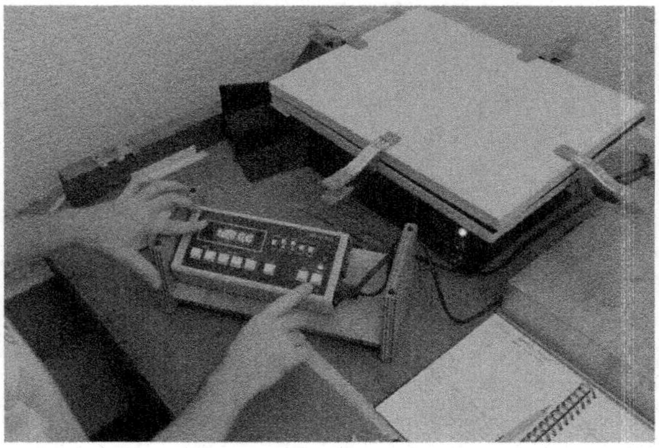

(image 7-19) Make the first exposure, using the shortest time listed for the experiment.

In this example, the first exposure is 12 minutes.

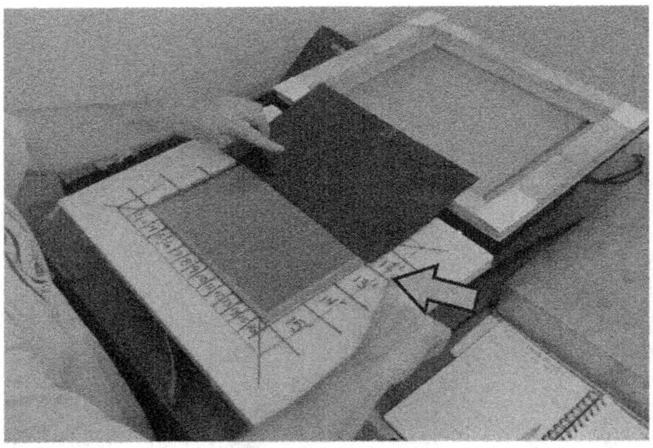

(image 7-20) After the first exposure, remove the glass from the contact frame, but keep the image transparency against the KM73 plate. Using a piece of thin opaque material, over the transparency and plate, cover the area that was marked for the first exposure.

In this example, the opaque material is a piece of the light-proof shipping bag for the KM73 plates. The first exposure time is 12 minutes, so that is the strip that is covered.

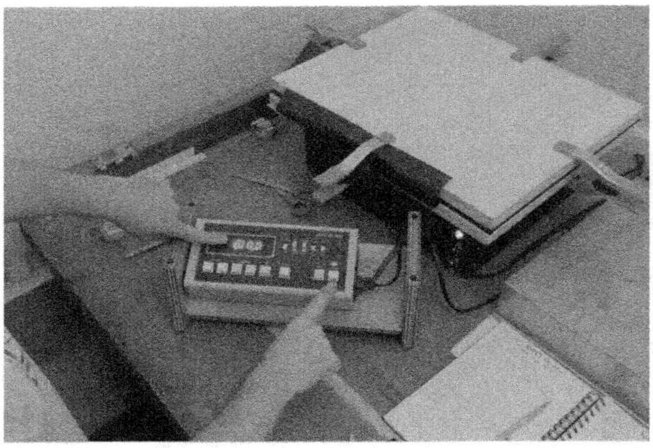

(image 7-21) Expose the plate for enough additional time to make the second exposure.

Since the first exposure was made to the entire plate, additional exposure times to parts of the plate/image that are not covered will add up to longer exposures. Anything covered will not be exposed.

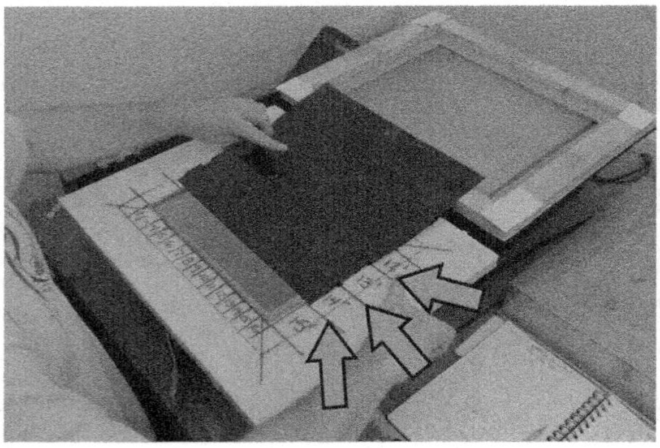

(image 7-22) Using the marks made on the contact frame as guides to cover sections after they received enough exposure.

In this example, the plate was exposed for 1 minute after each time the plastic bag was moved:
12 minute initial image exposure
covered a section, plus 1 minute exp. = 13'
covered another section, plus 1' exp. = 14'
covered another section, plus 1' exp. = 15'

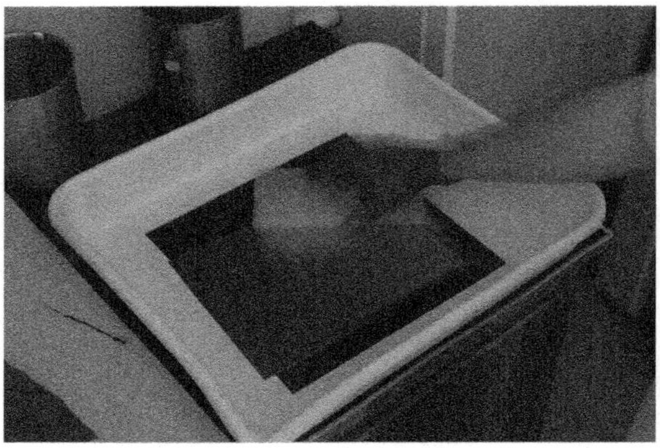

(image 7-23) When finished with all the exposure times, bring the plate to the wash-out tray. Let it sit, undisturbed for 1 minute. Gently brush the surface for 1 minute. (see chapter 1)

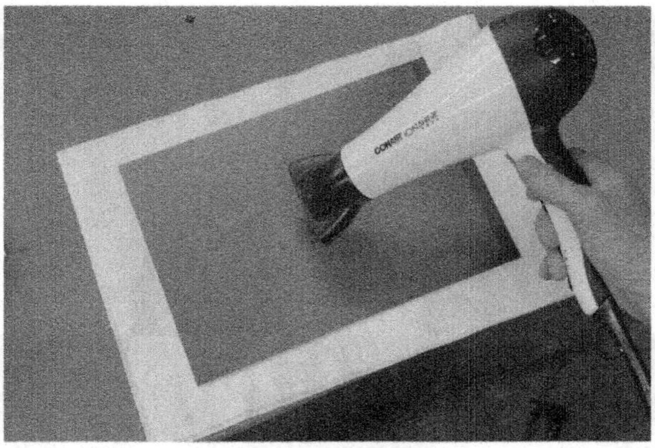

(image 7-24) Immediately blot the plate dry with paper towels to remove most of the water, then finish drying and heat setting the plate with a hair drier for at least 7 minutes.

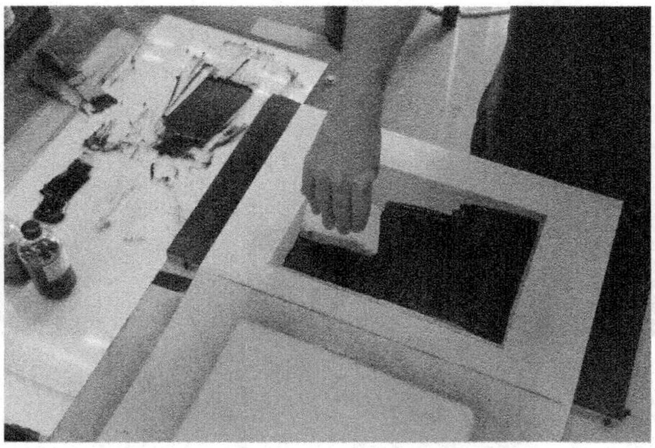

(image 7-25) Once the plate is fully dried, cured, and post exposed to UV light, ink the plate with the same color black ink you plan to use for most prints.

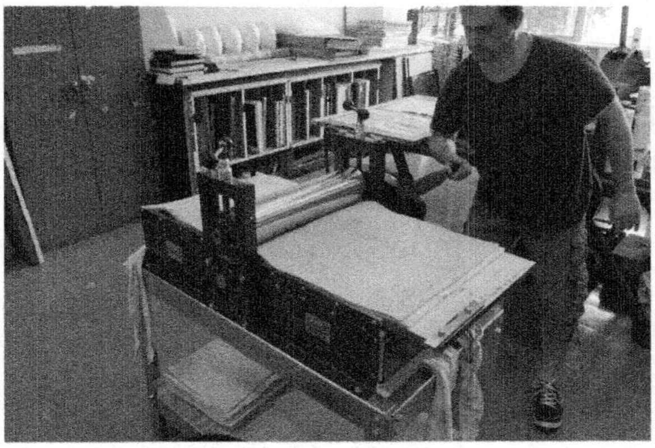

(image 7-26) Print the plate on the etching press using damp printmaking paper.

(image 7-27) Look closely at the result to find the best exposure time. Look at both the plate and resulting image to determine the best times. Different zones on the image may look similar, but the plate will reveal inconsistencies in the aquatint matrix that might exist in different times. Choose a time that has the finest grain aquatint pattern.

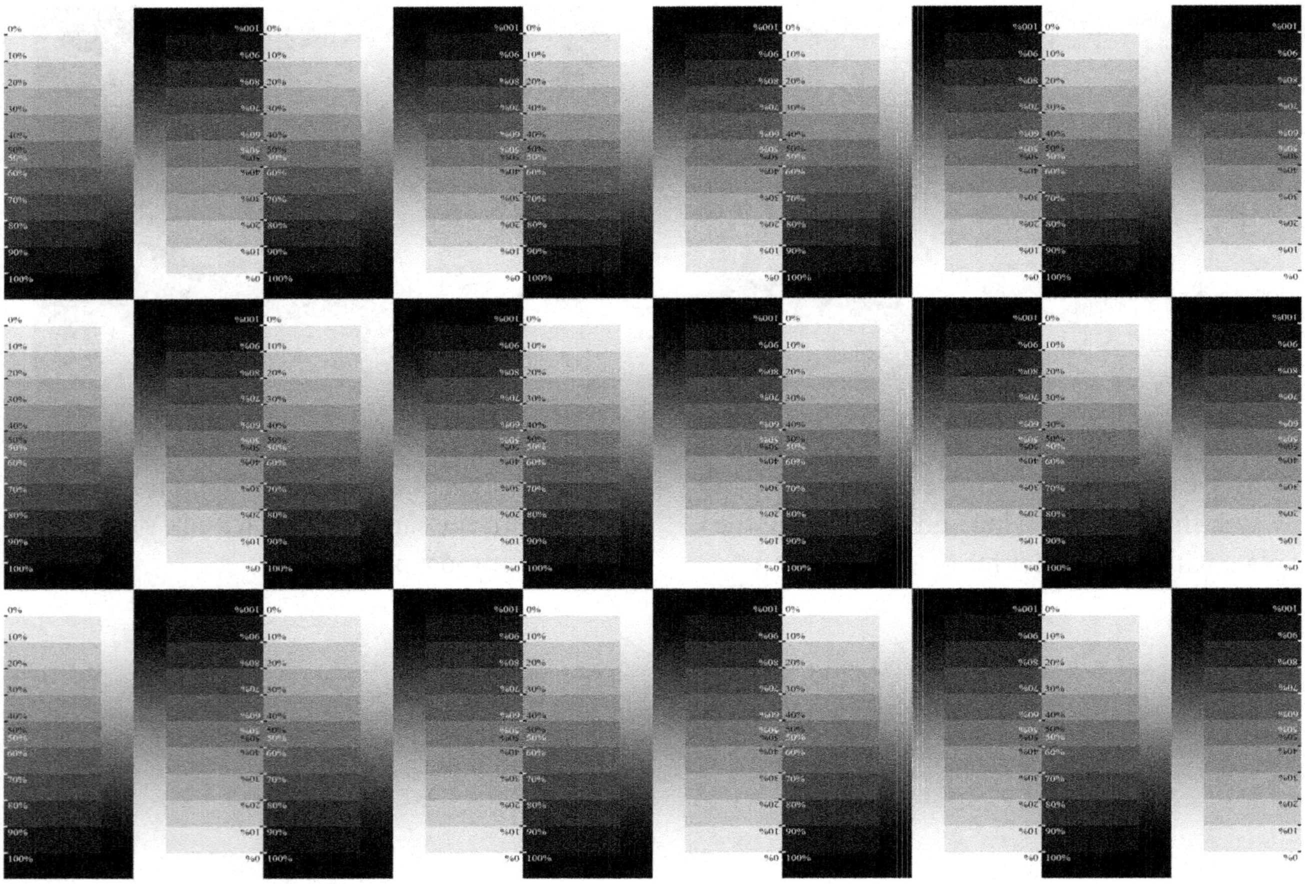

Advanced Option

(image 7-28) The advanced option uses the same principle as the previous option, with the addition of variable Base Exposure Times ("screen"). Above you see a series of step wedges, lined up in a grid. The step wedges are paired in opposite directions. Each opposing pair will sit at the intersection of a specific Base Exposure Time ("screen") and Image Exposure Time ("image").

The following example shows "screen" times of 12, 13, 14 minutes and "image" times of 11, 12, 13, 14, 15 minutes using the Aristo Platinum Printer.

The resulting print reveals 15 possible screen/image exposure times (in minutes).

screen/image	screen/image	screen/image	screen/image	screen/image
12' /11'	12'/12'	12'/13'	12'/14'	12'/15'
13' /11'	13'/12'	13'/13'	13'/14'	13'/15'
14' /11'	14'/12'	14'/13'	14'/14'	14'/15'

A later experiment (not shown in this book) was run with the new Ryonet RXP 16x20 UV exposure unit, in which this same image above was exposed with "screen" times of 5, 6, 7 minutes and "image" times of 5, 6, 7, 8, 9 minutes. The results of this later experiment was used to make new adjustment curves using the technique demonstrated in chapter 8.

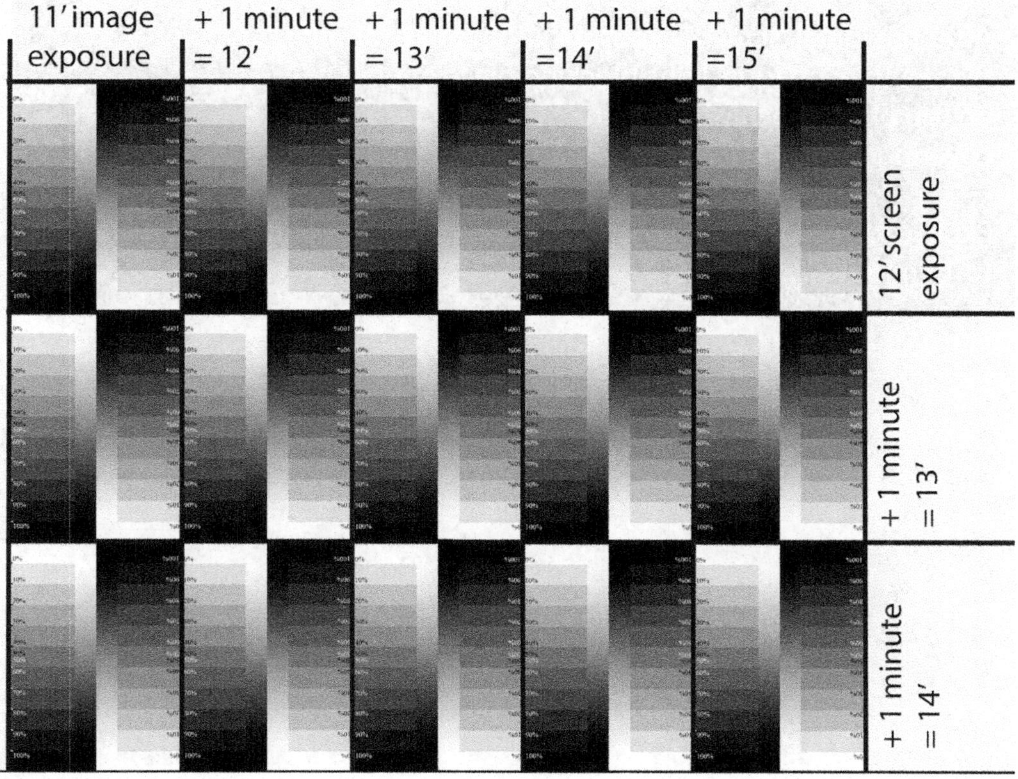

(image 7-28) Put the printed transparency on top of a polymer plate. Mark both the plate and the backing of the contact frame with screen and image times.

(image 7-29) Replace the transparency with the stochastic screen. Leave 2 edges of the plate uncovered by the screen so you can see the exposure time notes that were made. Make the initial exposure to the entire plate.

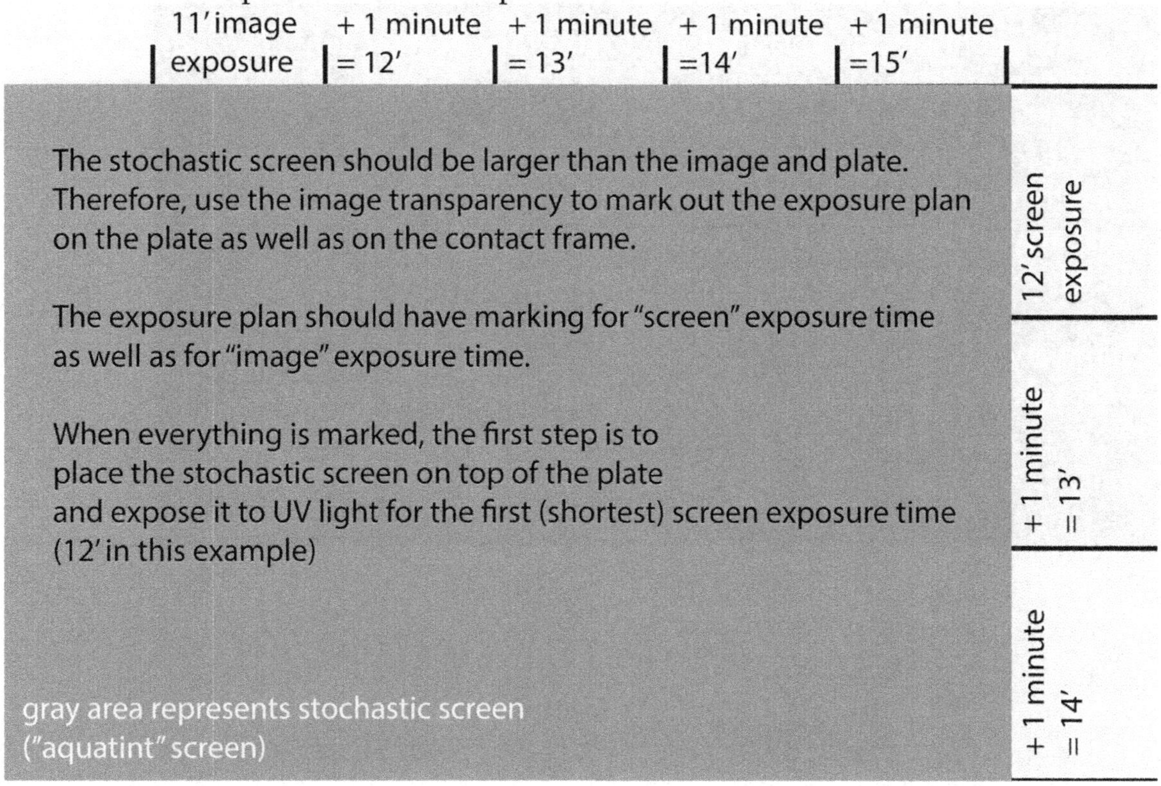

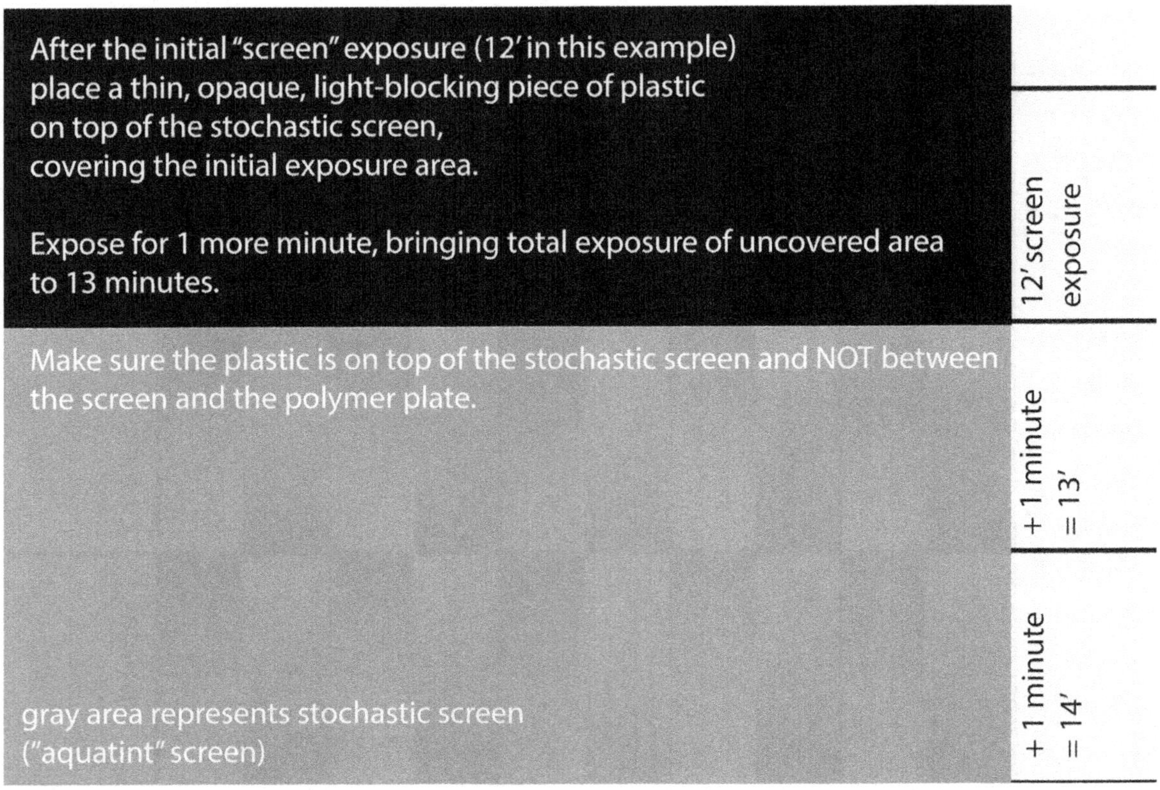

(image 7-30) After the first exposure, cover part of the screen/plate with an opaque piece of plastic. Expose for 1 more minute.

(image 7-31) After exposure, move the plastic so it covers the next zone and expose again for 1 more minute.

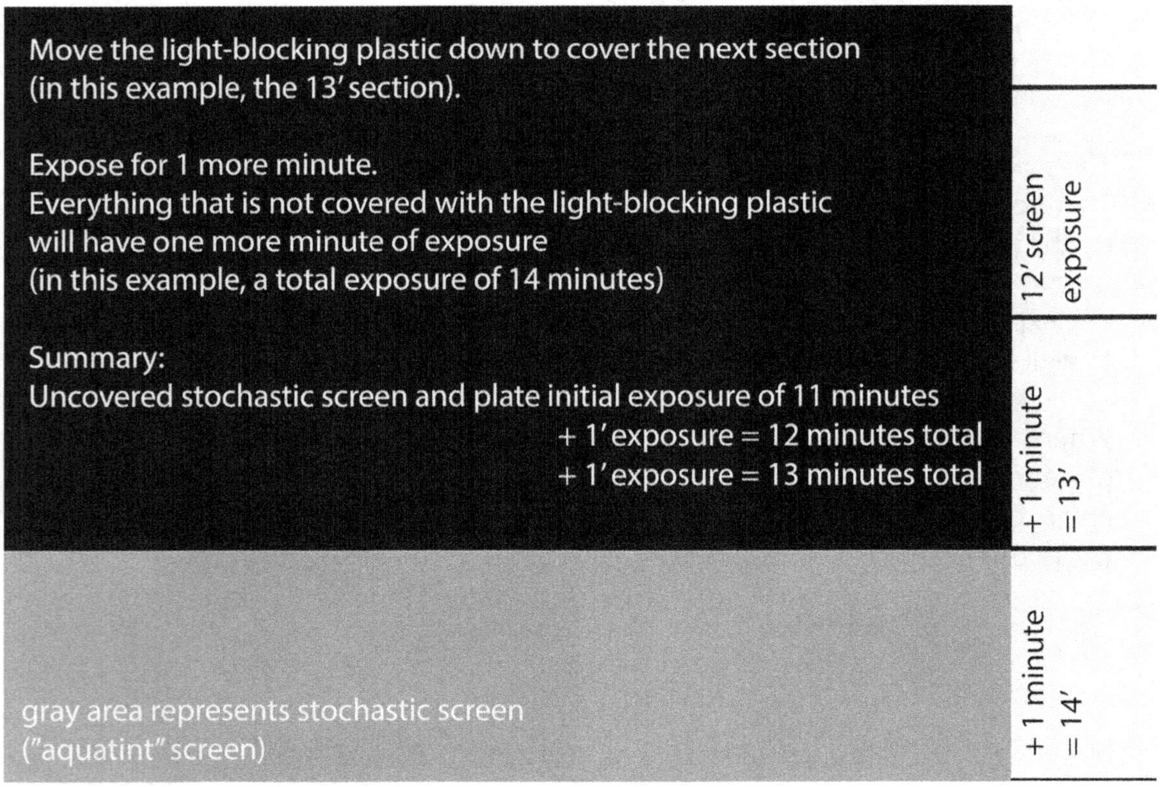

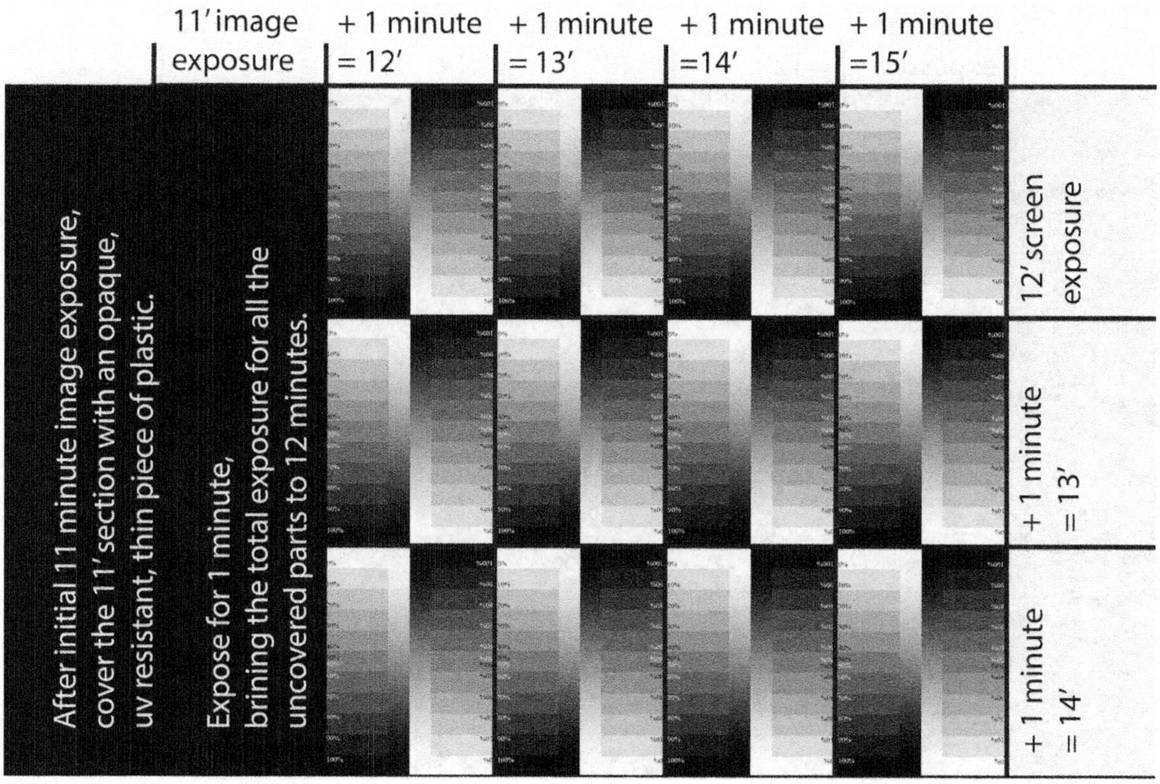

After all screen exposures, replace the stochastic screen with the image transparency. Use the registration marks to line everything up. Make the initial exposure. (11' in example)
(image 7-32) Cover one strip with opaque plastic and expose for 1 more minute.
(image 7-33) Move the opaque plastic over to the next strip and expose again for 1 minute.

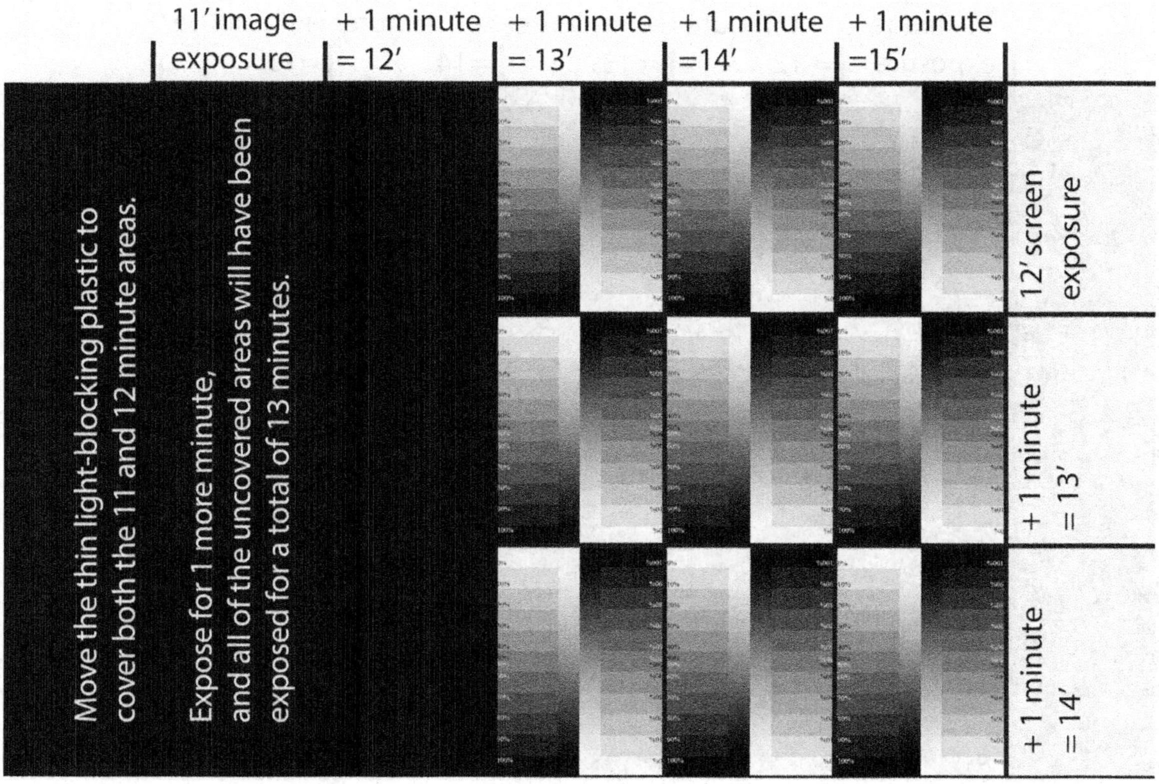

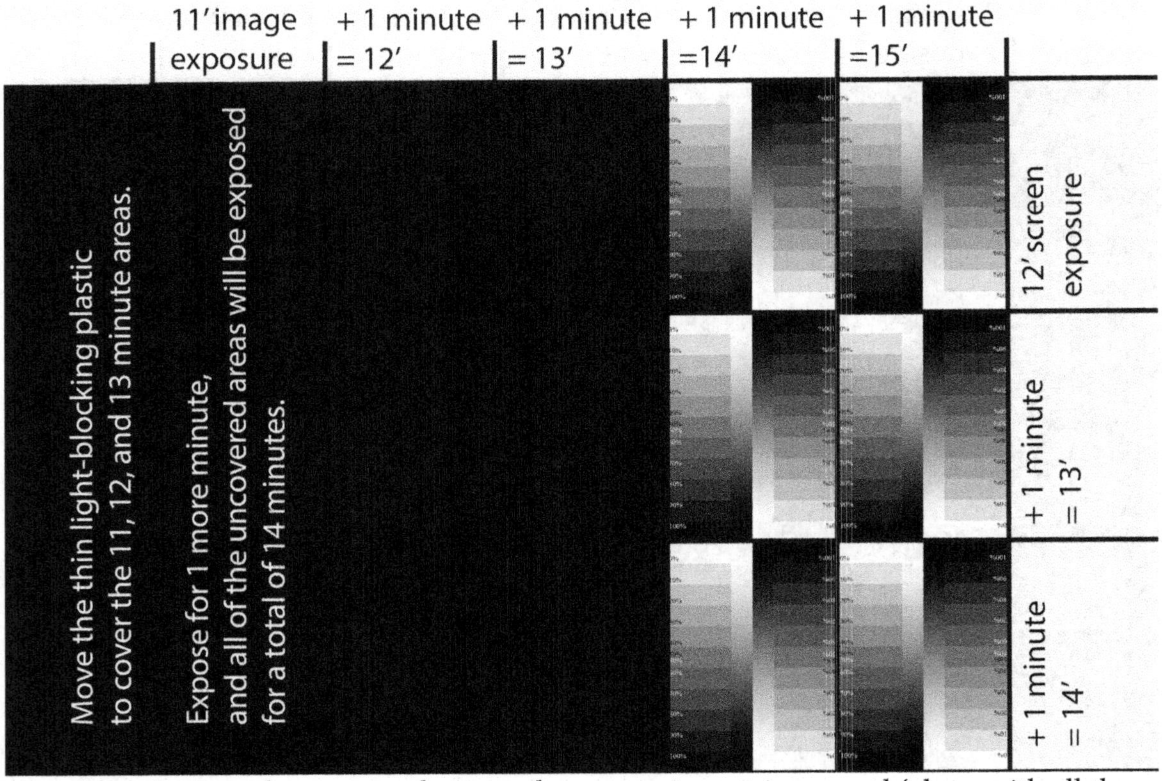

(image 7-34) Move the opaque plastic to the next strip so it is covered (along with all the previous strips) and expose for 1 more minute.

(image 7-35) Repeat the process of moving the opaque plastic from strip to strip, making sure that, once covered, a strip stays covered. Keep track of all the additive exposures that are made so that times can be accurately tracked.

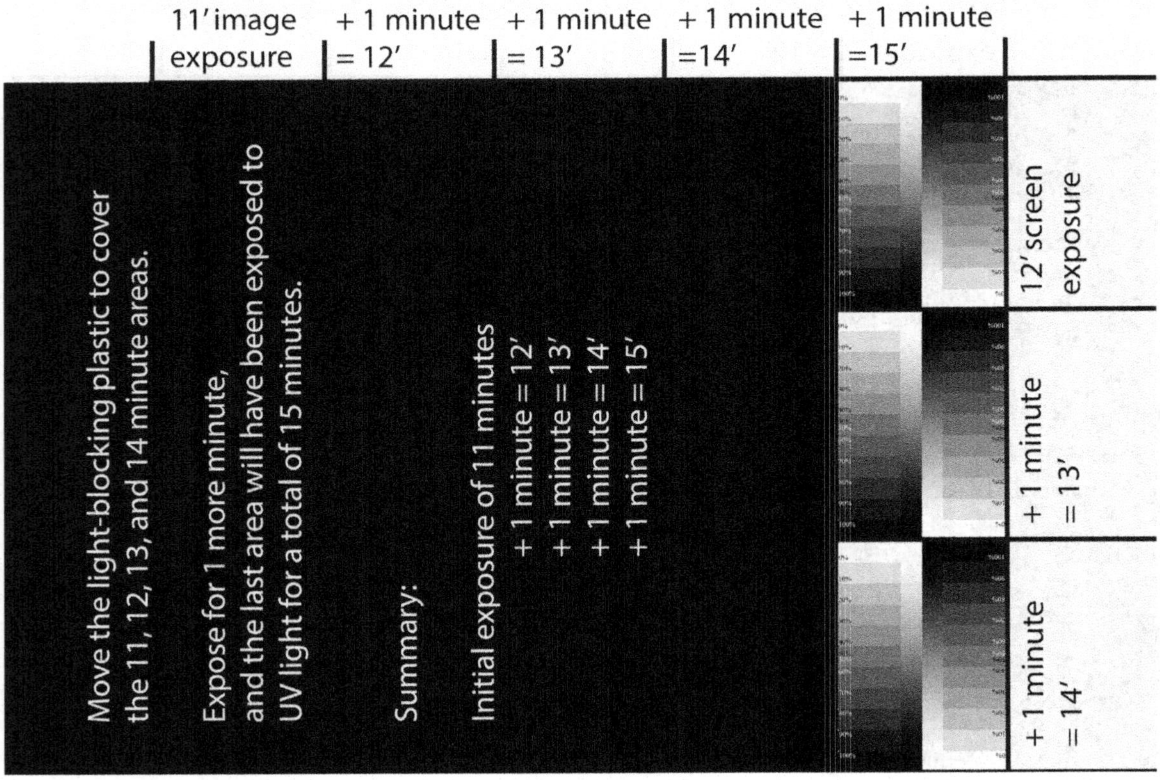

*The previous images showed graphical representation of this **advanced option** experiment. The next images will show real photos of the experiment being performed.*

Screen exposure times are made in horizontal strips while image exposure times are along vertical strips.

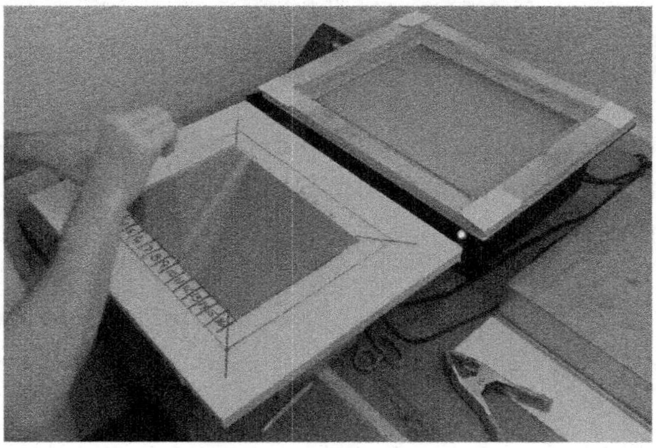

(image 7-36) Place the KM73 plate on the contact frame and remove the protective film from the polymer side.

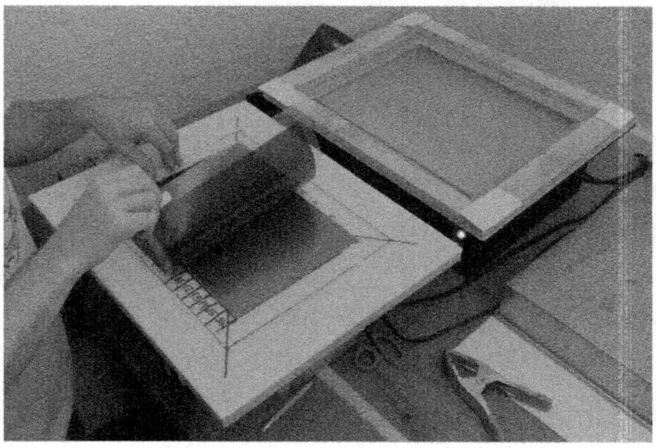

(image 7-37) Place the stochastic screen on top of theplate. Printed side of the stochastic screen goes against the polymer side of the plate.

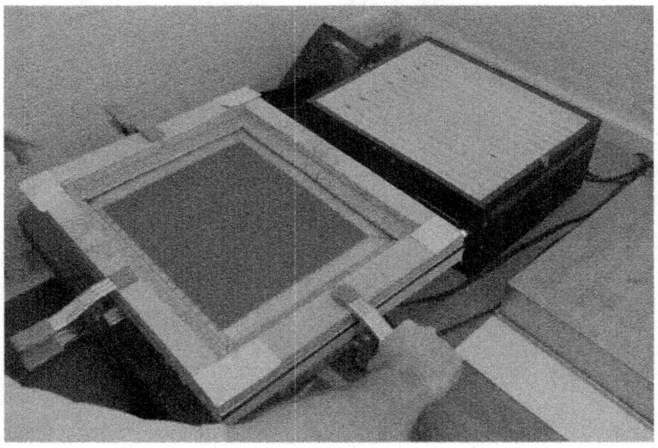

(image 7-38) Assemble contact frame with KM73 plate and stochastic screen inside.

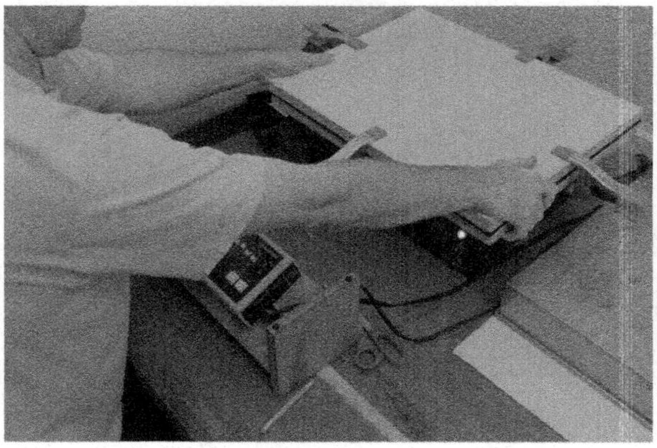

(image 7-39) Put the contact frame on the UV exposure unit.

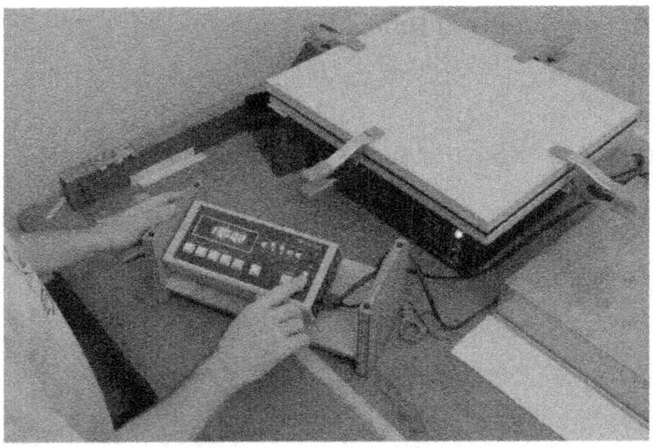

(image 7-40) Make the initial "aquatint" exposure to the plate, using the shortest time planned for the stochastic screen.

In this example, the shortest "screen" time is 12 minutes, so that is the first exposure made, to the entire plate with the stochastic screen.

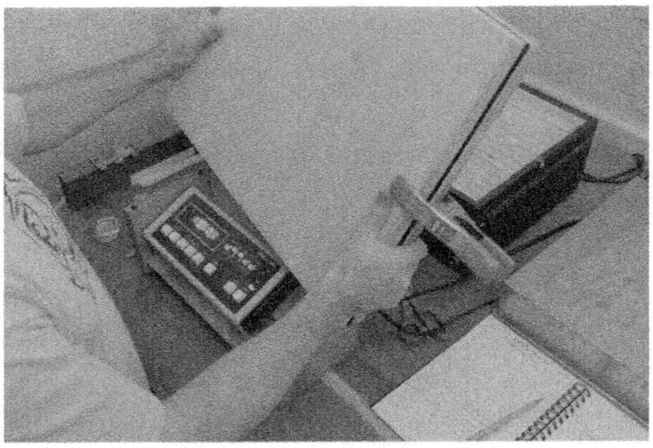

(image 7-41) After initial exposure, remove the contact frame from the UV exposure unit.

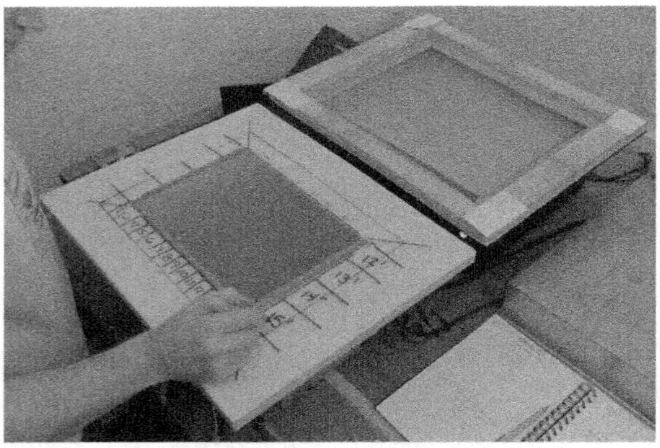

(image 7-42) Make sure that registration marks (with exposure times) exist on both the polymer plate and the base of the contact frame. Writing on both surfaces will help line up the stochastic screen, image transparency, and the light-blocking plastic. This parity of notation also insures against lost information during the experiment.

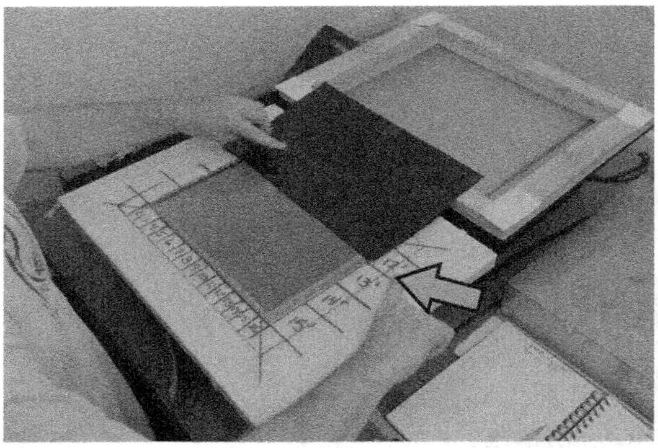

(image 7-43) After the initial exposure, cover the first horizontal strip, and make another exposure of 1 minute.

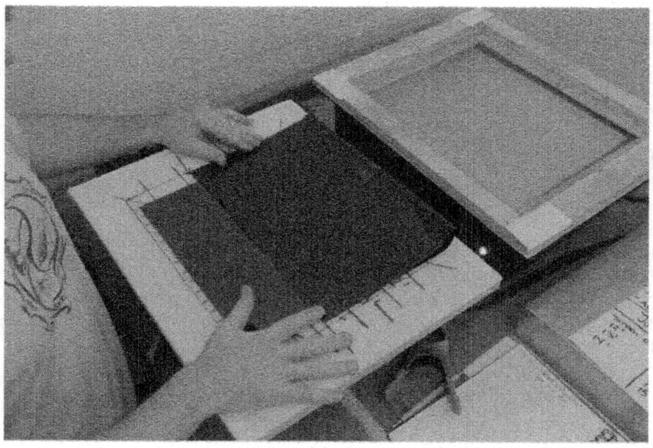

(image 7-44) Cover the first and second horizontal strips with the opaque plastic and make another exposure of 1 minute.

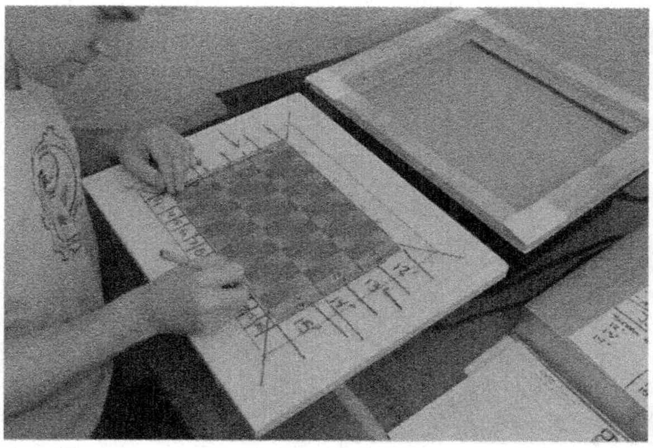

(image 7-45) When all of the screen exposures have been made, remove the stochastic screen and replace it with the image transparency. Carefully line it up with the registration marks made earlier.

The experiment shown in these images had screen exposure times of 12', 13', and 14 minutes.

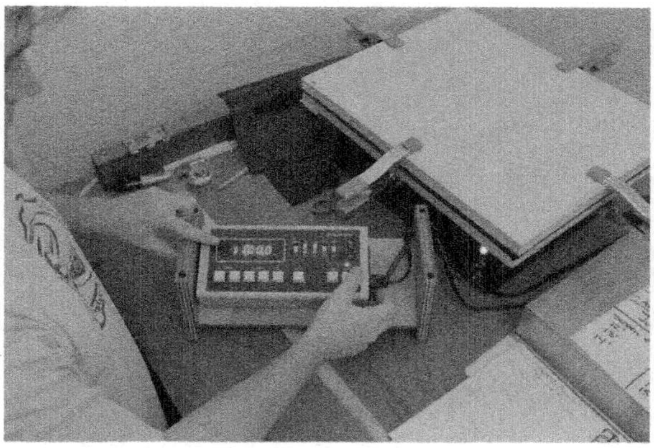

(image 7-46) Make the initial exposure to the entire plate. The initial exposure is the lowest total desired exposure planned for the experiment.

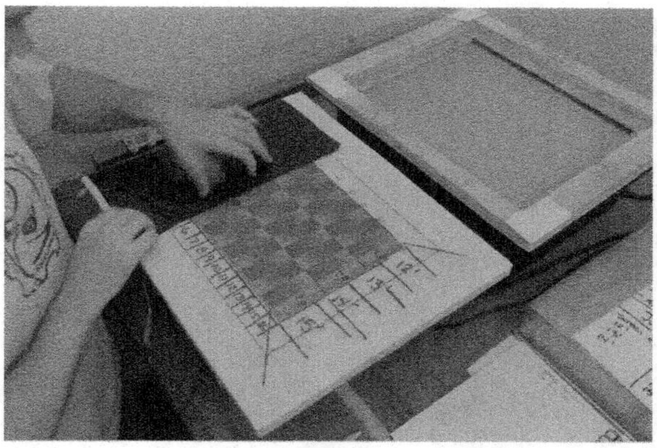

(image 7-47) After the initial exposure, cover the first vertical strip, and make another exposure of 1 minute.

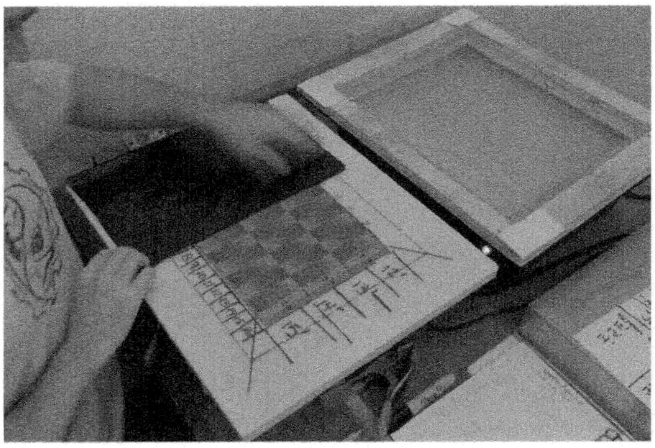

(image 7-48) Cover the first and second vertical strips with the opaque plastic.

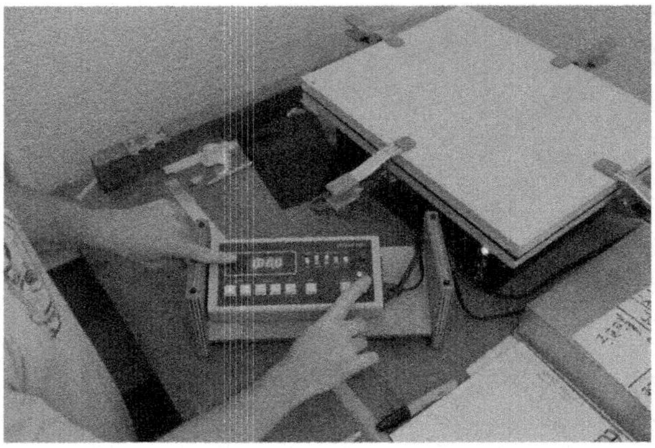

(image 7-49) Expose for 1 minute.

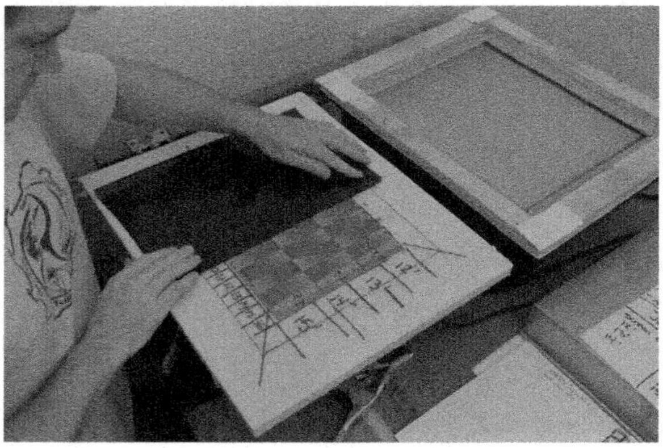

(image 7-50) Cover the first, second, and third vertical strips with the opaque plastic.

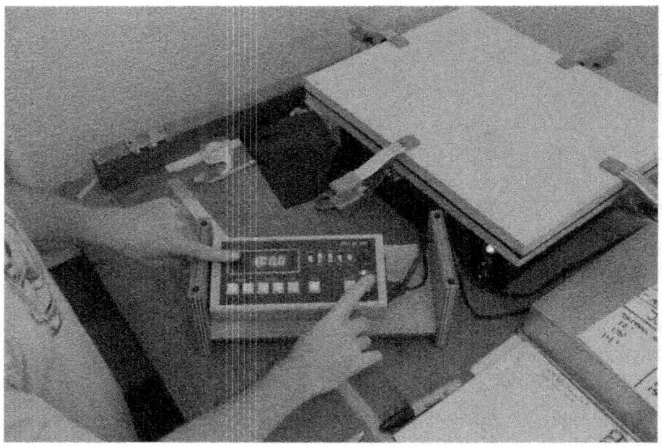

(image 7-51) Expose for 1 minute.

Repeat this process of covering vertical strips and making 1 minute exposures until all of the zones have been exposed.

The image exposure times in this experiment are 11', 12', 13', 14', and 15 minutes

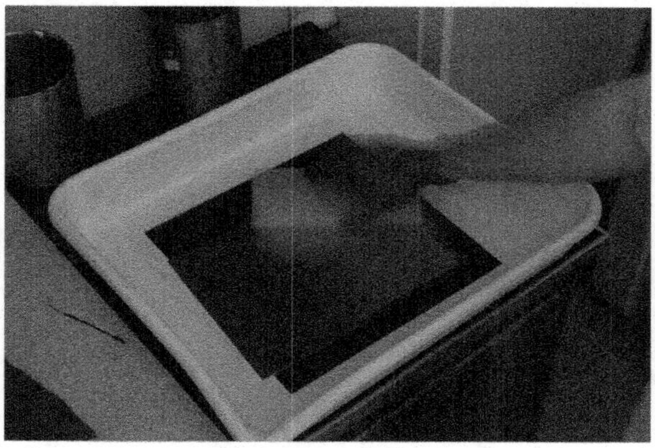

(image 7-52) After all screen and image exposure have been made, wash out the plate.

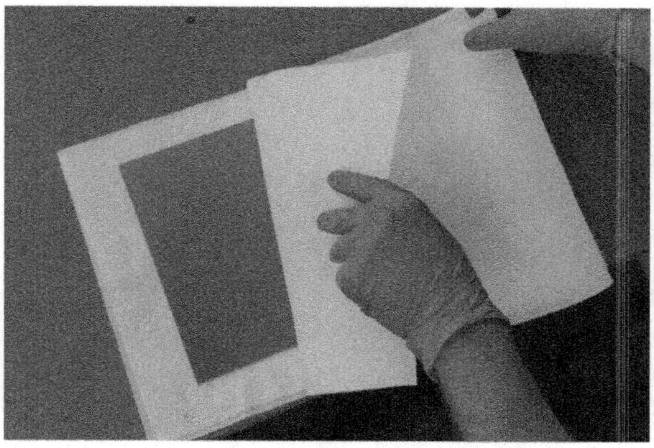

(image 7-53) Gently, and quickly absorb water after washout.

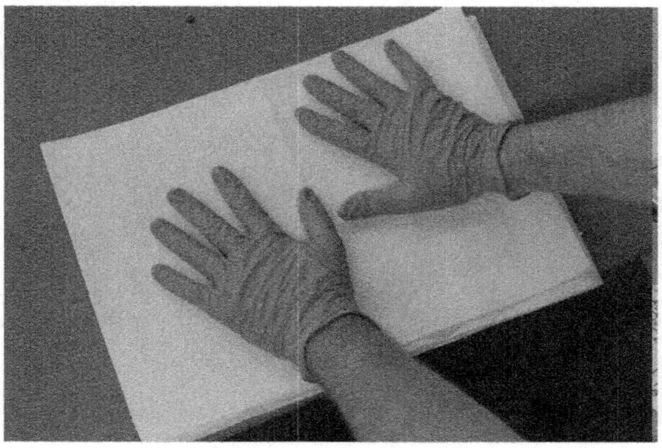

(image 7-54) Do not apply much pressure. Work quickly and only use the weight of your hands. Do not push.

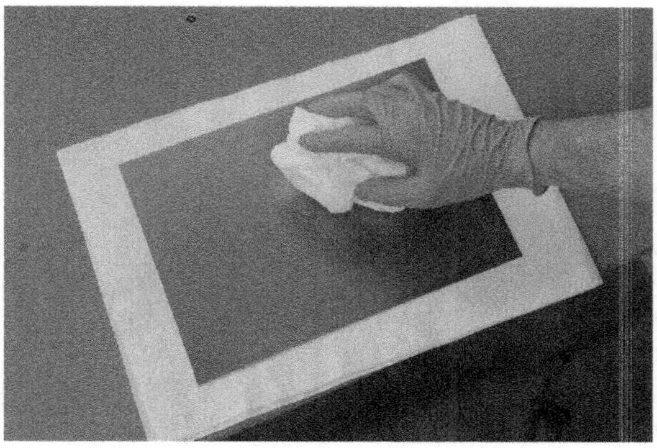

(image 7-55) Blot quickly. The entire drying process with paper towels should only take 5 - 15 seconds.

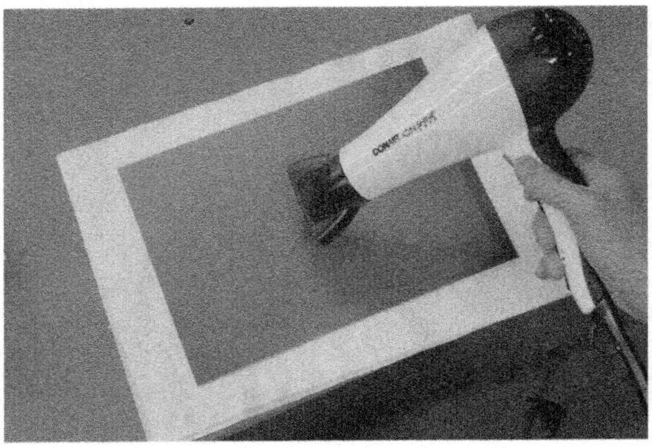

(image 7-56) Immediately move to drying the last bit of water with a hair drier set on the highest setting. Keep moving the hot air across the entire surface of the plate for at least 7 minutes. This will heat cure the plate.

Remember to post-expose the plate with UV light, after heat curing with the hair drier, for at least as much time as the Base Exposure time.

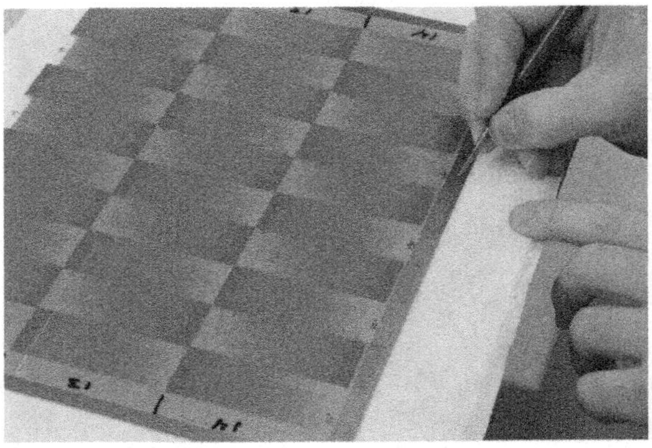

(image 7-57) Polymer scratches easily. Exploit this tendency to make sure that exposure information can easily be read on the plate. Use a sharp stylus (or even a safety pin) to write exposure times that may have not been recorded (before they are forgotten).

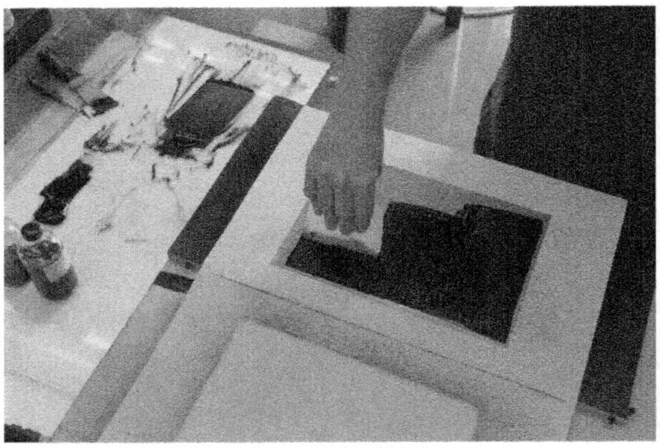

(image 7-58) Prepare printmaking paper and ink the plate with the standard black etching ink you have chosen to use.

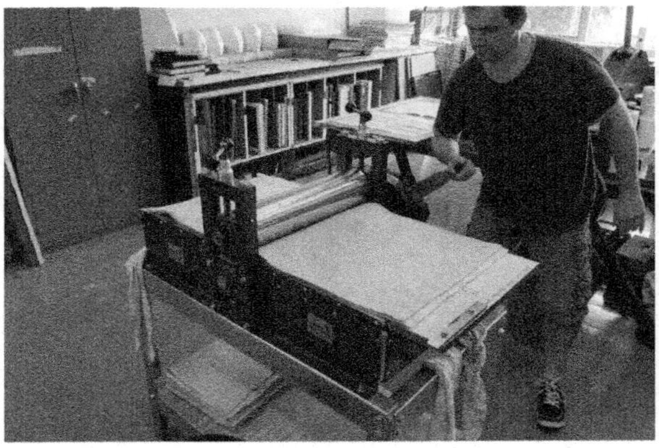

(image 7-59) Print the plate with the etching press.

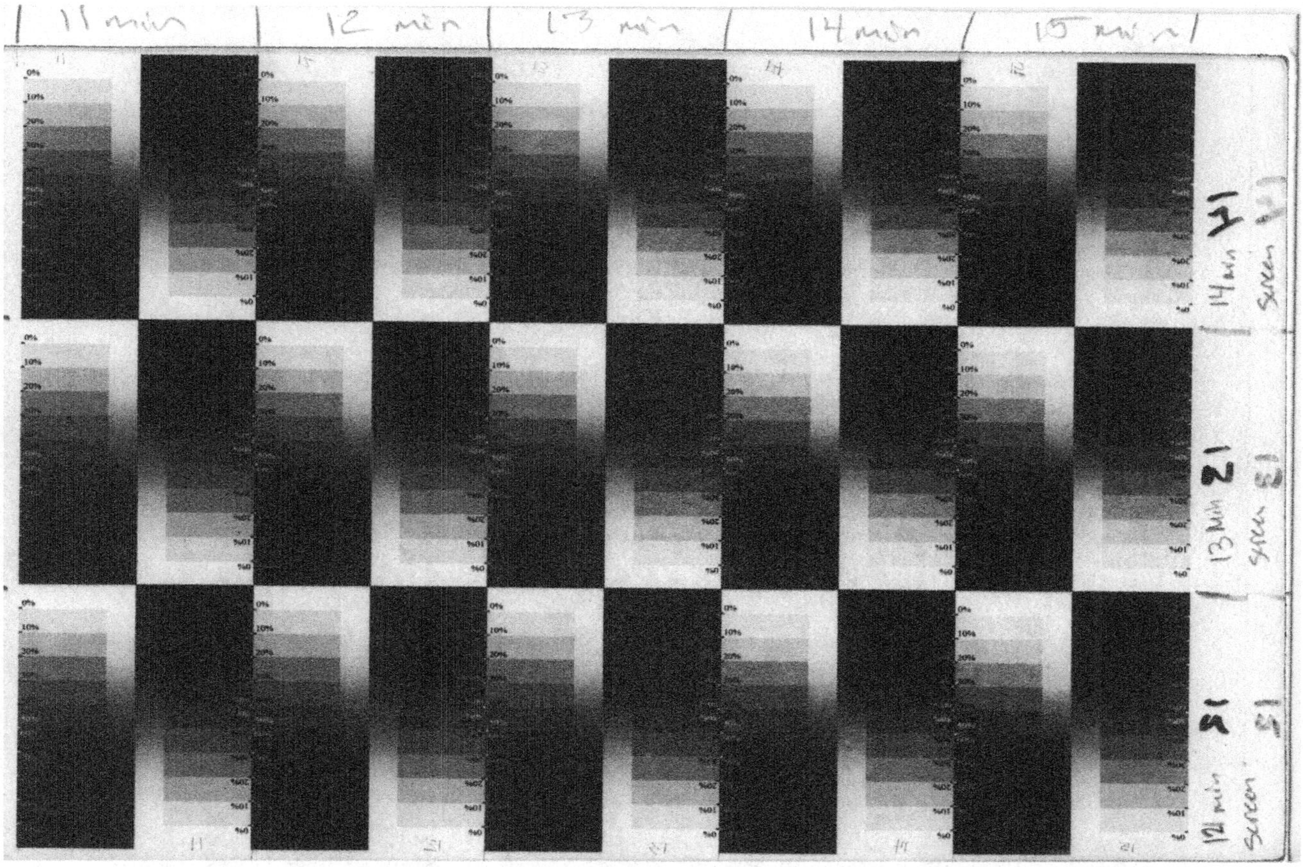

(image 7-60) Let the print dry before examining it. Contrast changes slightly as the print dries. After it is dry, however, take a close look at the grid of step wedges. Choose the one that has the largest tonal range. Write down the screen and image times that work best, and use those to make some real photographs with this technique. Save this print (along with all other experiments) for future reference.

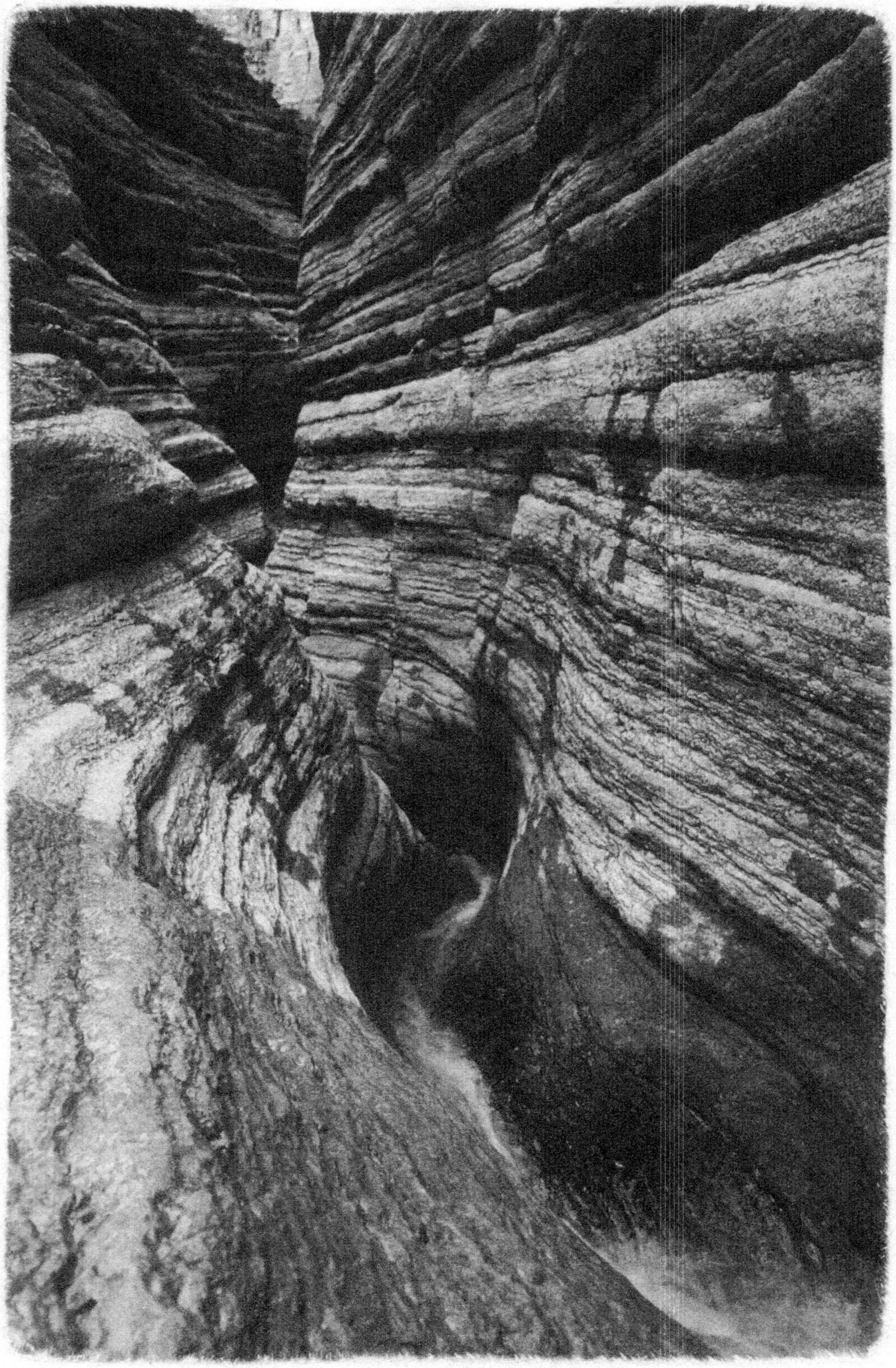

"Matkatamiba 3"

photogravure

Scott Barnes

Chapter 8

Making Adjustment Curves

After you have found the ***base exposure time*** (chapter 5) for the stochastic screen (a.k.a. "aquatint" screen) and ***image exposure time*** (chapter 7), you'll need to construct an adjustment curve. The adjustment curve is applied to your image before printing. It compensates for the discrepancies between the digital and analogue processes used to create a useful printing plate.

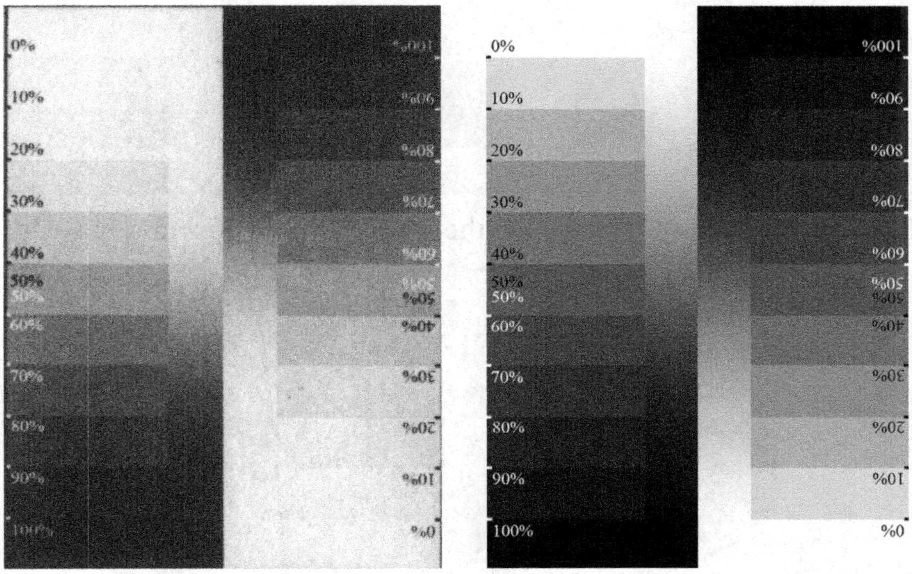

(image 8-01) The digital image on the right is what was printed on the transparency. The analogue image on the left is the result after exposing that transparency to the photopolymer plate (and making from that plate with an etching press). The digital image shows an even progression of gray steps, from pure black (100% density) to pure white (0% density). The analogue image is not as smooth, and seems to be missing information at the ends.

note*: Some of this can be adjusted during the printing process. More accurately, poor intaglio printing techniques will increase the difference between the theoretical gray tone scale (digital) and the actual tonal range found in the print (analogue). The final prints will have higher contrast, with fewer gray steps and some awkward transitions. I recommend spending a lot of time focusing on the physical practice of making prints with the etching press, using the plate you made in chapter 7. As your printmaking skills improve, you may find that a better tonal range emerges from the same plate. If you do find this happening, then you should repeat the steps in this chapter to create a more refined adjustment curve.*

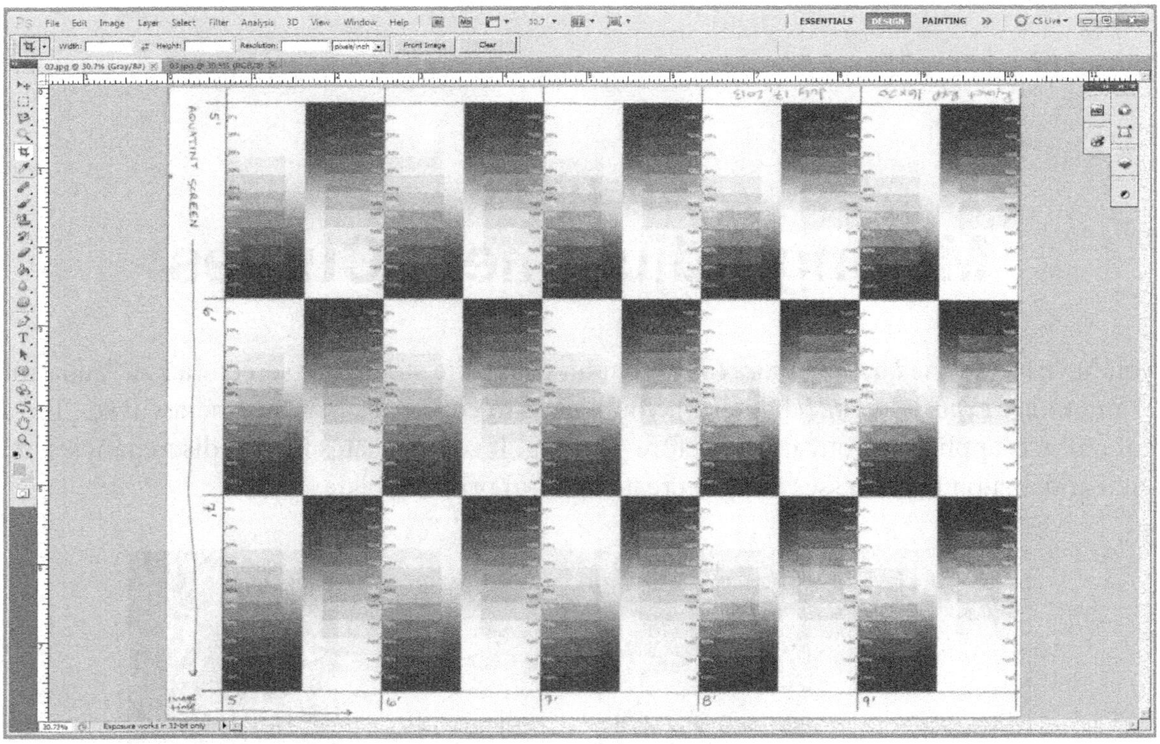

(**image 8-02**) Launch Photoshop and open the scanned image of your step wedge print.

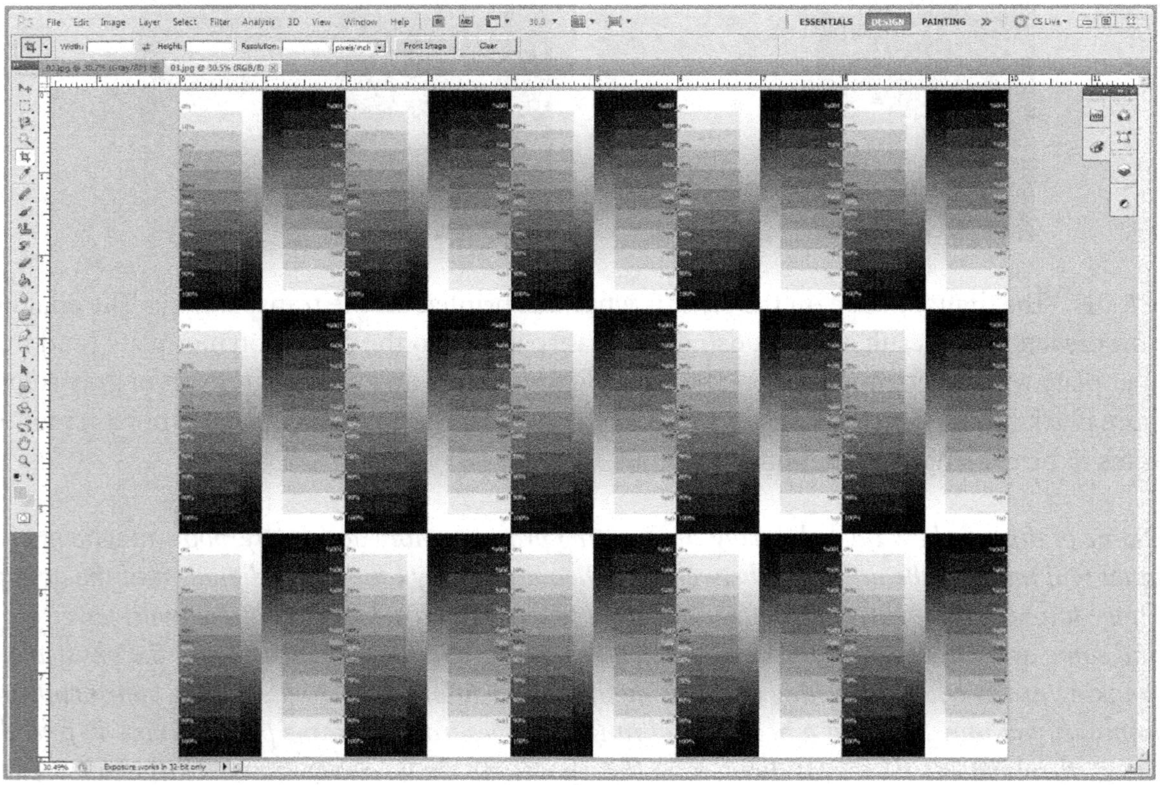

(**image 8-03**) Also open the digital image used to make the transparency.

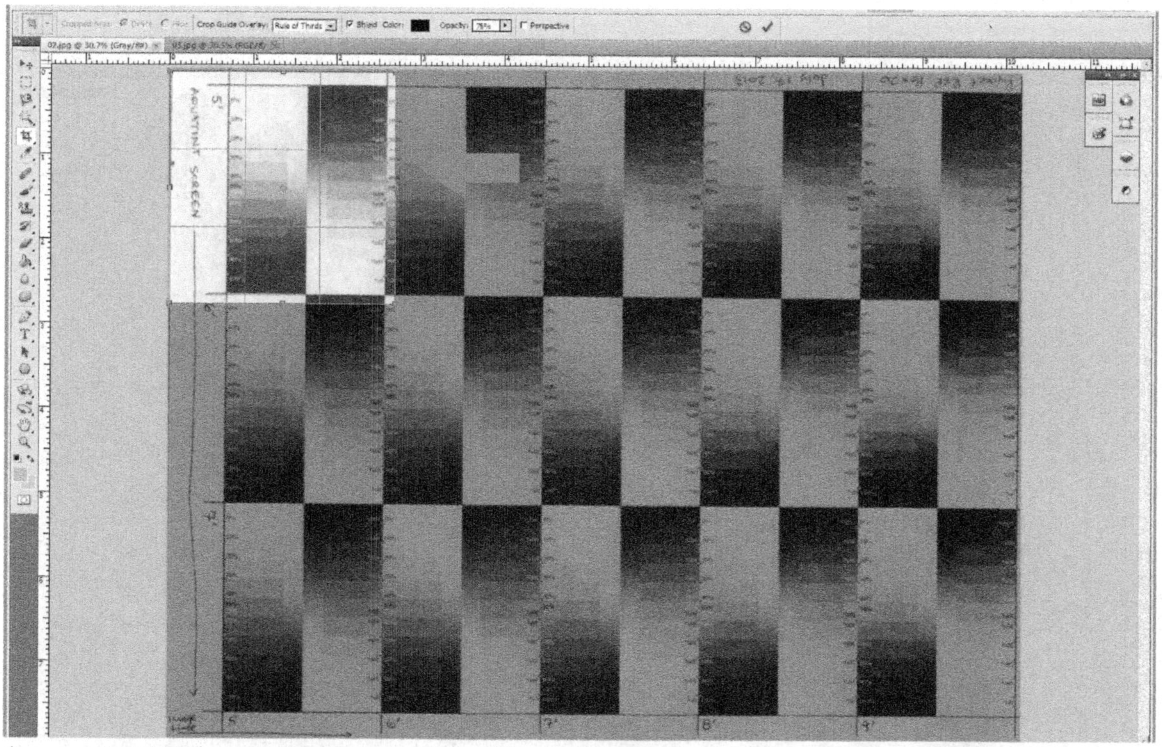

(image 8-04) Choose the step wedge with the best exposure times, that reveals the best looking tonal range, and crop the image to fit just that section. The best step wedge in this example is the one with a 5 minute aquatint exposure (stochastic screen) and a 5 minute image exposure using the RXP 16x20 exposure unit from Ryonet.

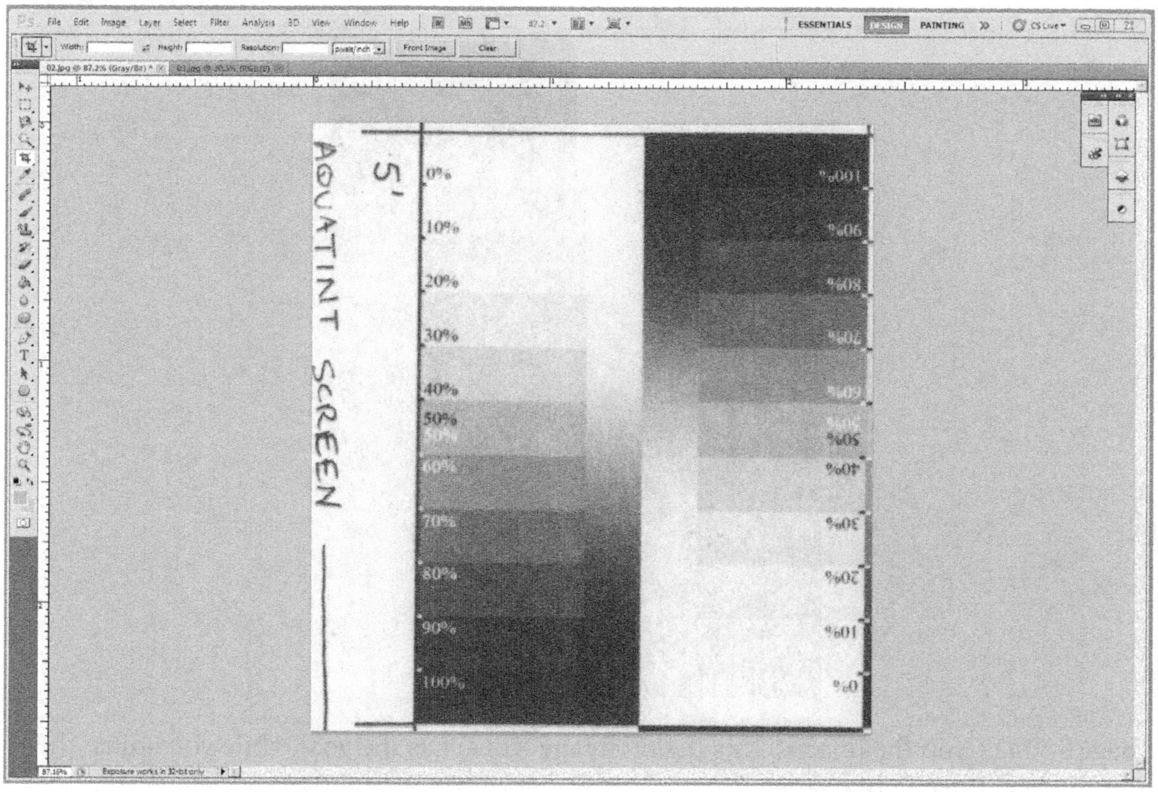

(image 8-05) The cropped step wedge will need to be cropped and straightened.

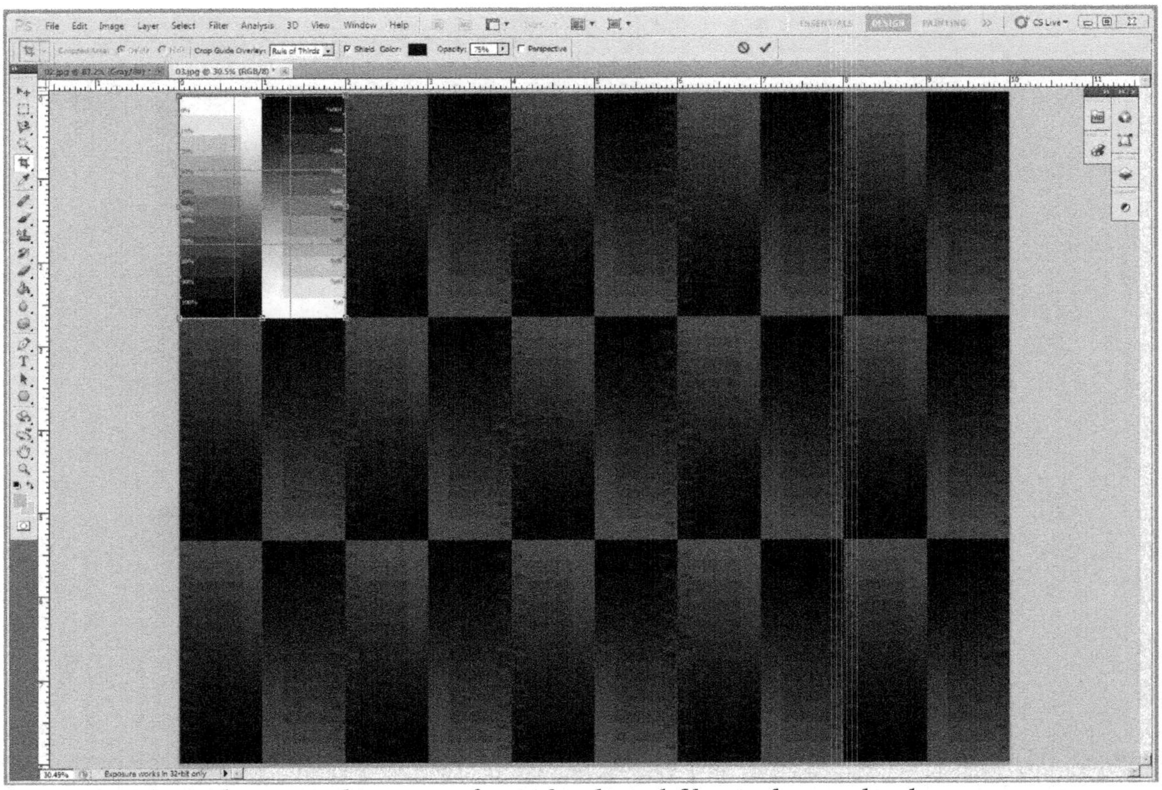

(image 8-06) Isolate a simlar image from the digital file used to make the transparency.

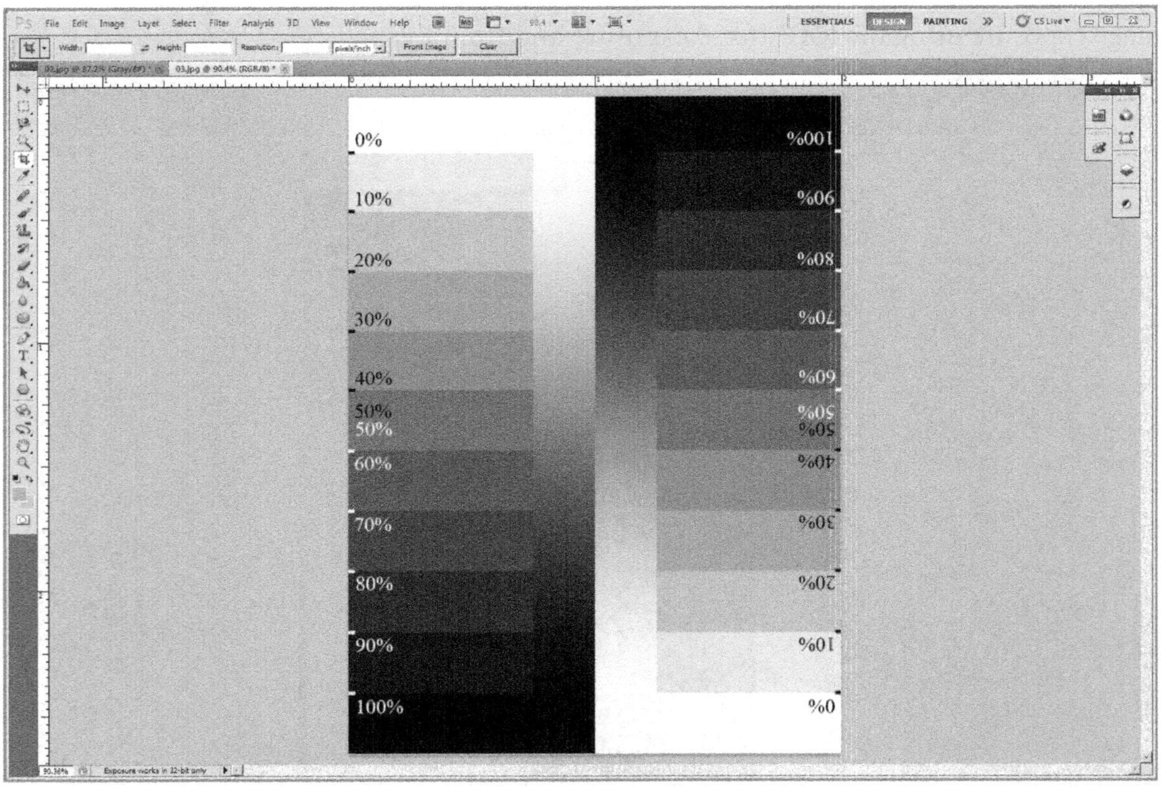

(image 8-07) Crop the image. This digital image will act as the goal while you adjust the print made at the end of chapter 7.

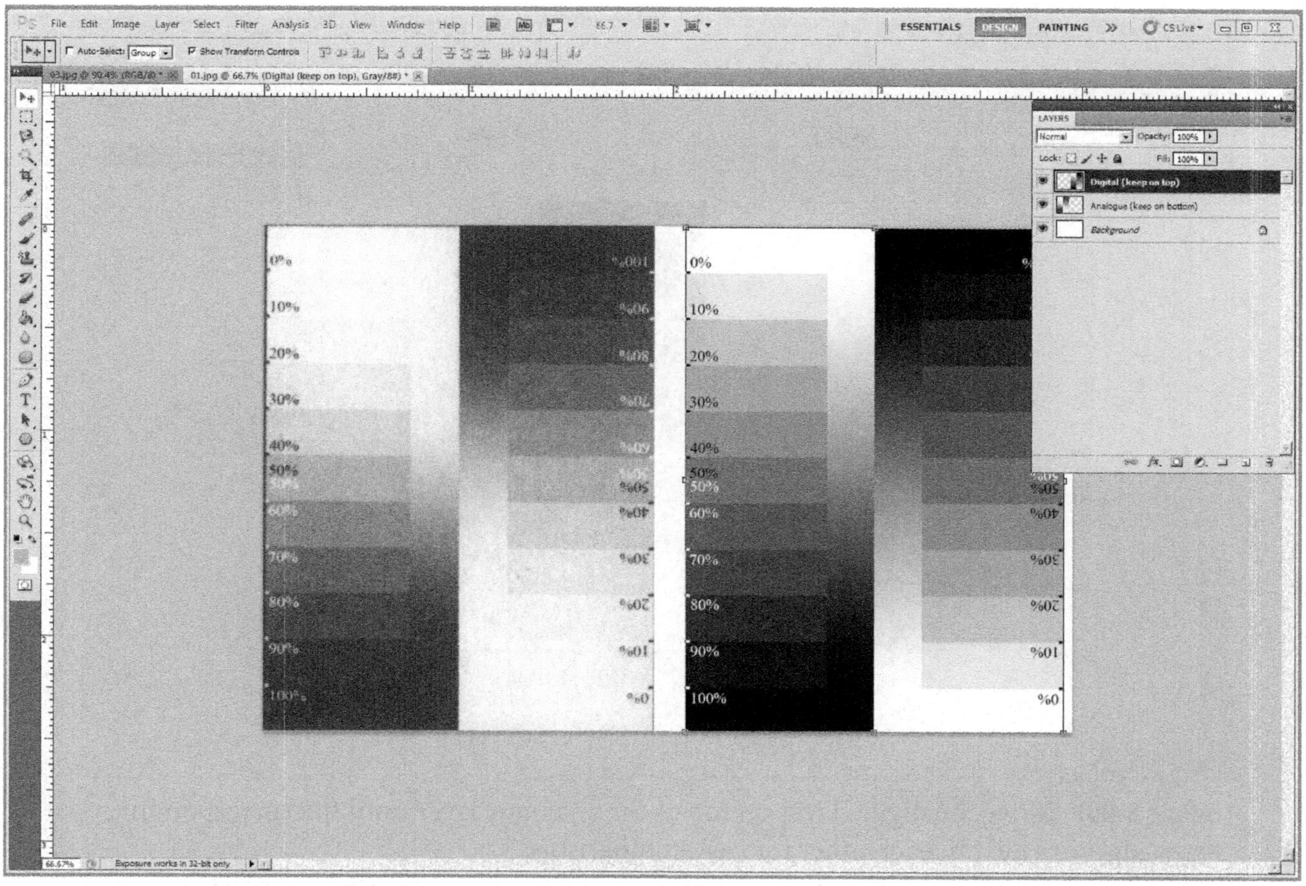

(image 8-08) Cut and paste both the analogue and digital step wedges into a new image. This is very important! Be sure that the analogue layer (scan of print) is on the bottom of the layers stack and that the digital layer is on the top of the layers stack. Also, switch to 16 bits/Channel. It will make a much more accurate curve for you. You can do this by clicking on Image --> Mode --> 16 Bits/Channel.

Labellng layers is useful so that you don't forget what they are (and where they are supposed to be) later in the workflow. By default, Photoshop is set up so that every layer effects the ones below it. With this workflow, you are making adjustments to the analogue print while using the digital layer as the goal of that adjustment. Keeping the digital layer at the top will allow you to add adjustment layers below it that will effect the analogue layer but not the digital layer.

The analogue layer (scan of intaglio print, step wedge that appears on the left) has not been adjusted yet. It is just the raw scan, with all automated adjustments turned off in the scanner.

The differences between 8 Bits/Channel, 16 Bits/Channel, and 32 Bits/Channel is beyond the scope of this book. What is worth mentioning here, however, is a simple maxim of "more bits per channel equals more information and finer adjustments". I tend to visualize the differences like a calculator. 8 Bits/Channel is like a calculator that only uses whole numbers (no fractions or decimal points). 16 Bits/Channel is like a calculator that has the capacity to use two places beyond the decimal point (working in 10ths and 100ths). 32 Bits/Channel is like a calculator that can use five places beyond the decimal point. It is very accurate, but not needed for most applications.

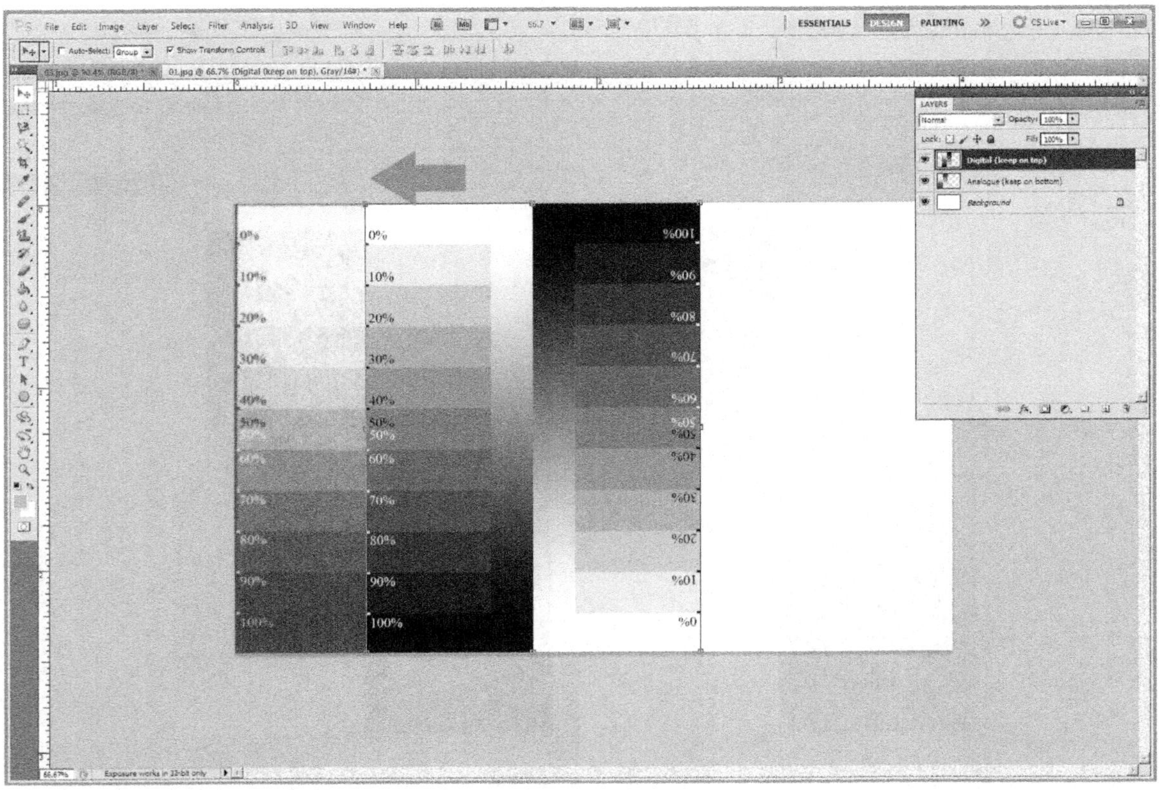

(image 8-09) Move the digital layer on top of the analogue layer until the corresponding step wedges are next to each other for easy comparison.

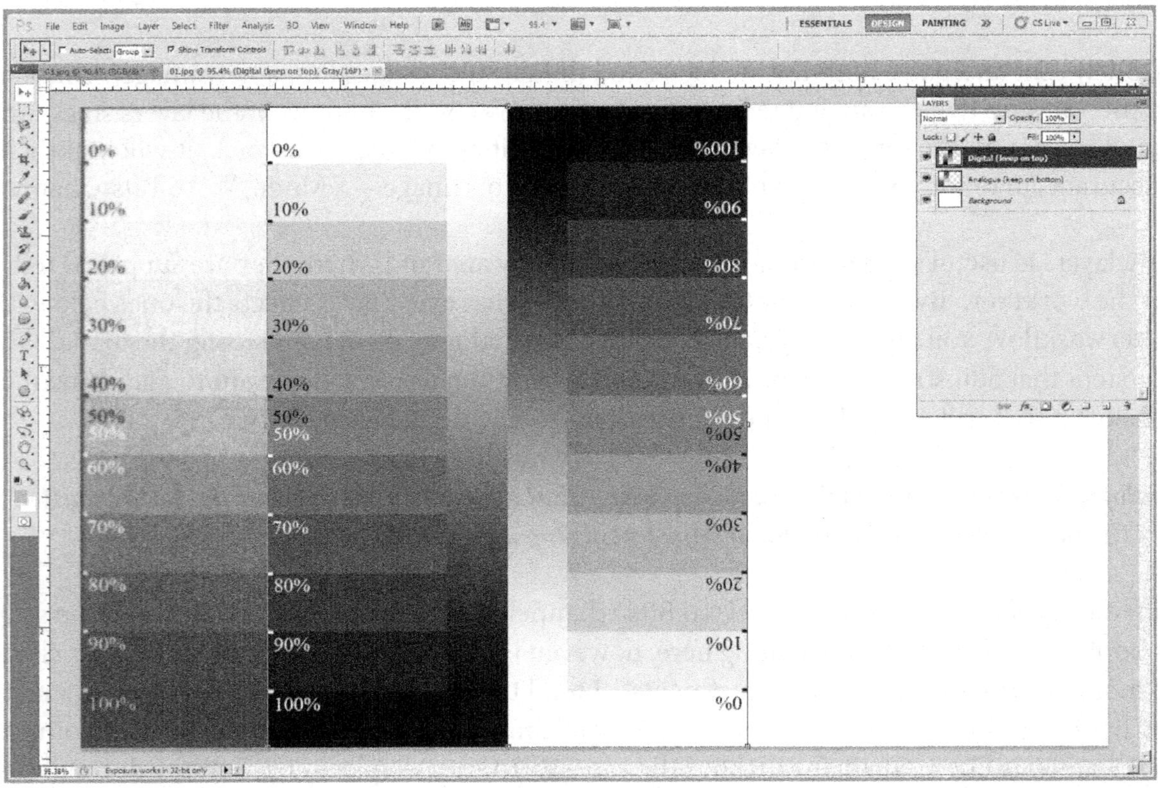

(**image 8-10**) Press Ctrl/0 so that the image will fit on the screen as large as possible making it easier to see the work you'll be doing.

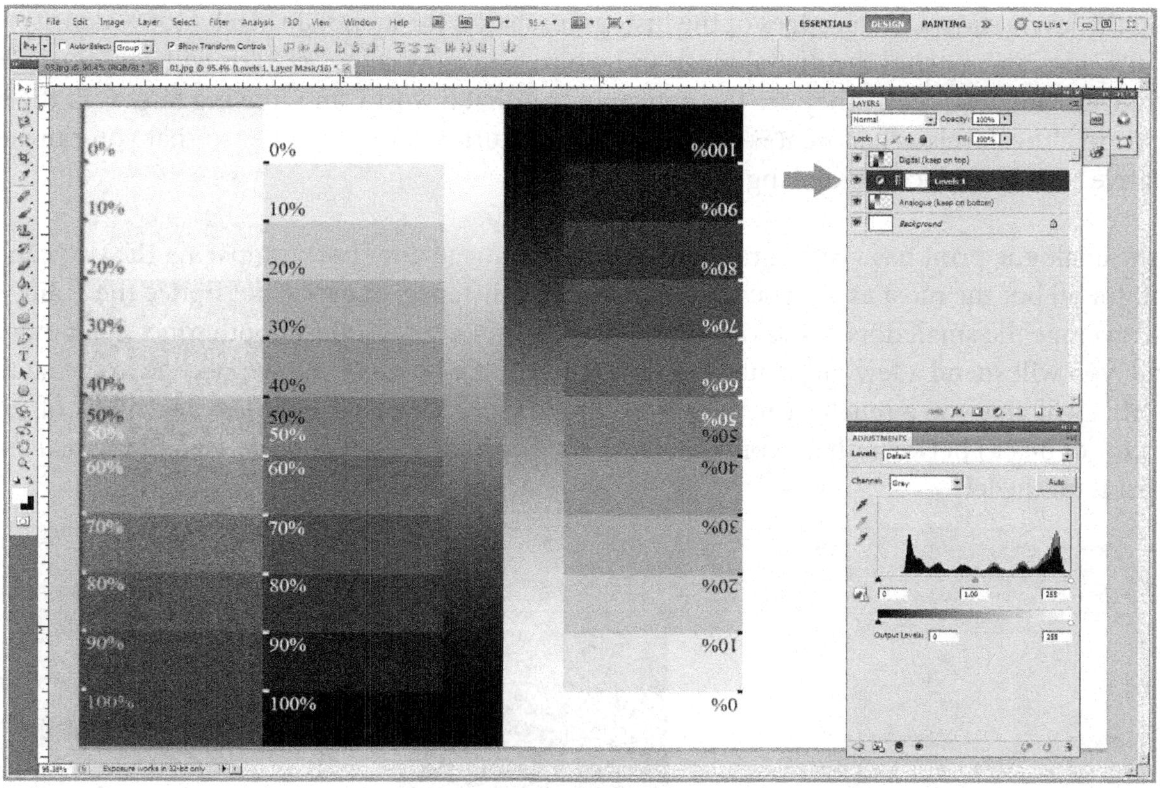

(image 8-11) Create a Levels layer. Make sure it is above the analogue layer but below the digital layer in the stack soit effects the analogue layer, but not the digital layer.

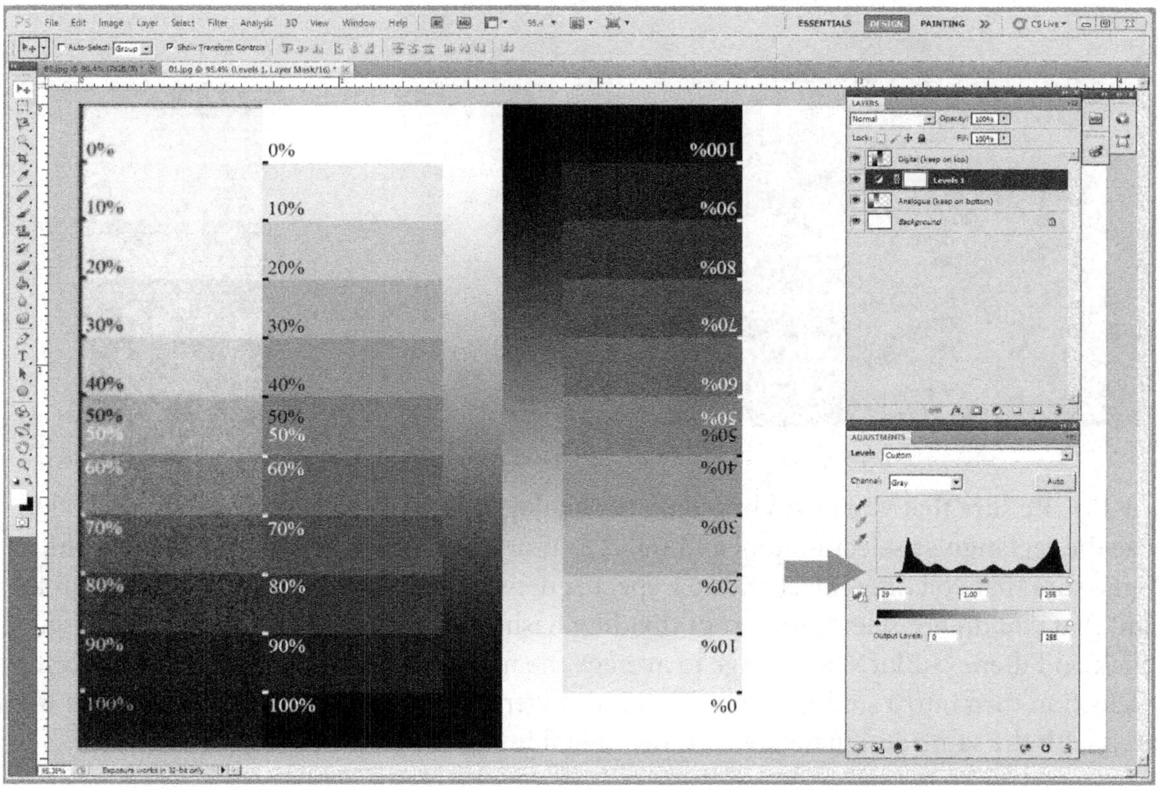

(**image 8-12**) Move both the black and white sliders on the levels layer until they just barely touch the outside of the histogram.

Moving the levels sliders to the edges of the histogram makes the analogue black (100% density) and white (0% density) matches the digital black and white. The gray steps between will shift too. Black and white are not absolutes. They are theoretical in the digital world, and moving targets in the analogue world. This levels adjustment is bringing the two worlds closer together so that you can adjust the relative scale from a common language.

Since the analogue print has visible grain and the digital image does not, comparing the two can be difficult for all but the most experienced viewer. From a distance, one may not notice the grain. The eye will average the small dots of dark and light gray so they read as one smooth tone. Keeping this in mind, you will spend a few moments averaging each of the boxes of the step wedge in the analogue print. This will give you a much easier way to compare specific densities of black (each box of gray is a "density" of black) between the theoretical digital image on the right and the scan of the real analogue print on the left.

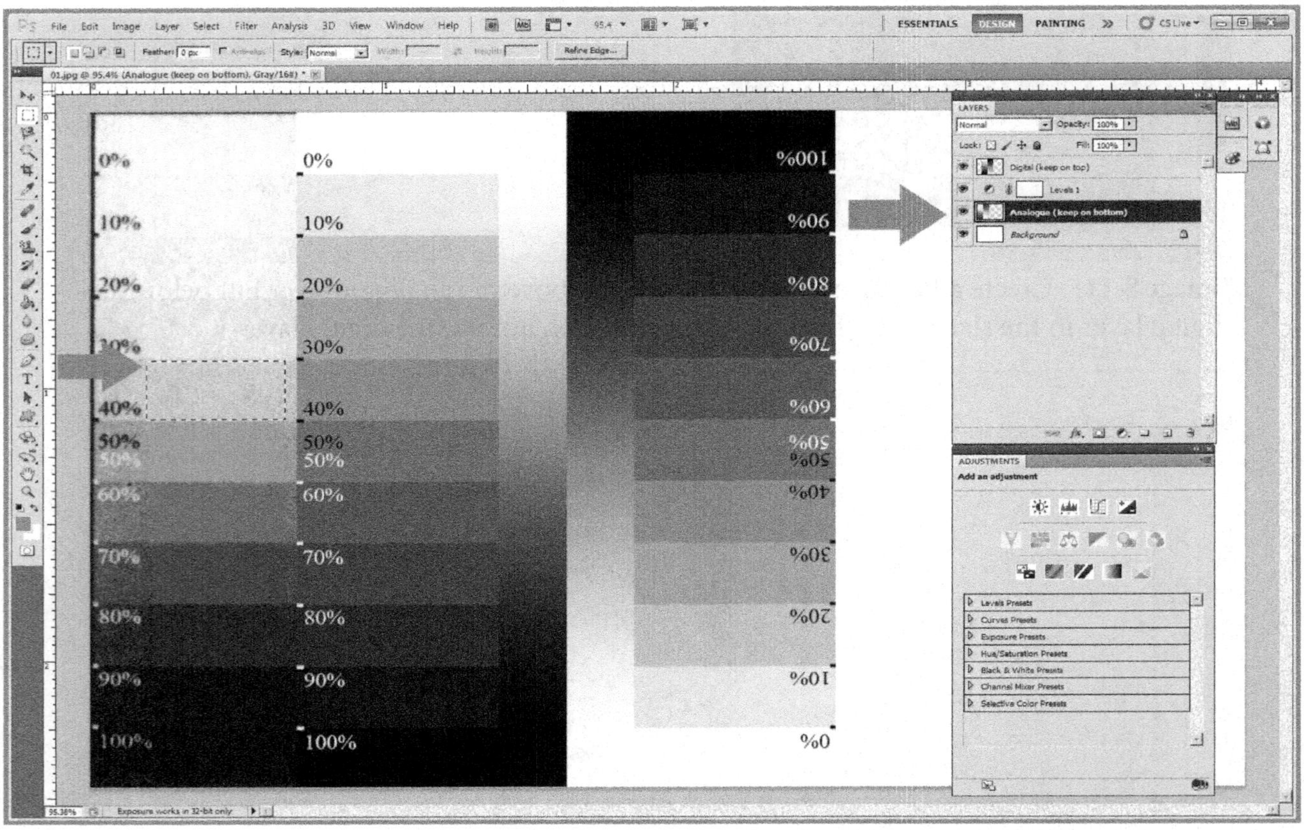

(image 8-13) Be sure that you have clicked on the analogue layer so all action will be applied to it. Next, use the rectangular selection tool and select as much of a gray box in the analogue print as you can. Make sure that you only select within a specific density (this image shows a selection in the 40% box), and that you do not select any text or dividing hash marks. Once you have the selection you want, click on Filter --> Blur --> Average to average the information in the box. You should see a grainy selection turn into a smooth tone. That is the average density of that selection which will be compared with the same designated box on the digital image later.

Repeat these steps on all 11 boxes (or "steps") on the analogue image until you have a smooth tone for each one.

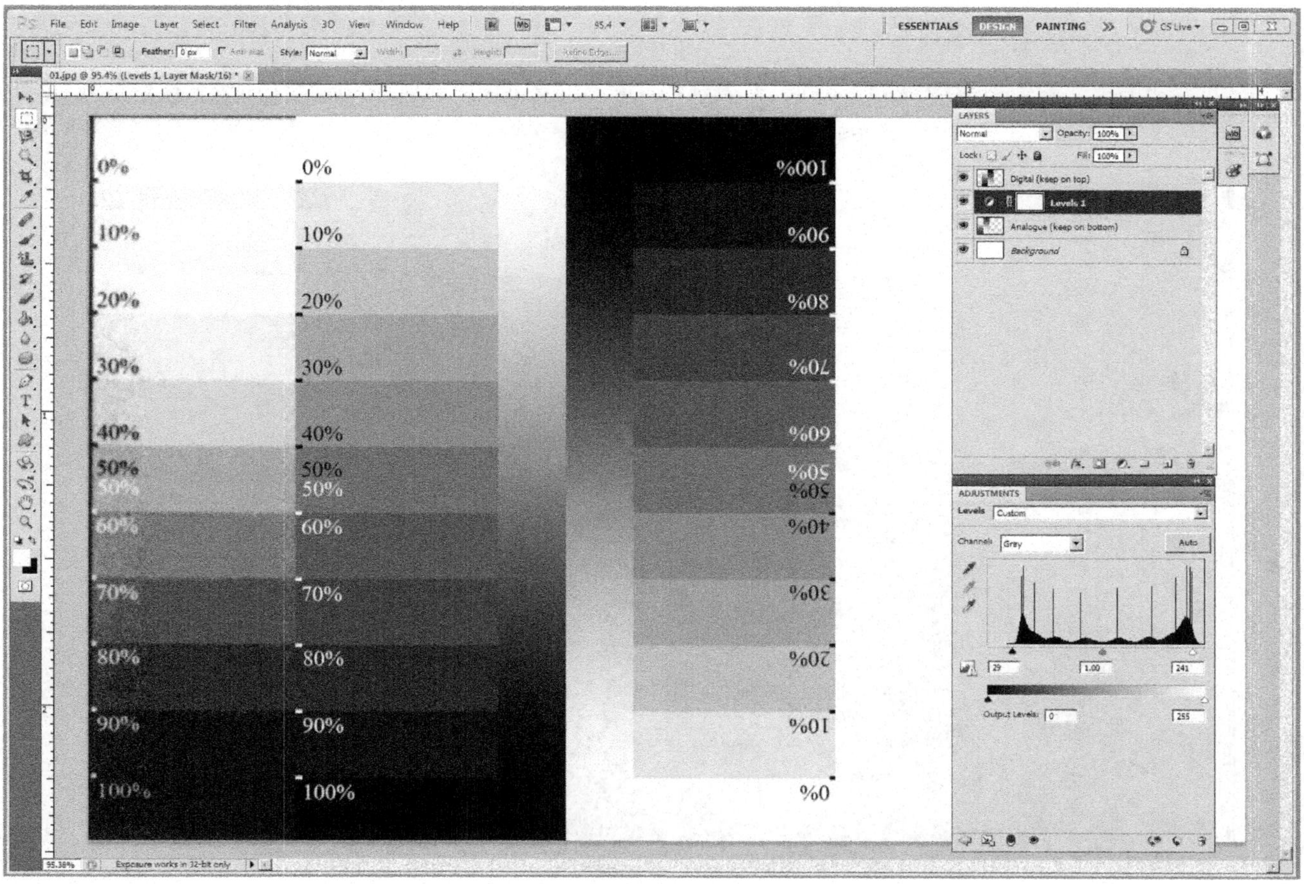

(image 8-14) Once you have the averaged boxes in the analogue step wedge (left side), you may want to revisit the levels adjustment layer to make sure that 0% is as white as can be and 100% is as black as can be.

Some words of caution: do not do this at the expense of making 90% go completely black and 10% go completely white. If there was information in those boxes, you need to treat them with extreme care. The analogue print will never perfectly match the theoretical densities of the digital image. The intent is to get as close as possible without losing information. In some workflows, 0%, 10%, and 20% will already be dropped out to look completely white, while 80%, 90%, and 100% will already be completely black. If that is the case, then the adjustment curve you are about to make will help. In the example used here, however, there was some information in the 10% and 90% boxes, so I need to be careful. Look to see where the information begins, and where there is a difference in density. Noting the location of 100% and 0% are important. Making sure that differences exist between steps is what actually makes the steps. Even if 80% is not a perfect 80%, it does need to be more dense than 70%. If they are same, then information is lost and the picture will be flat. The next steps in this process address these concerns.

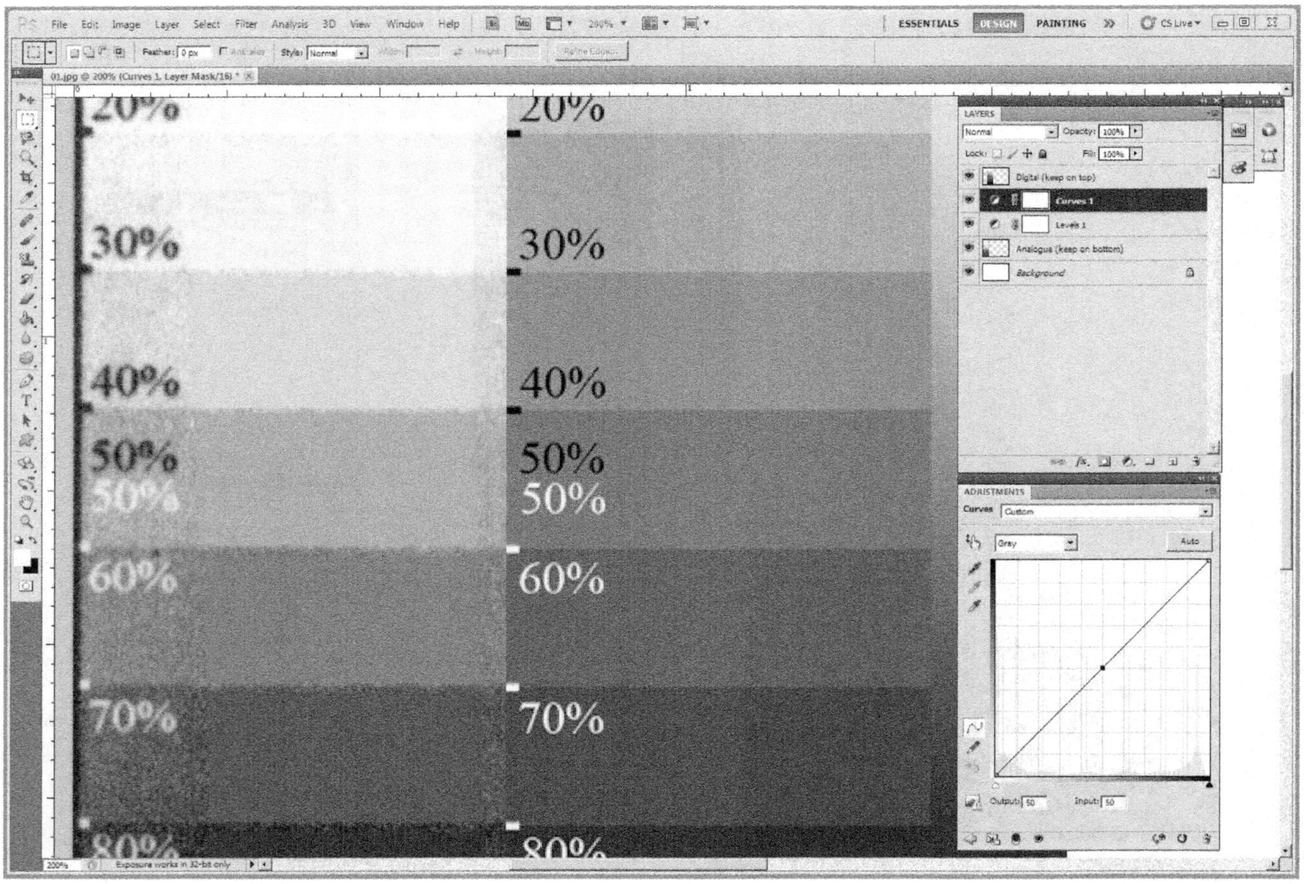

(image 8-15) Zoom in so that you can see both the analogue and digital image's rectangles for the 50% density value.
Create a new Curves adjustment layer, making sure that it is above Analogue & Levels in the layers stack, but below the Digital layer.
In the Adjustments window, you are going to start manipulating the Curves layer. Start by clicking in the center of the line, where the values are Output: 50 and Input: 50. As long as you get close, it will work because you can reassign the value to both be 50 and have a good starting point.

In the curves adjustment layer, the vertical axis represents the density value (in % black) that is input from the image or application. The horizontal axis represents the density value that is output. In this case, you must consider the output as what ends up happening in your final print. With so many steps from computer to final print, the output is not going to match the input.

In this example, 50% was input to the computer and only 42% ended up being output in the final print. So, when you put in (input) a value of 50%, how much more needs to actually be put out (output) by the computer to result in a real value of 50%?

(Useful Tool: click on Window --> Info and a box will appear that will allow you to see the black value [K] for any part of your image expressed in 0 - 100%. Click on the Move Tool and move that arrow around the screen. You should see the value of K [black] change)

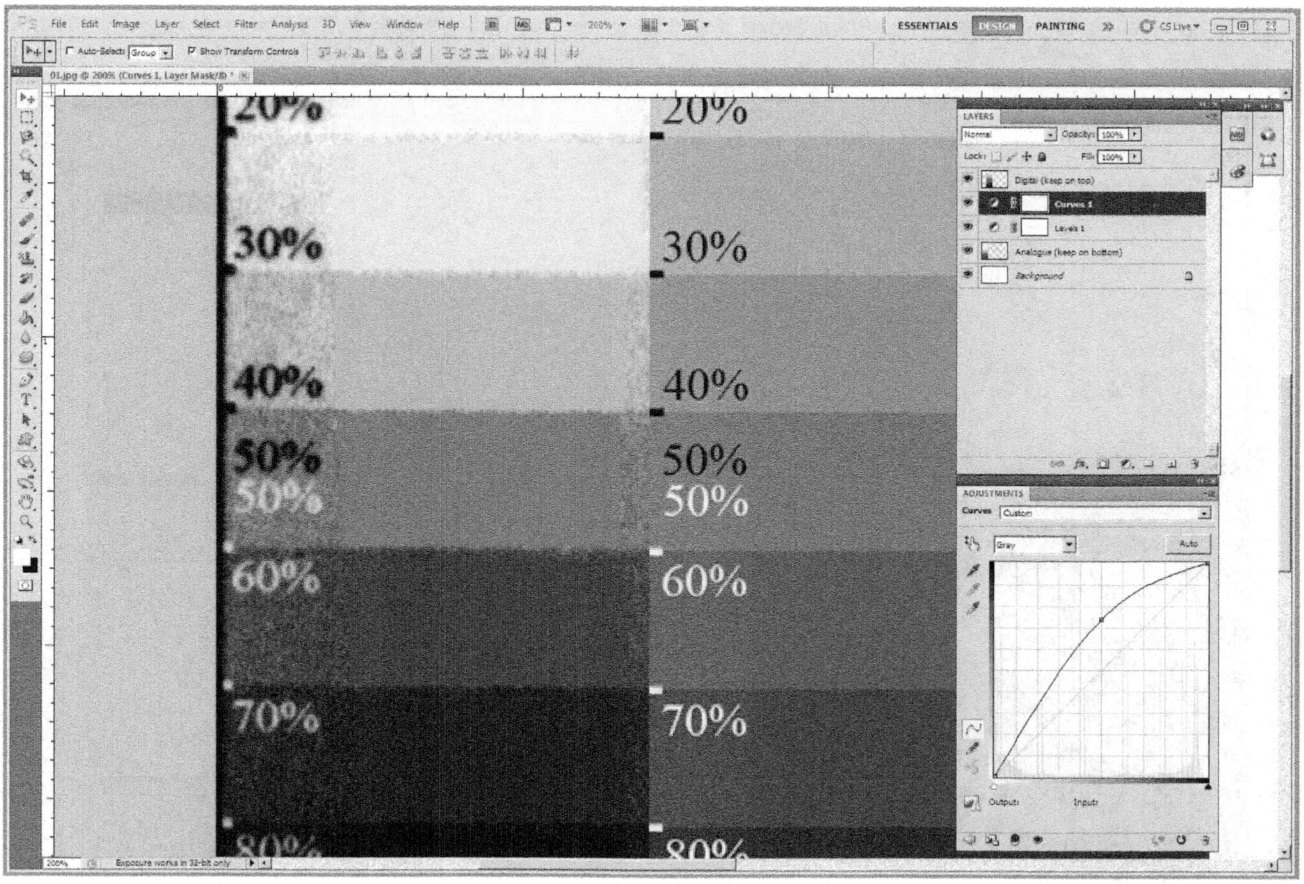

(image 8-16) Be sure that the point you plotted at Output:50/Input:50 in the Adjustments window is active. If it is not, just click on it with your mouse. Use the keyboard arrow keys to move that point straight up or down until the 50% rectangle in the analogue image (left side) looks like the 50% rectangle in the digital side. In this image, the point had to be moved up until the Output was 74%.

Work only on the 50% value. Do not pay attention to the other values at this point. The other values (except 0% and 100%) will change significantly. The other values will be modified in the next few steps.

Get in the habit of writing down the results of the Input and Output windows. If you have the data, you can reconstruct a curve if you make any mistakes or if something get's lost. At this early stage, this example has the following:

Output	Input
0	0
50	74
100	100

To get a final output of 50%, we must input a value of 74%.

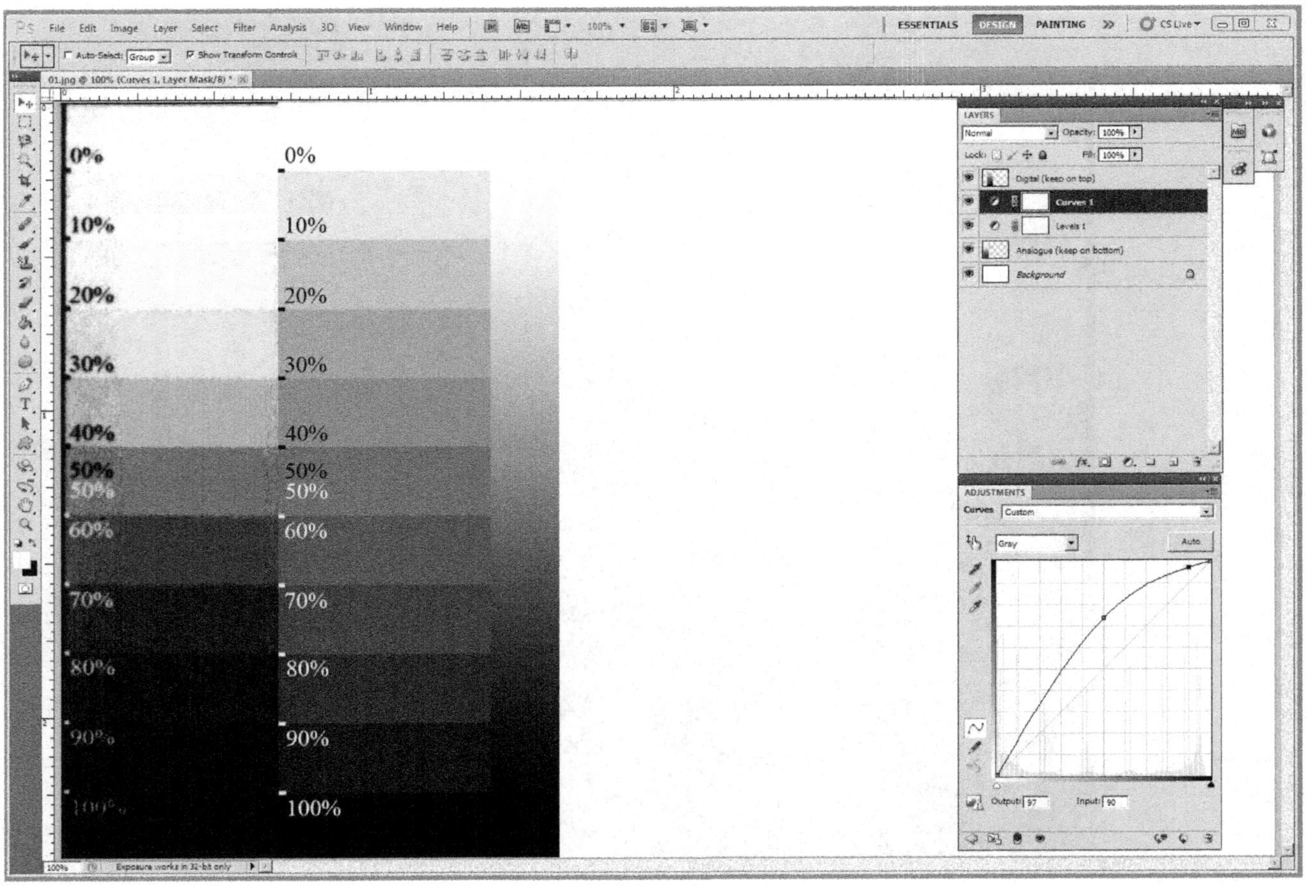

(image 8-17) In the Adjustment window (where you are working the plotted curve), click on any neutral gray area to make the Output and Input windows not active. The numerical value windows will disappear when they are not active. This means that you are no longer working on the 50% point and can choose a new point with the mouse.

This example had a good 90% density before we ruined it with the 50% adjustment in the last image. Let's see if we can get 90% back to a good place.

Click on a point, as close as you can, along the plotted curve to the 90% value. If it's 92%, or something close, it's ok. Simply reassign the value of Input to 90% to make sure you are in the right place. Do not worry about the Output value yet, since that will be adjusted in the next step.

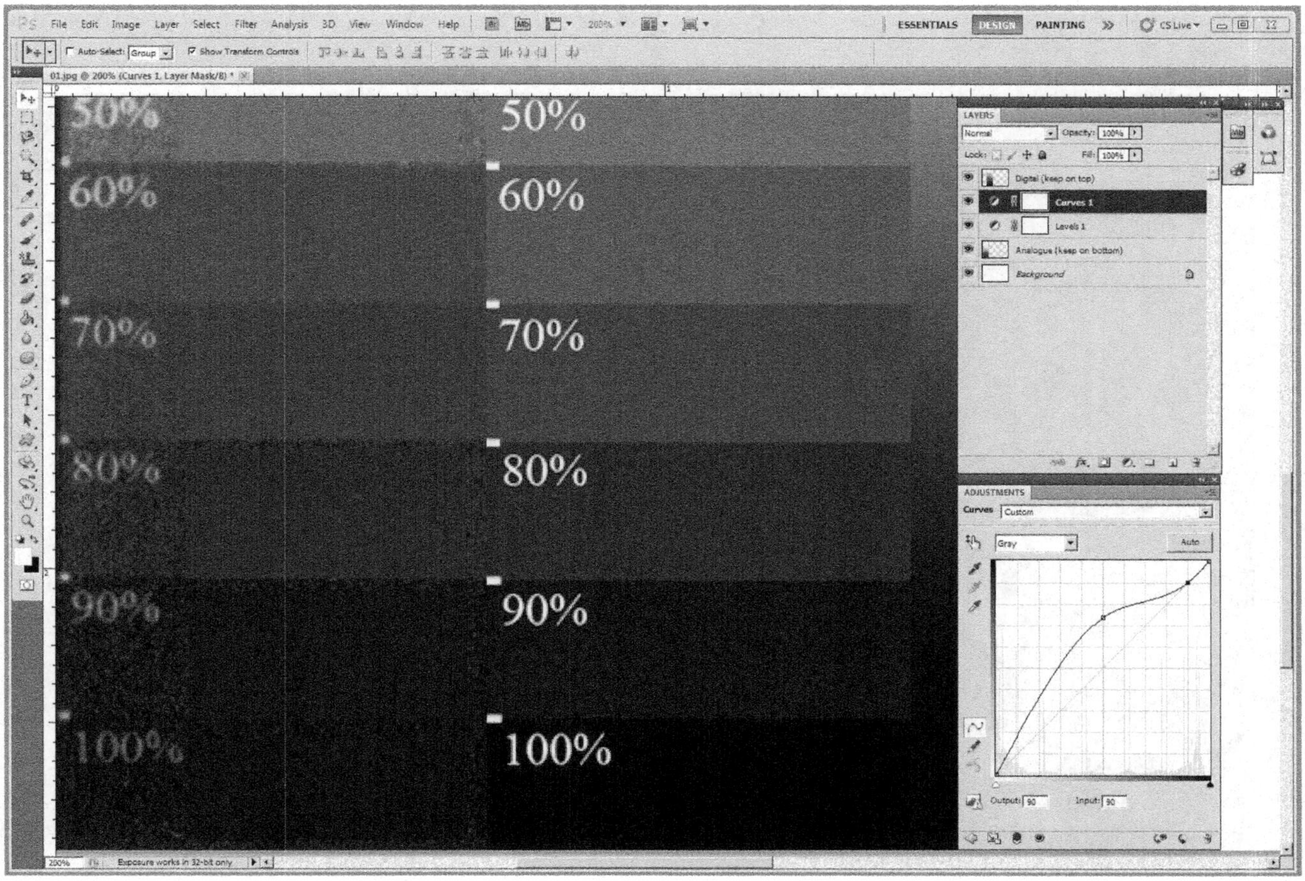

(image 8-18) With the 90% plotted point active, use the up/down arrows to move it along the vertical axis. The horizontal axis is the Input axis, and you do not want to move that. You only want to move the vertical axis that shows the output.

Using the zoom tool to enlarge the work area is a good way to ignore the rest of the step wedge and focus only on the step that is being worked on for the moment. I suggest that you get in the habit of zooming in and out to check your work.

In this example 90% input ends up being 90% output. That does not always happen.

Remember to write down the data you are getting.

Output	Input
0	0
50	74
90	90
100	100

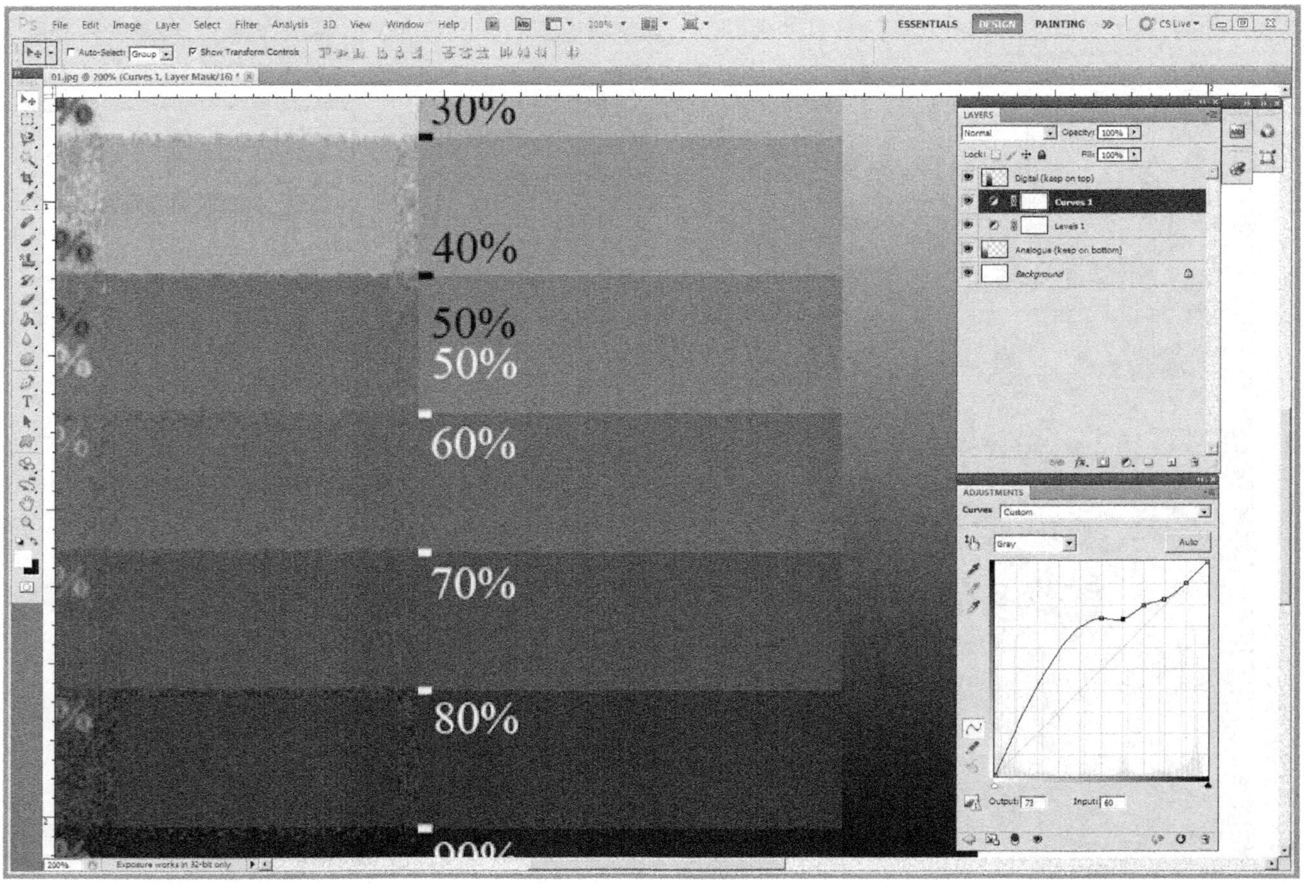

(image 8-19) Go through the same process with 80, 70, 60%, manipulating the plotted points with the up and down keys, attempting to match the tone of the analogue image to the digital image.

The curve will not look graceful, and you may discover one point that ends up being plotted lower than it's lower-value neighbor. Every adjustment you make on the curve effects the overall curve, which is why the simple adjustments we are making don't perfectly reflect the real math of these types of curves. It does work, however, because ultimately we are working in the realm of perceived light and dark values, which are filtered through out eyes and brains to create relative impressions of light and dark.

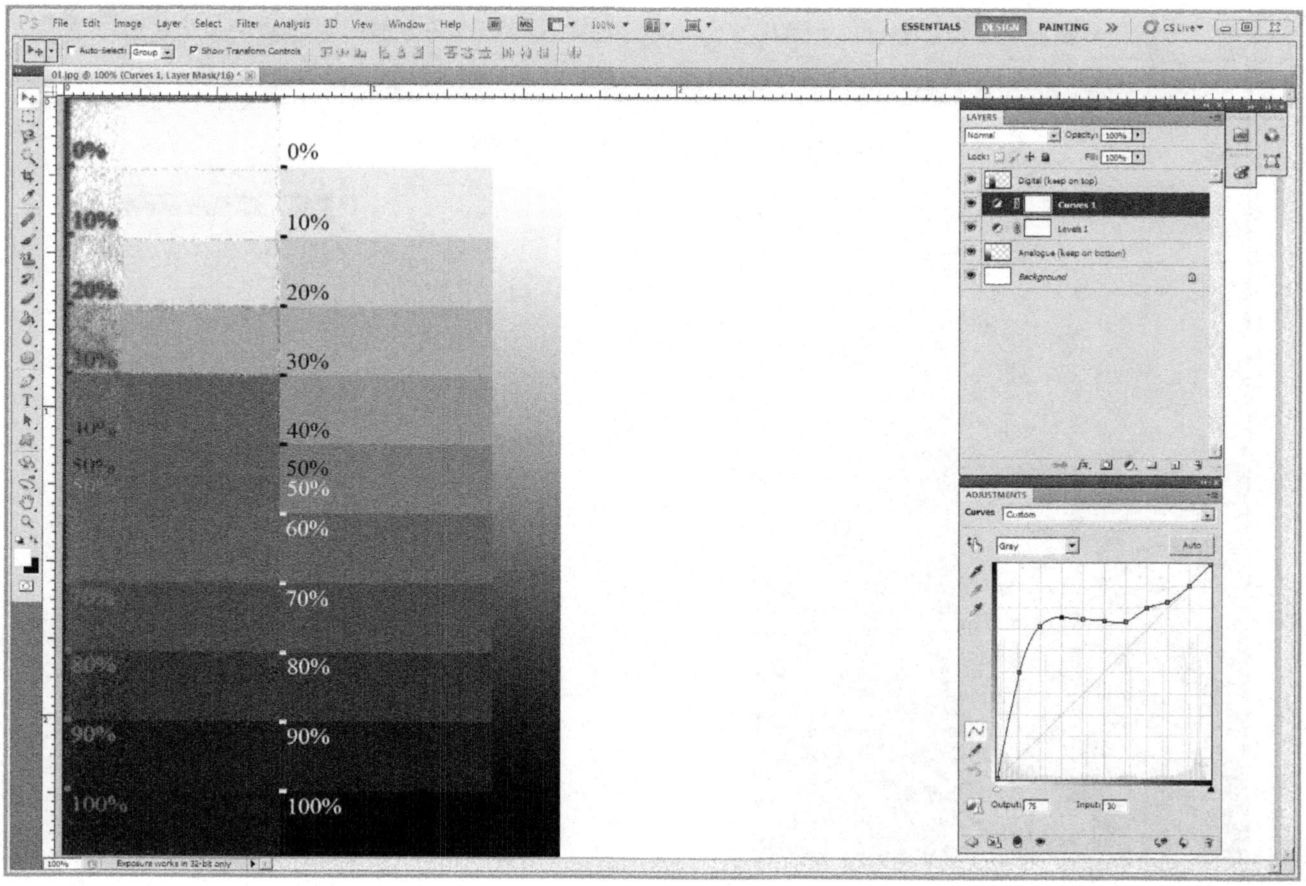

(image 8-20) Keep going through all the points from 10% - 90%. At least get all the points plotted. In this example, the image is starting to get flat and look funny.

Once all 11 Input points are plotted in 10% increments (from 0% - 100%), you can begin to fine tune the curve. Start by looking for crooked parts of the curve, or reversals. This example has both.

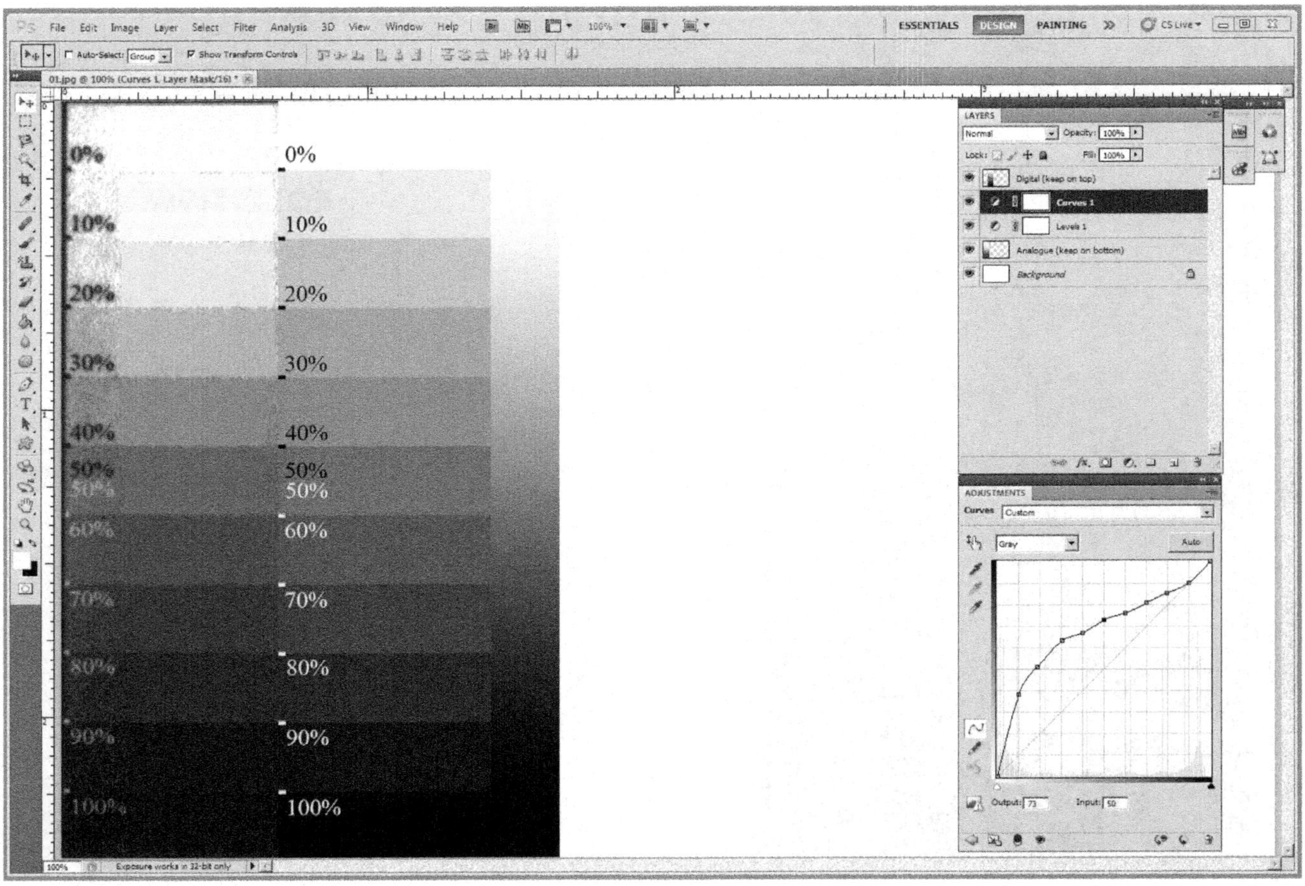

(image 8-21) First, click on one of the points that is reversed (an anomaly that is lower or higher than the rest of the curve around it). See if adjusting that point up or down helps.

In this example, 40%, 50%, 60% need a lot of work, so that is where I started. I kept clicking back and forth on those points and trying to bump them up and down until the middle of the step wedge looked good.

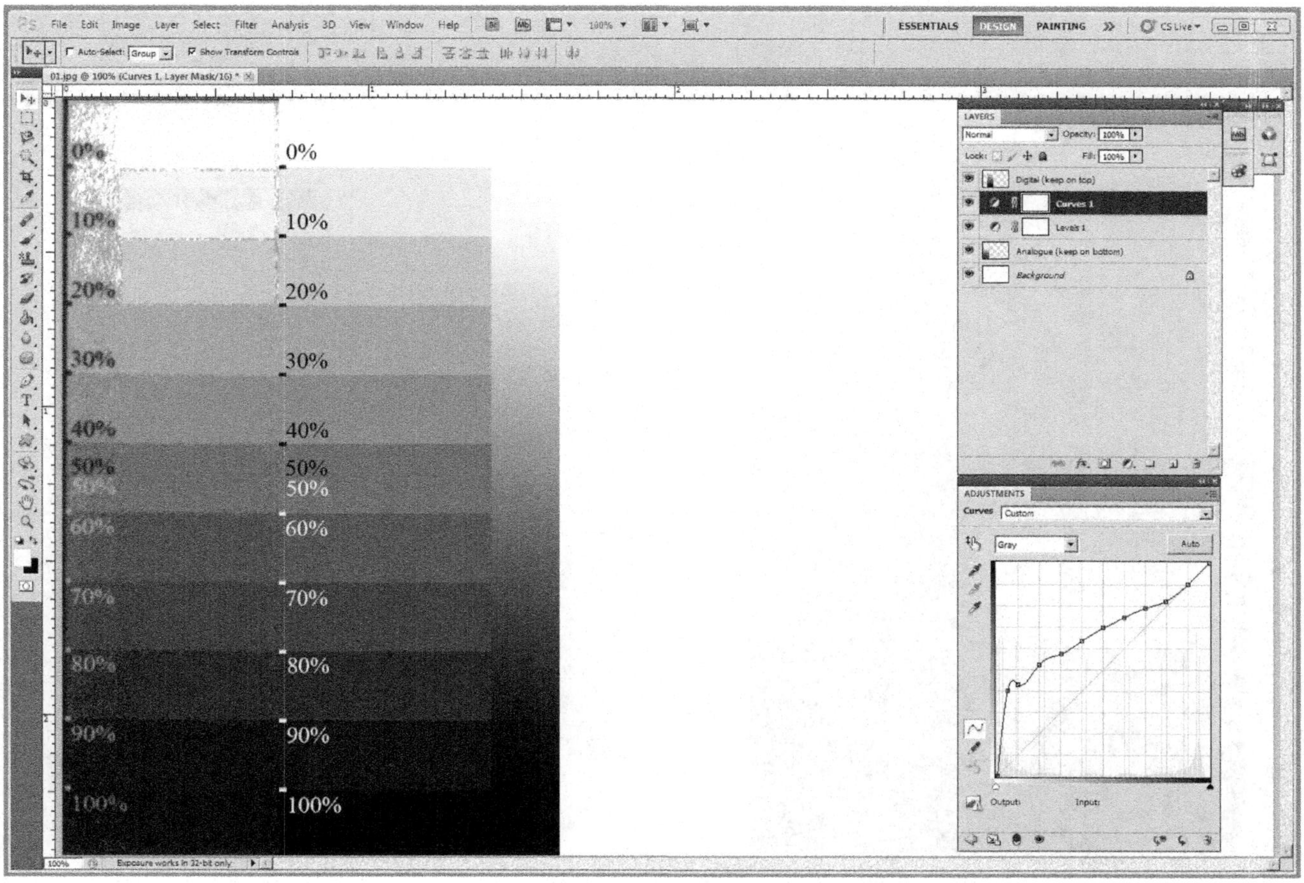

(image 8-22) You could keep going, but at some point you have to stop and accept how close you got. I am usually happy if 0%, 30%, 50%, 80%, 100% are a good match and the rest of the steps between those numbers show some progression from light to dark (and are not just all the same tone).

Having recorded all of the data, here is what the example has for Output/Input after overall tweaking:

Output	Input
0	0
5	40
10	43
20	52
30	57
40	63
50	69
60	75
70	79
80	82
90	90
100	100

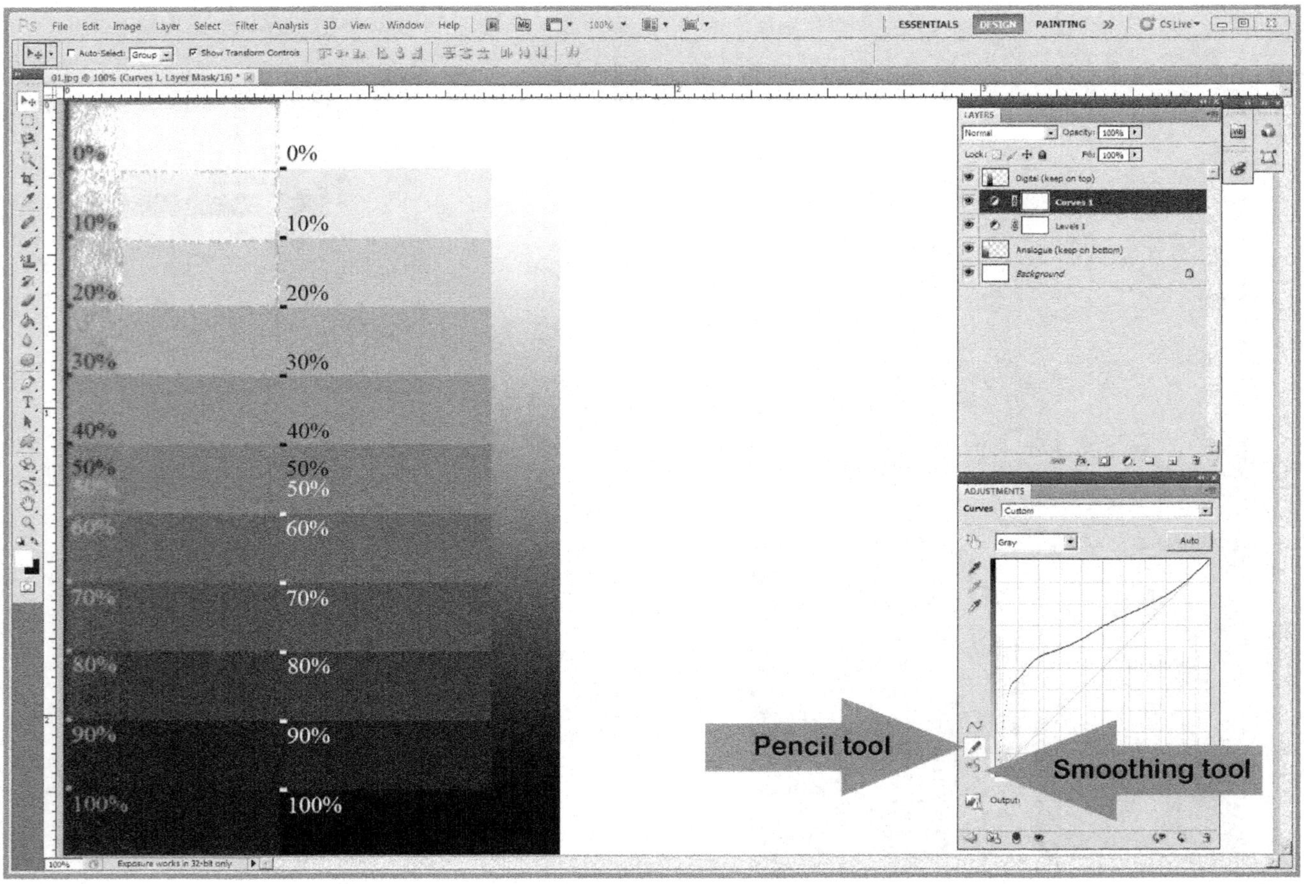

(image 8-23) The smoothing option is not always needed, but is worth trying.

In the lower left corner of the adjustments window, click on the pencil tool then click on the smoothing tool below it.

(If you hold your cursor over the pencil, it will say, "draw to modify the curve". If you hold your cursor over the smoothing tool, it will say, "smooth the curve values")

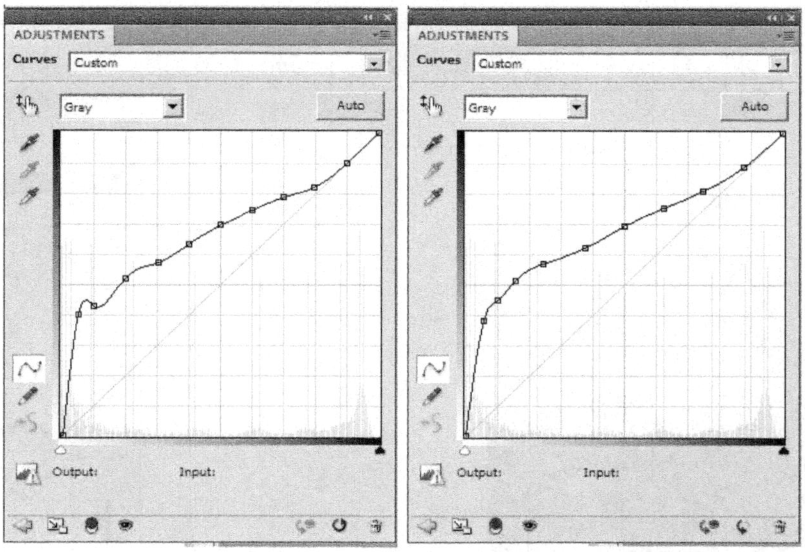

(image 8-24) These are the curves before smoothing (left) and after smoothing (right).

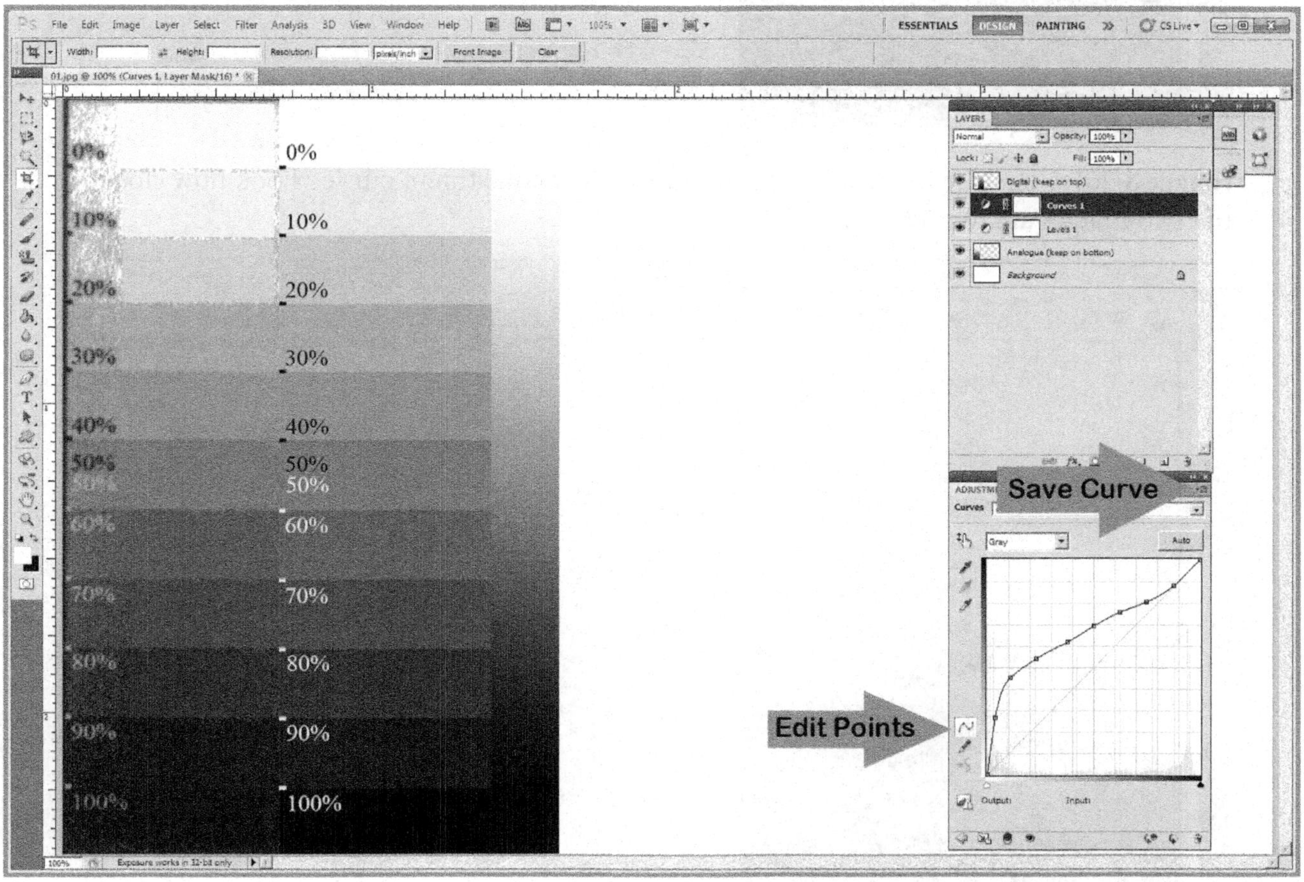

(image 8-25) Remember to save all of your hard work!!!

Be sure you are on the Edit Points mode (top box of the three; above the pencil tool and smoothing tool). In the top right corner of the adjustments window, pull down the menu and chose "Save Curves Preset". Name the curve and save it with .acv extension.

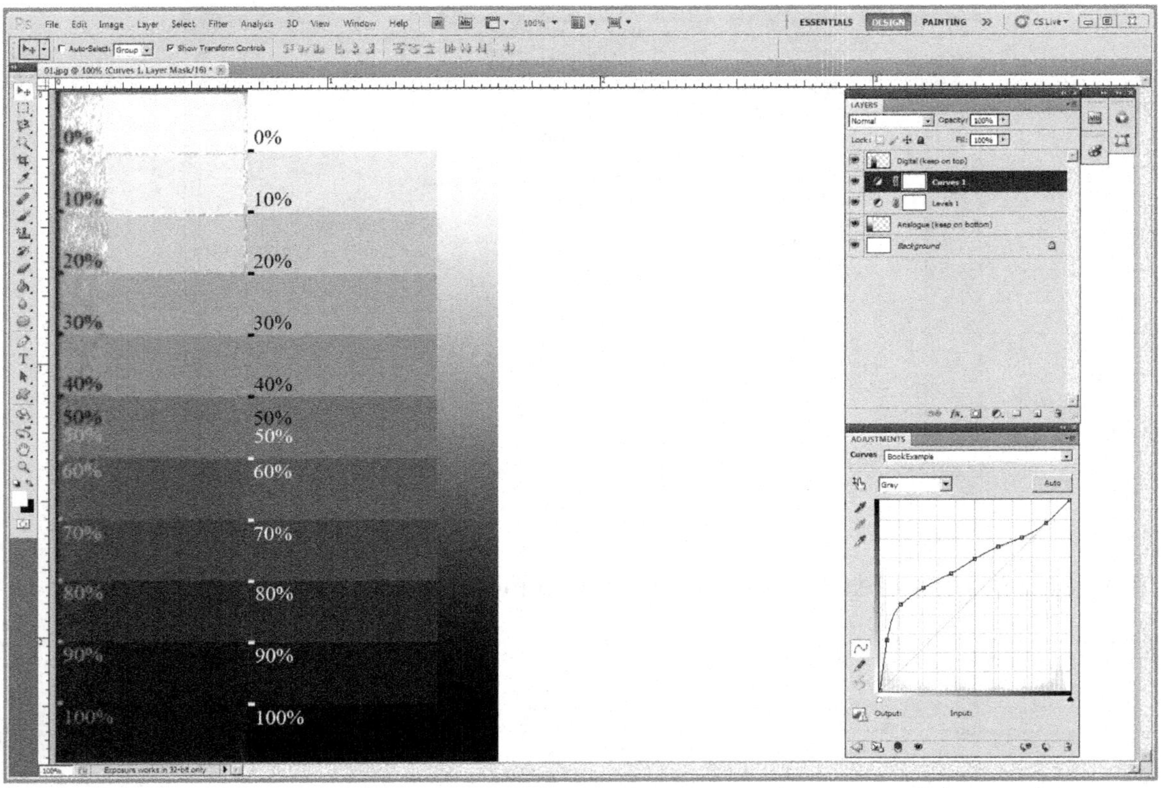

(image 8-26) Consider the work you just did with the adjustment curve. Look how close the two images are to each other.

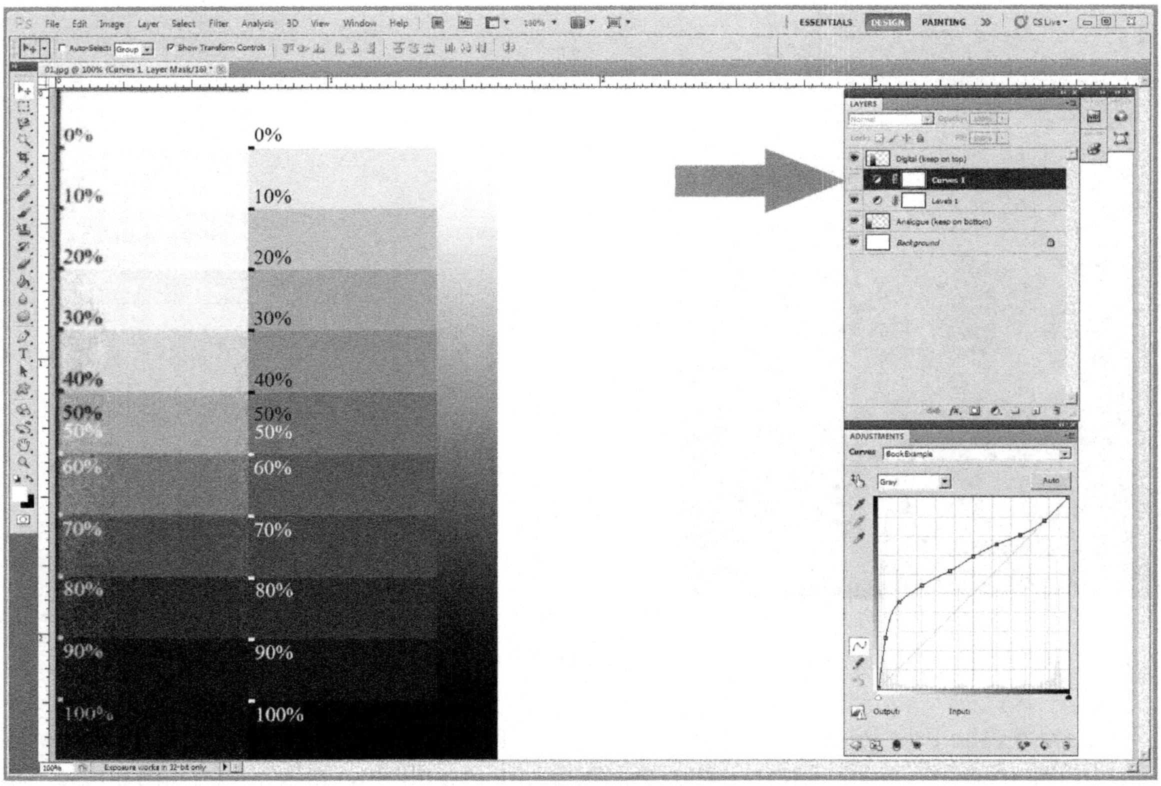

(image 8-27) Turn the adjustment curve off by clicking the eye symbol in the box next to the Curves layer. This shows you how the analogue image looked when you started.

Different conditions require different adjustment curves. Switching UV exposure units will require a new curve. Sometimes changing exposure lengths on the same UV unit will require a new curve. Too many variables exist to trust that the same curve is going to work forever. If you just want a basic image with black, white, and 3 steps of gray, then you can go through this process once and never have to do it again. If, however, you are looking for very refined images, then you will have to keep repeating the process of making new curves every time you change one variable in your workflow.

Here are some of the Output/Input values that I have used, and the equipment used with them:

Ryonet RXP 16x20 UV exposure unit
Contact frame with 1/4" tempered glass, acid etched one side
Fixxons Waterproof Silkscreen Positive Film
Epson Stylus Pro 3800
KM 73 photopolymer plate
5 minute stochastic screen exposure ("aquatint")
5 minute image transparency exposure

Output	Input
0	0
5	31
10	40
20	53
30	60
40	66
50	71
60	74
70	78
80	82
90	88
100	100

Aristo Platinum Printer
Contact frame with 1/4" tempered glass, acid etched one side
Fixxons Waterproof Silkscreen Positive Film
Epson Stylus Pro 3800
KM 73 photopolymer plate
12 minute stochastic screen exposure ("aquatint")
12 minute image transparency exposure

Output	Input
0	0
10	16
20	31
30	38
40	44
50	50
60	59
70	65
80	73
90	84
100	100

The system shown in this chapter is one that I developed after gaining an understanding of some of the underlying principles of adjustment curves. I have not yet seen this simple method on the internet or in books that I have read. My hope is, that by showing different system of finding adjustment curves, it will provide a contrast to all of the other methods and systems that are either in print or on the web.

Below you will find a list of resources that I have used with varying degrees of success. I encourage you to follow some of the links and try some other systems so that you can gain a deeper understanding of how adjustment curves work. All the systems work. They all have the same basic principles, with different workflows that appeal to different personalities.

"Digital Negatives for Palladium and other Alternative Processes" by **Ron Reeder**
ISBN 978-0-557-60468-5
This easy-to-follow book shows the basics of making adjustment curves as well as a more comprehensive technique that uses Quadtone Rip to control the printer's ink output.
www.ronreeder.com

Quadtone Rip is not only useful for making digital negatives and the associated adjustment curves, but it is a terrific application for fine tuning black and while photos with an inkjet printer.
http://www.quadtonerip.com

"Making Digital Negatives for Contact Printing" by **Dan Burkholder**
ISBN 0-9649638-6-8
www.danburkholder.com
This is an old book that is still full of exceptionally useful information. Dan Burkholder is also offering a new book on his website that is certainly worth checking out.

Michael Koch-Schulte has an excellent website for his RNP Array system.
http://www.inkjetnegative.com/images/RNP/quick_guide_to_making_digital_ne.htm

Chart Throb is a script for building curves. It was made by **Kevin Bjorke**, and is quite effective.
http://www.botzilla.com/blog/archives/000544.html

Clay Harmon has taught many people how to make adjustment curves for transparencies, both in workshops and through his easy-to-understand systems that he has shared on various alternative photography sites.
http://www.clayharmon.com

Mark Nelson's precision digital negatives (PDN) is a complex and thorough system that has worked well for many people. The one catch to the system is that it is expensive. But, if you have a chance to take a workshop with the author of this system, I'd suggest it. You'll surely learn a great deal about image control in both the digital realm and during output (printing).
http://www.precisiondigitalnegatives.com

Chapter 9
Paper

Use thick cotton printmaking paper.
100% cotton paper (sometimes called "rag") is very strong and naturally acid free. It is the best choice for beginners and experts alike. It can withstand the pressure of printing. It will last a very long time without becoming yellow and fragile.

Do not use alpha cellulose paper.
Be wary of less expensive paper, that has wood pulp (alpha cellulose), even in the smallest amount. Wood pulp is not strong, and it contains a lot of acid. Papers that contain wood pulp are often marked "acid free". This is a purposely deceiving marketing tactic in which enough buffer is mixed into the paper so that it tests pH neutral. The buffer eventually breaks down and the natural acid of the wood pulp will make the paper yellow and brittle.

Other acceptable sources for paper exist. Bamboo can be good. Kozo makes nice prints. However, until you develop better knowledge about art papers, keep using 100% cotton printmaking paper. My go-to paper is Rives BFK. I have used others, but Rives BFK is the one I return to most frequently.

Paper needs to be damp so that it can be flexible enough to reach into the recesses of the aquatint matrix and pick up the ink. Damp paper also has wicking properties, allowing the ink to spread evenly across the surface, making smoother tonal transitions. Other than the resolution of the image transparency, two factors play important roles in creating smooth tones: pressure setting on the etching press, and paper that is evenly damp.

While the paper needs to be damp, it should not feel like a sponge, or have any excess water on its surface. The paper should feel cold to the touch, but should not make your hand feel like it is wet.

All of the examples in this book show the use of a tub of water to soak the paper for 30 minutes or more. After the paper is evenly soaked throughout, it is removed from the water and pressed between pieces of blotter paper. Blotter paper removes excess water through a wicking action, and is assisted by the pressure applied with your hands. Many people use a kitchen rolling pin to press the blotter paper against the printmaking paper. I find that using my hands works enough for me.

Many printmakers create what they call a "wet pack" of paper the day before a print run. They dunk printmaking paper in water, then place it flat on top of a piece of cotton blotter paper. Alternating layers of wet printmaking paper and dry blotter paper are assembled into a stack. The stack is stored, flat, in a plastic bag, sandwiched between straight boards with some weight on top until the next day, when the print run requires a piece of paper.

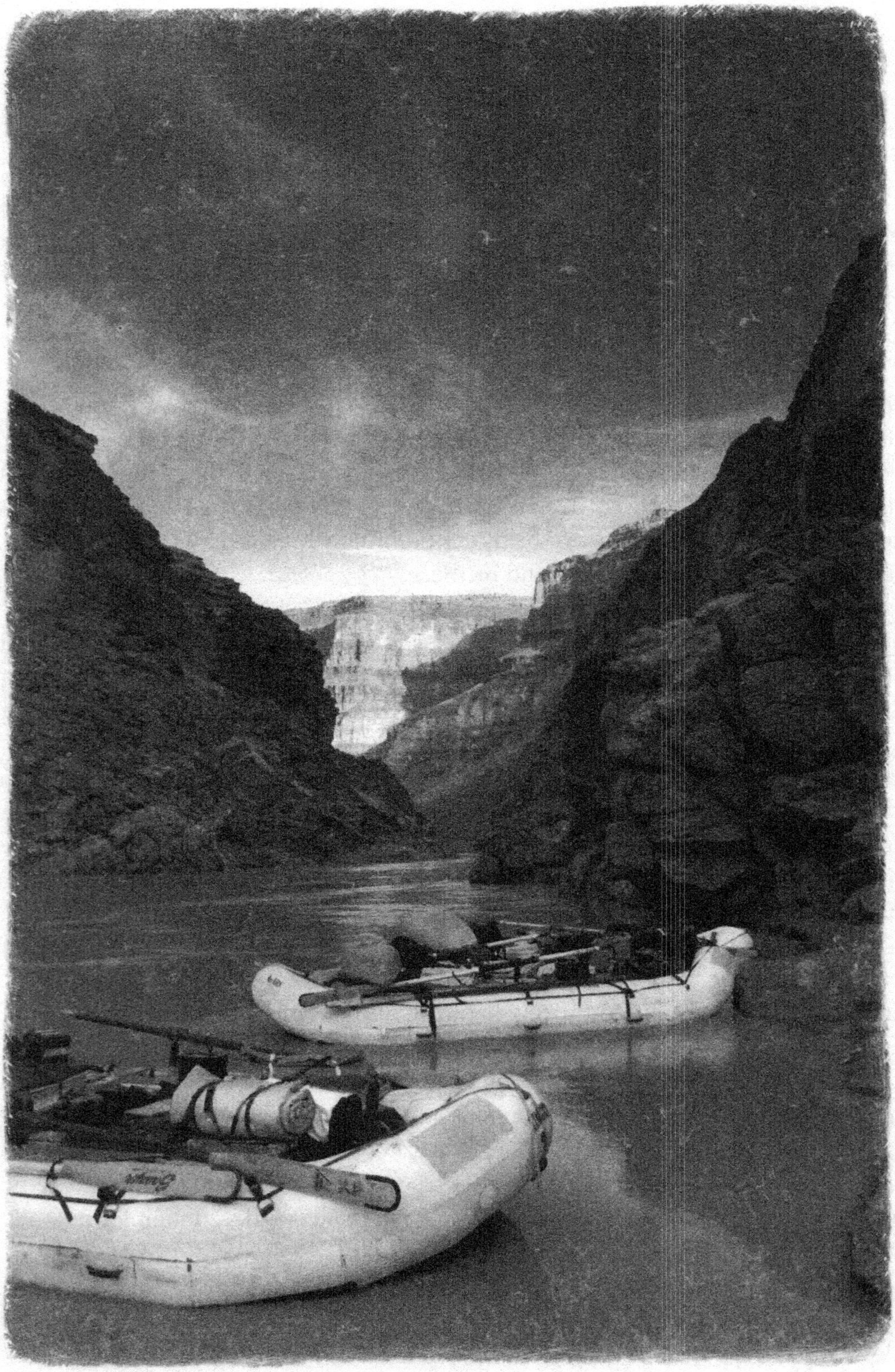

"Paul & Ringo"

photogravure

Scott Barnes

Chapter 10
Setting Press Pressure

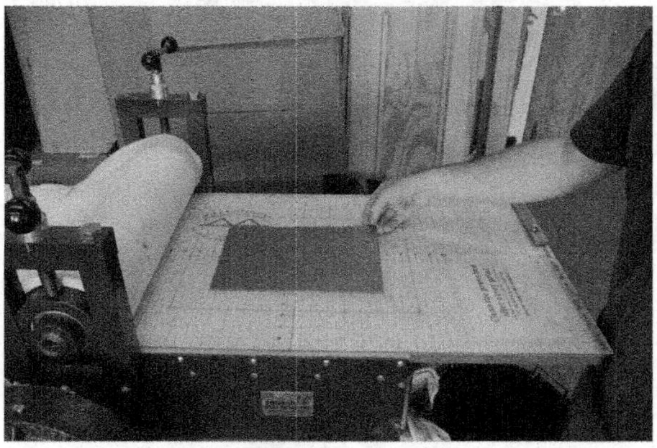

(**image 10-01**) Place one of the photopolymer plates on the bed of the press.

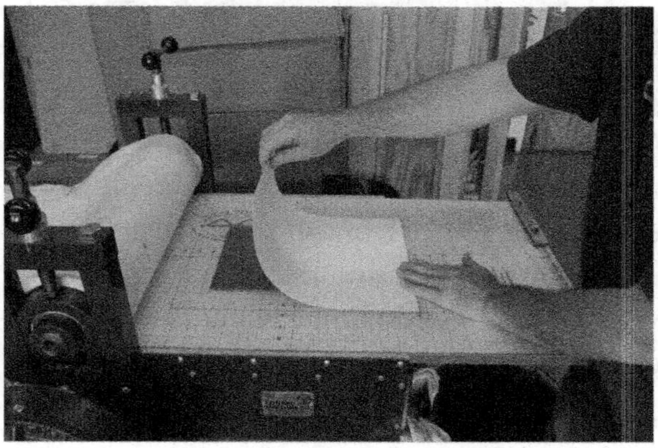

(**image 10-02)** Put a piece of dry printmaking paper on top of the plate.

Making sure that the plate is centered, and that the paper is centered over the plate will yield the best results because you are duplicating the printing workflow that you normally use. Dry paper is recommended because it will show too little or too much pressure better than damp paper. Remember, this is just a test to set the press pressure. Damp paper is required when actually making prints.

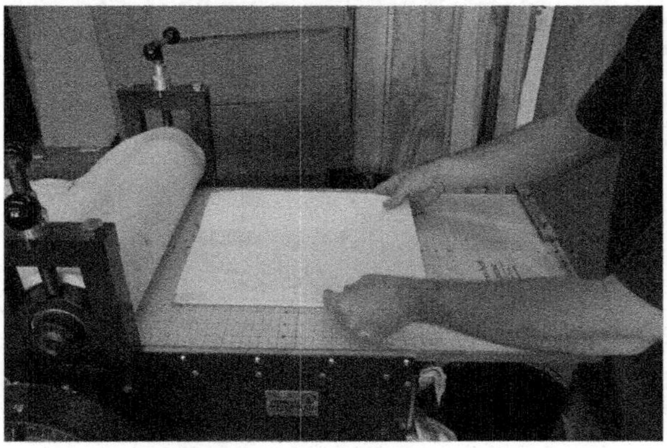

(**image 10-03**) Place a second piece of printmaking paper on top of the first.

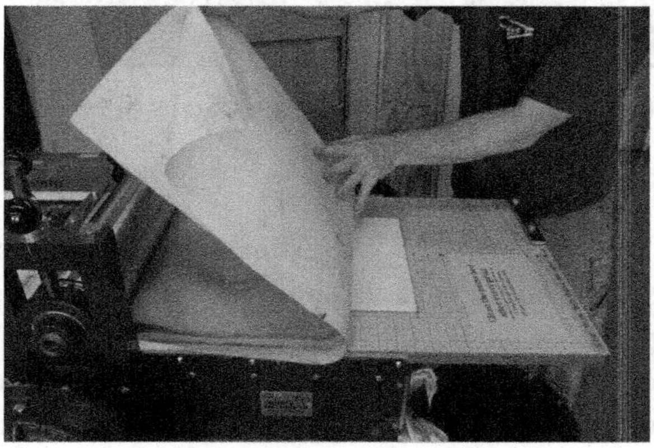

(**image 10-04**) Gently place the wool blankets over the plate and paper.

The second piece of printmaking paper acts as another blanket, spreading the pressure of the press evenly. Using the same type of printmaking paper for the last blanket will help make sure that texture or impefections from the wool blankets are not transferred to the print.

Make sure that the blankets are straight and do not have any wrinkles that will make marks or create uneven pressure.

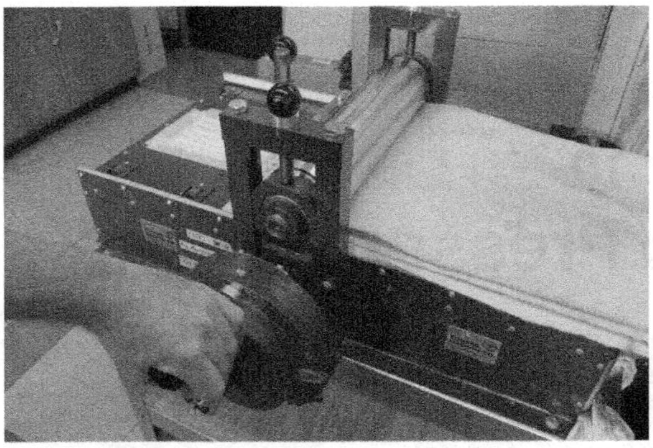

(**image 10-05**) Run everything through the press at a pressure setting in which you feel enough resistance from the plate that you notice when it picks up the top drum, and when it has passed completely under the top drum.

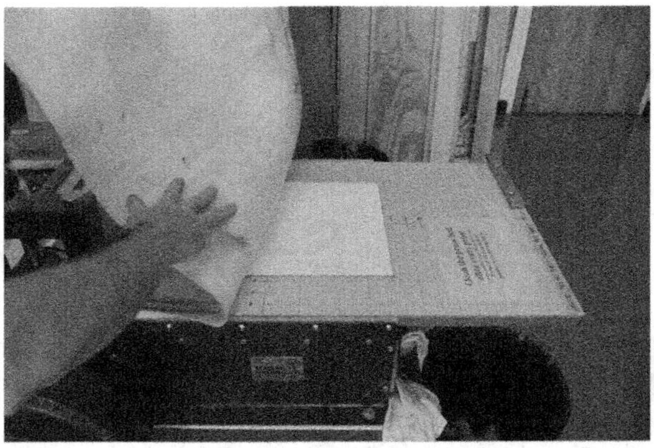

(**image 10-06**) Gently pull back the blankets to access the paper that has been embossed by the plate.

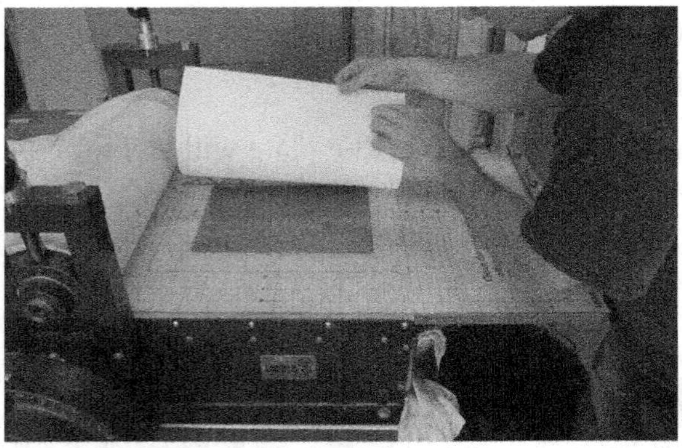

(**image 10-07**) Pull back both pieces of paper.

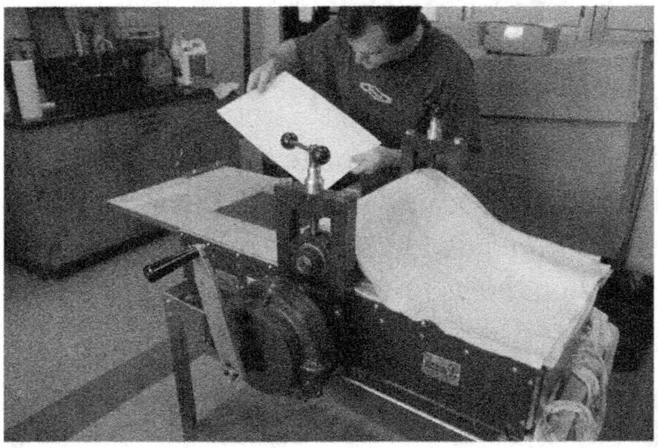

(**image 10-08**) Inspect the piece of paper that was in contact with the plate.

The paper will have left some kind of impression on the dry paper. If it did not, then the pressure setting on the press is much too light. If the pressure was too high, then the corners of the impression will have wrinkled paper. The goal is to have a distinct impression around all four sides of the rectangle made from the plate, and hopefully some indication of the image. The indication of the image from the plate will be very faint, mostly likely only showing up in the pattern that has been etched the deepest.

This photogravure process requires a lot of pressure to get the fullest tonal range possible. High pressure will make sure that the very light gray areas will print. Too much pressure, however, will make the dark areas block together into 100% black. Using dry paper for the intitial tests allows you to see when you have the pressure set too high.

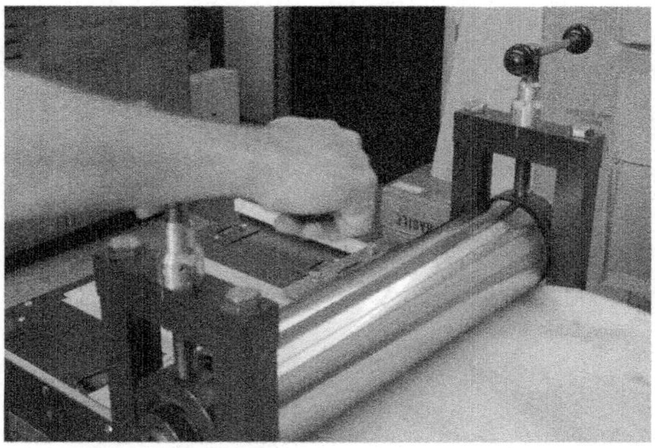

(**image 10-09**) Based on the results of the first pass, adjust the pressure settings on the press.

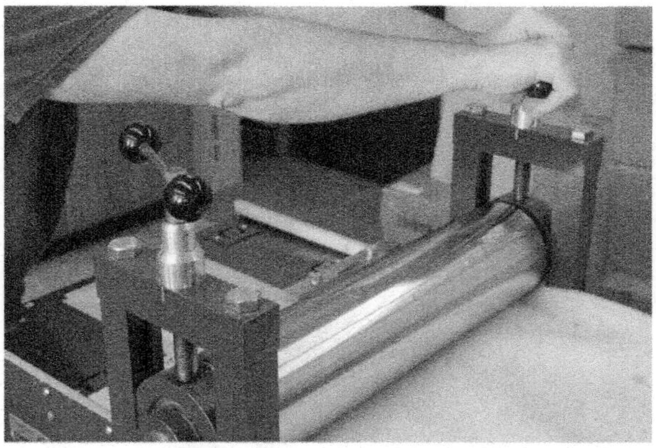

(**image 10-10**) Make sure to adjust both sides of the drum so that the pressure is applied evenly across the print surface.

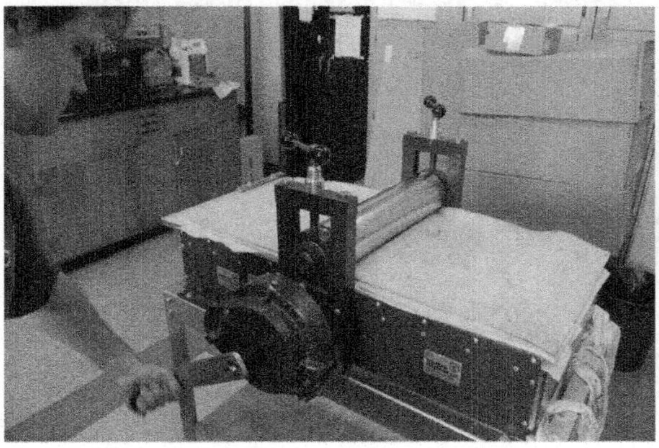

(**image 10.-11**) Run new paper through the press with the new pressure settings.

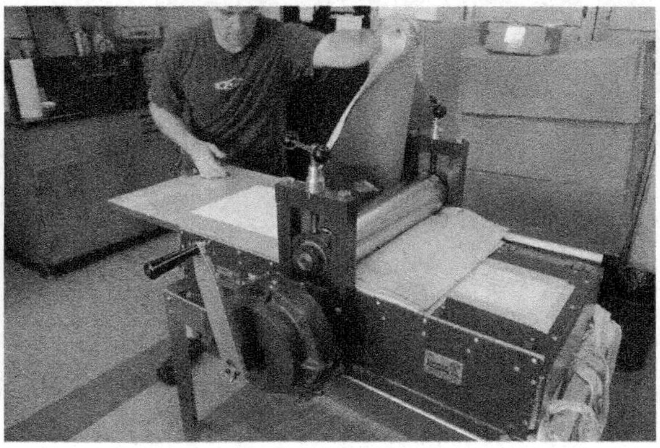

(**image 10-12**) After running everything through the press, with the new settings, remove the blankets and inspect the result.

The paper upon which you intend to print (if the plate were inked) must be new with each pressure test. The extra piece of paper that acts as a buffer to blanket patterns, however, can be reused since it is not in direct contact with the plate.

Some fine tuning may be needed once you start printing with ink, but this test should give you a good place to start.

Be sure to take notes. Write down the pressure settings you decide to use. Keeping a daily printing log will help you troubleshoot in the future, and allow you to fine tune your process quickly. The more data that you record, the less guessing you'll have to do in the future.

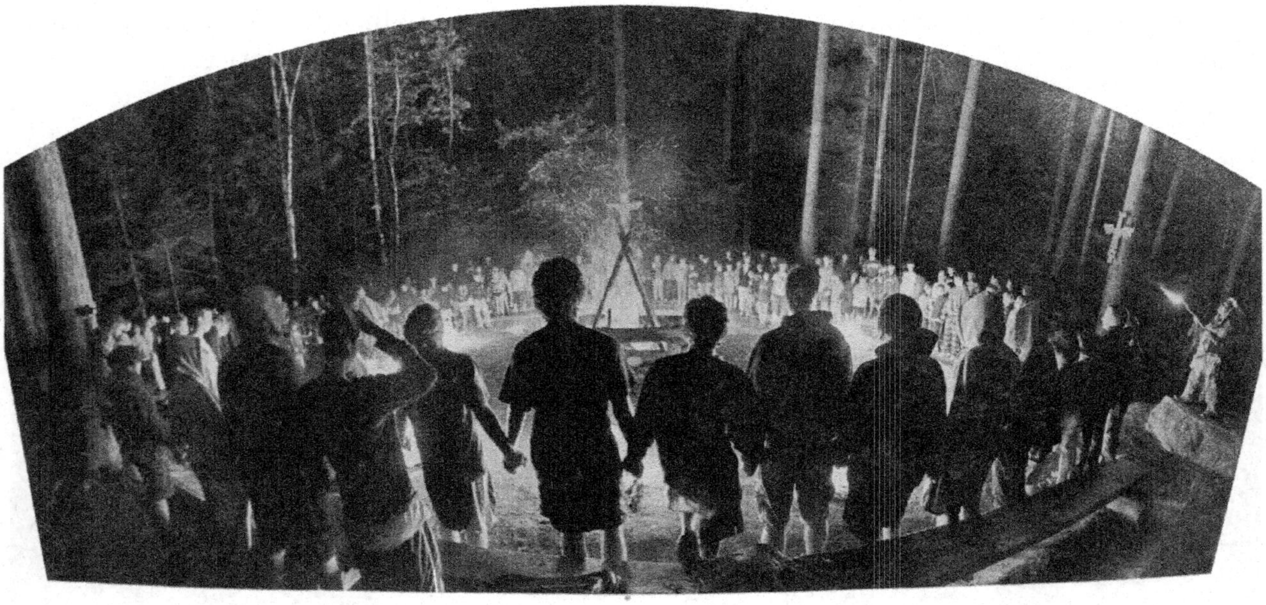

“Chief Kawanhee”

photogravure

Scott Barnes

Chapter 11
Preparing Ink

High quality printmaking ink is made with burnt plate oil and pigment. Very few (if any) additives are used to make the ink. This means that most ink is thick, and will be somewhat difficult to apply to the print plate. Depending on the pigments used, different colors of ink will be more "**stiff**" (*feels thick and pasty, has **high viscosity***) or "**loose**" (*thinner, with a more buttery feel, has **low viscosity***). All ink has to be prepared so that it has a viscosity appropriate for the intaglio technique employed.

Ink that is packaged in both tubes and tins is exposed to air. When ink is exposed to air it starts to become harder through a curing process. Cured ink cannot be reconditioned so must be removed. Take steps to minimize ink's exposure to air before it is used to make prints. Tubes of ink should never be left without caps, and the ink should be level with the opening of the tube. Tins of ink require some extra care. Remove ink only with a flat scraper or palette knife. And, remove ink evenly, without digging into the ink. Making sure to leave a smooth flat surface will expose only that flat smooth surface to air. A thin hard film will form on that surface, but it is easily removed later. If the palette knife digs into the ink it will expose the deeper layers of ink to air, curing more of the unused ink.

Warming ink will lower its viscosity. If the studio is warmer than 65 degrees, most ink can be warmed up without an external heat source. Simply drawing the ink across the palette, several times, with a scraper will start to warm it up. ("Drawing" ink means smashing it with the scraper and pulling it down across the palette) On colder days, ink needs a hot plate, or some other source of low heat to help change the viscosity. *I have had success with placing a cheap oil heater next to my inking table, allowing the glass palette to hang off the table and over the heater.*

Adding burnt plate oil will change the viscosity of intaglio printmaking ink. Burnt plate oil #000 has a very low viscosity. Burnt plate oil #2 has a viscosity that is close to the oil used to make ink. Higher numbers have higher viscosity (they feel thicker).

Printmaking ink is sticky. For the most part, this is a good thing. But, too much tack (stickiness) makes wiping ink out of the highlight areas difficult. Every ink manufacturer makes their own tack reducer. Most ink conditioners will work regardless of brand, as long as the inks are traditional intaglio printmaking inks. I prefer Easy Wipe by Graphic Chemical, but have been using Gamblin's Tack Reducer with some success recently. A little bit of tack reducer goes a long way. Add small amounts at a time.

Like so much in printmaking, an explanation of preparing ink can only get you started. Making useful ink takes practice. Different viscosities will yeild different results. While you are learning this photogravure process, make sure you consistently mix the same ink and conditioner combinations. Every variable that you change will effect the entire workflow.

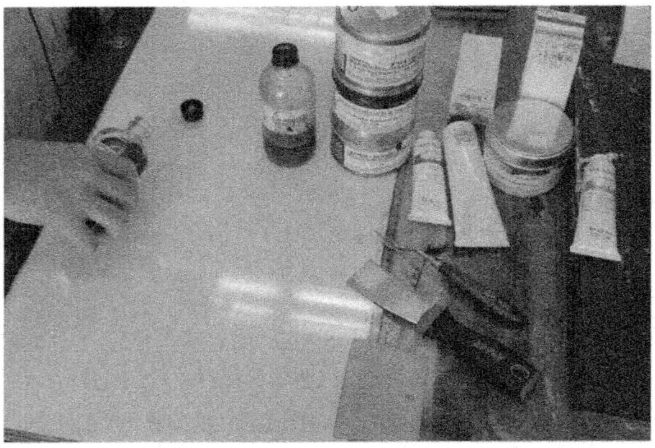

(image 11-01) Pour out a small drop of burnt plate oil #000.

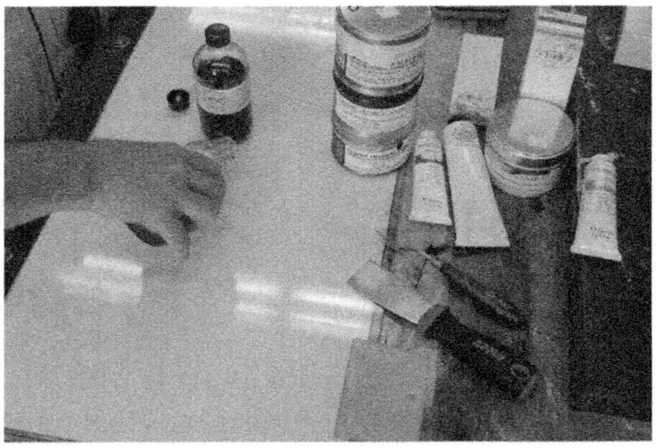

(image 11-02) Pour out a small drop of burnt plate oil #2.

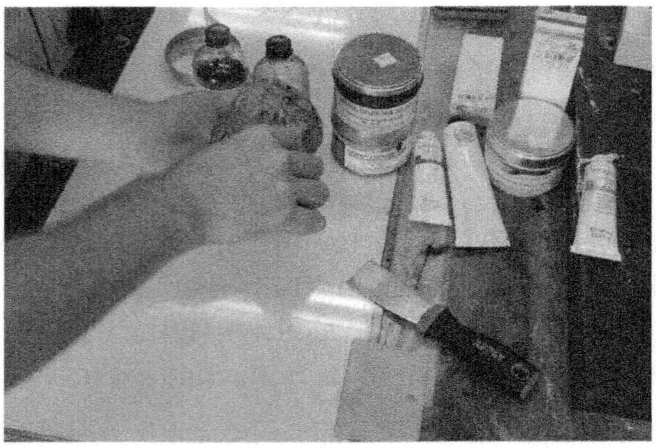

(image 11-03) Take out a small amount of easy wipe (or other tack reducer) from the container.

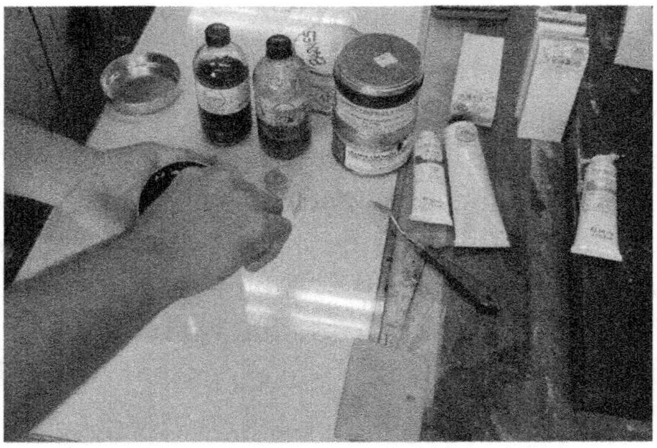

(image 11-04) Use a flat scraper to remove ink from the tin. Be sure to take an even layer from across the top of the ink. Do not dig down into the ink. Exposing the ink to air will make it start to cure, and the ink will not last as long in the can.

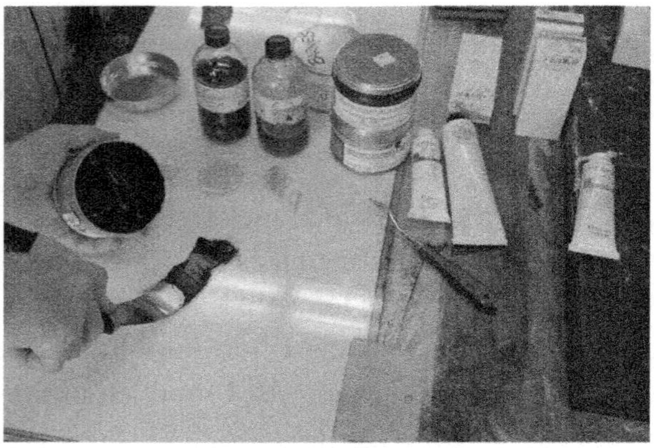

(image 11-05) Spread the ink on the palette. Look for dirt and small pieces of dried ink. It will be visible when the ink is drawn down flat along the palette.

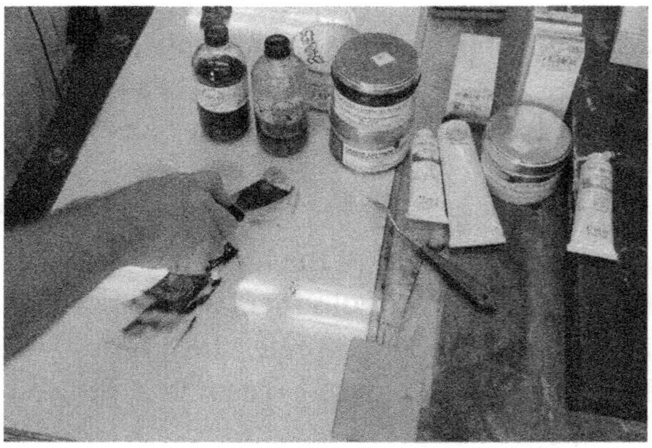

(image 11-06) Add a little bit of easy wipe.

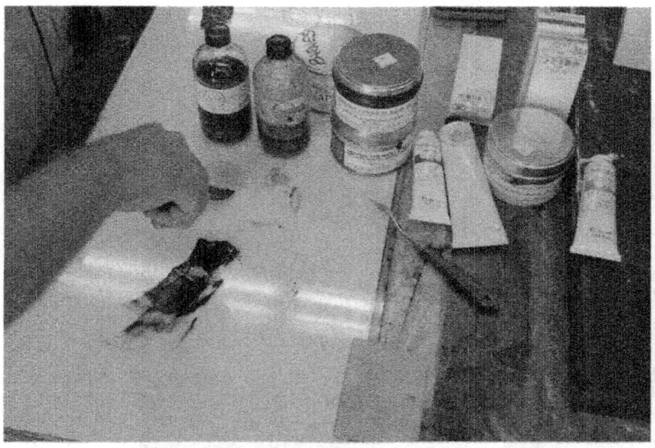

(**image 11-07**) Add a small amount of burnt plate oil #000 and even smaller amound of burnt plate oil #2.

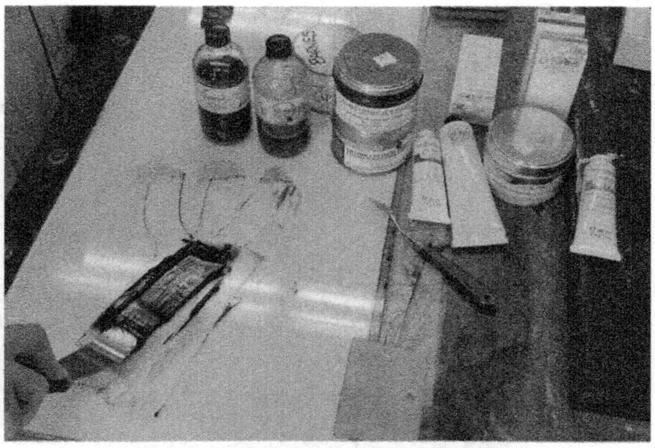

(**image 11-08**) Draw the scraper down acros the ink to start mixing everything together.

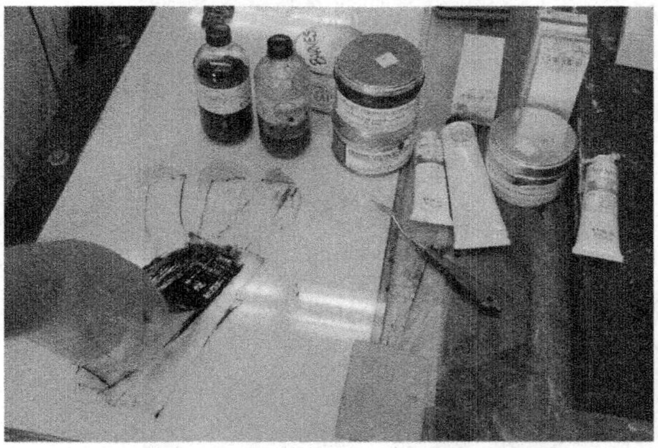

(**image 11-09**) Scrape up the drawn out combination of ink and conditioners.

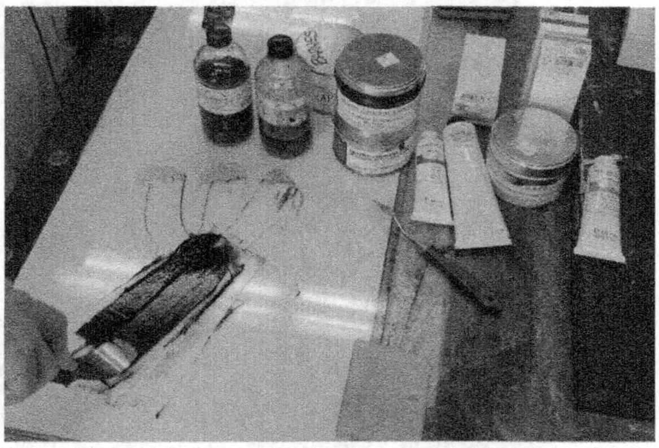

(**image 11-10**) Draw the ink down again. This will continue mixing the ink and conditioners as well as start to warm up the ink.

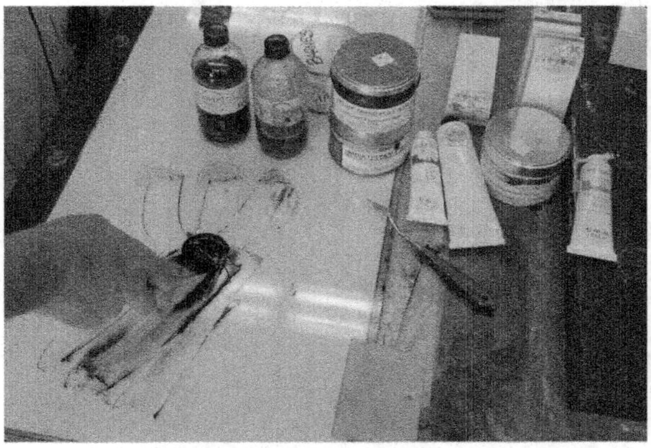

(**image 11-11**) As the process of drawing down and gather up the ink mixture continues, all the parts will be blended more evenly. An added bonus to this process is that dried ink and dirt can be found (and removed).

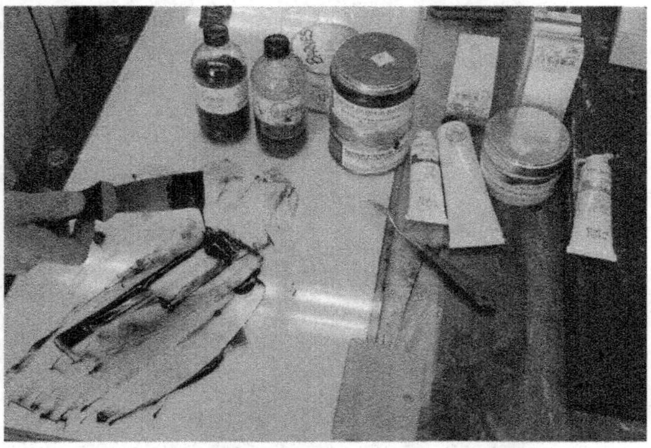

(**image 11-12**) The goal is to make ink that will run off the tip of the scraper like thick, cold honey. Finding the right balance of ink and conditioners takes practice.

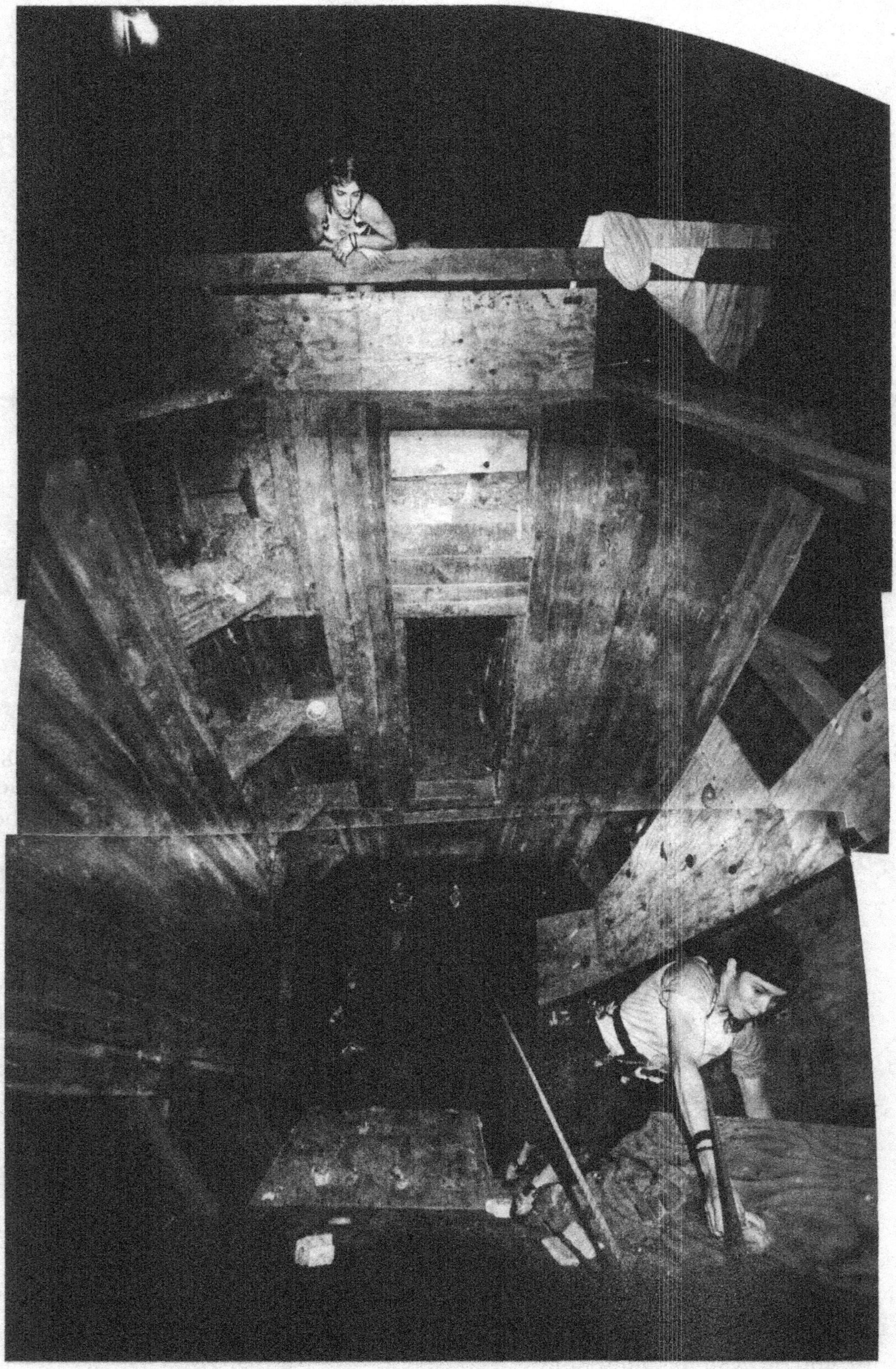

“Barn Party (Silo)”

photogravure

Scott Barnes

Chapter 12
Folding Tarlatan

Tarlatan is cheesecloth with sizing added to make it stiff. Some distributors offer regular tarlatan and stiff tarlatan. I have tried both and don't notice enough difference to have a strong preference. Tarlatan is used to wipe the majority of the ink off the surface of the printing plate, while leaving ink in the recessed aquatint area. It must be folded into a tool that will wipe the surface of the plate, but not dip into the recesses and remove ink from the areas that you intend to print. Some printmakers fold tarlatan into a square. I prefer to make a ball, then flatten out the smooth side.

Talatan is inexpensive. Intagio printmaking processes use a lot of it. I suggest that you buy several yards at a time.

How you fold tarlatan will become unique as you become a better printmaker. No single method is perfectly correct. The intent is to get a smooth wiping surface that does not have any dried ink or any other debris that can scratch the plate. You will get better with experimentation and practice.

I have found that fresh tarlatan almost removes too much ink, thus have to be careful with the first print with that tarltan. As it gets charged with ink, the tarlatan tends to wipe more predictably. It does have a limit. Once it is full of too much ink, it must be folded again around another clean spot.

Many printmakers keep progressively cleaner balls of tarlatan in their workspace during a print run. The ones with the most ink are used for an initial wipe to remove large amount of ink. The cleaner ones are used towards the end of the wiping process, with less pressure. I have a habit of using only one, and end up re-folding it many time.

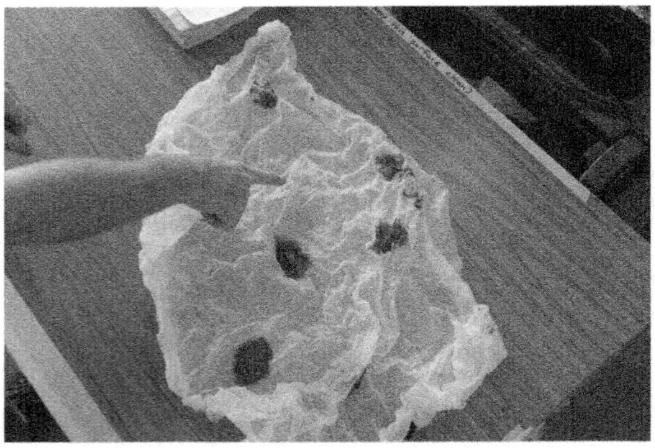

(**image 12-01**) Spread the tarlatan out on a clean surface. Look for an area of the tarlatan that does not have any ink. That will become the outer layer of the tarlatan ball.

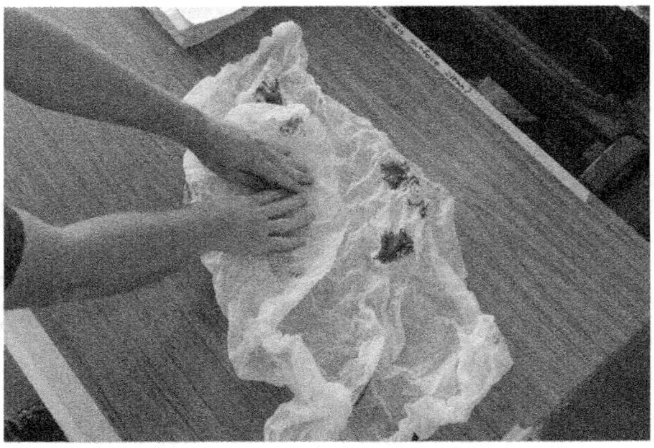

(**image 12-02**) Fold another clean point of the tarlatan to the first one, so that you have two layers of tarltan that are clean.

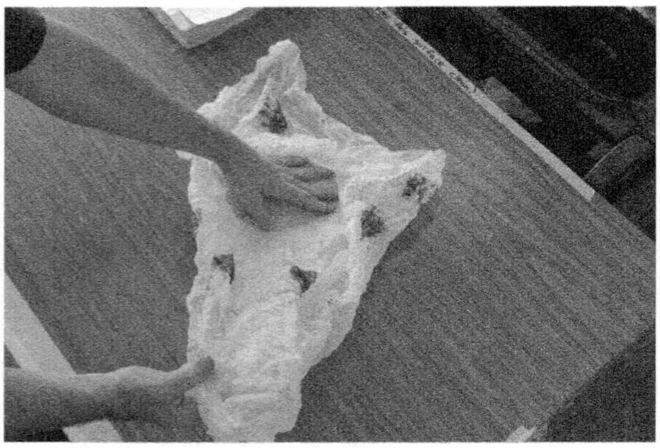

(**image 12-03**) Find a third area of tarlatan that is clean and fold it on top of the previous two.

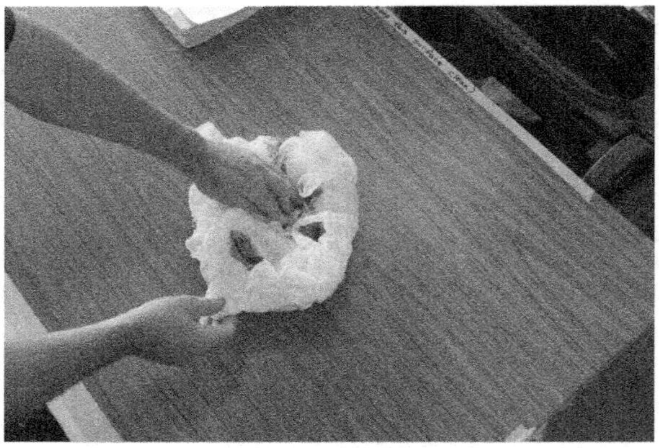

(**image 12-04**) Repeat the folding process, working around the outside so that the first clean point is the center of a rough circle, with layers of tarlatan folded on top of it.

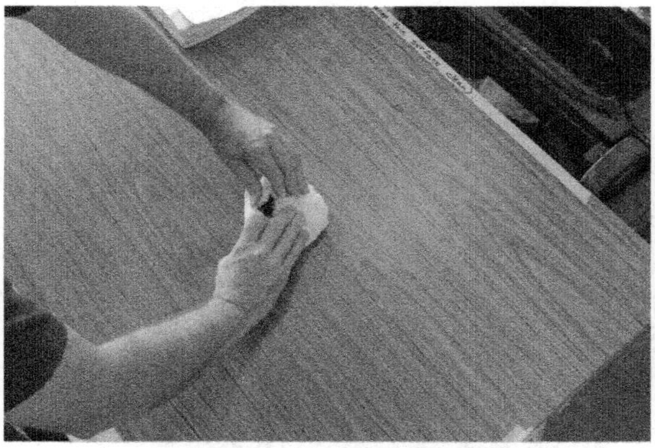

(**image 12-05**) At some point the ball is going to fold in on itself. It won't look perfect. The key to this is to make sure that the two outside layers (the first two steps) do not have any folds or tears in them. Any folds or tears will dip into the recessed aquatin areas and pull up ink that you did not intend to remove.

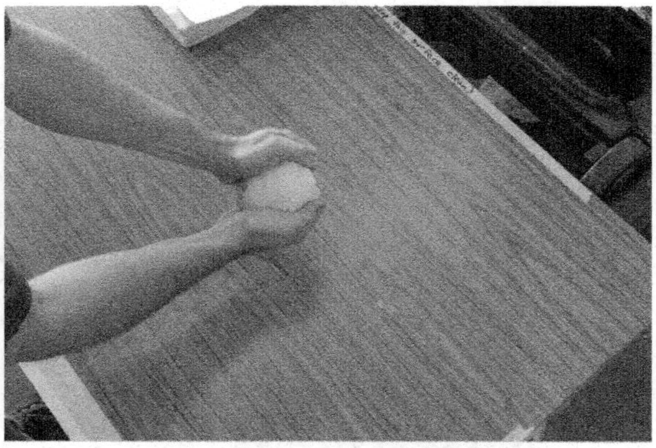

(**image 12-06**) Turn the tarlatan ball over so the smooth part is facing you. Using your fingers on one side and palms on the other, make as tight a ball as you can, ensuring that one side is smooth and clean.

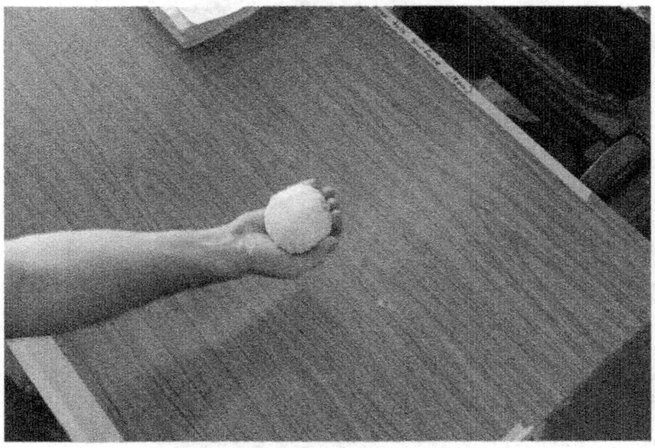

(**image 12 -07**) You need to flatten the smooth side of the ball. Hold it by the folded side, so that the smooth side is exposed.

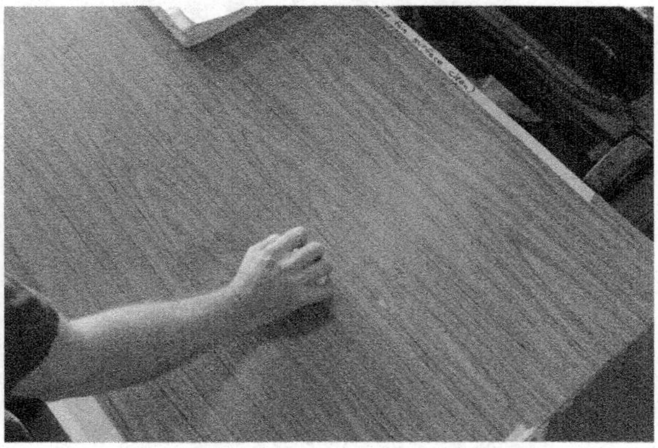

(**image 12-08**) Knock the smooth side of the ball against a flat clean surface a few time. This will create a flat spot. That flat spot is what will come in contact with the printing plate as you wipe ink from that plate. The smooth flat spot will remove ink from the surface, and leave ink in the recesses to print.

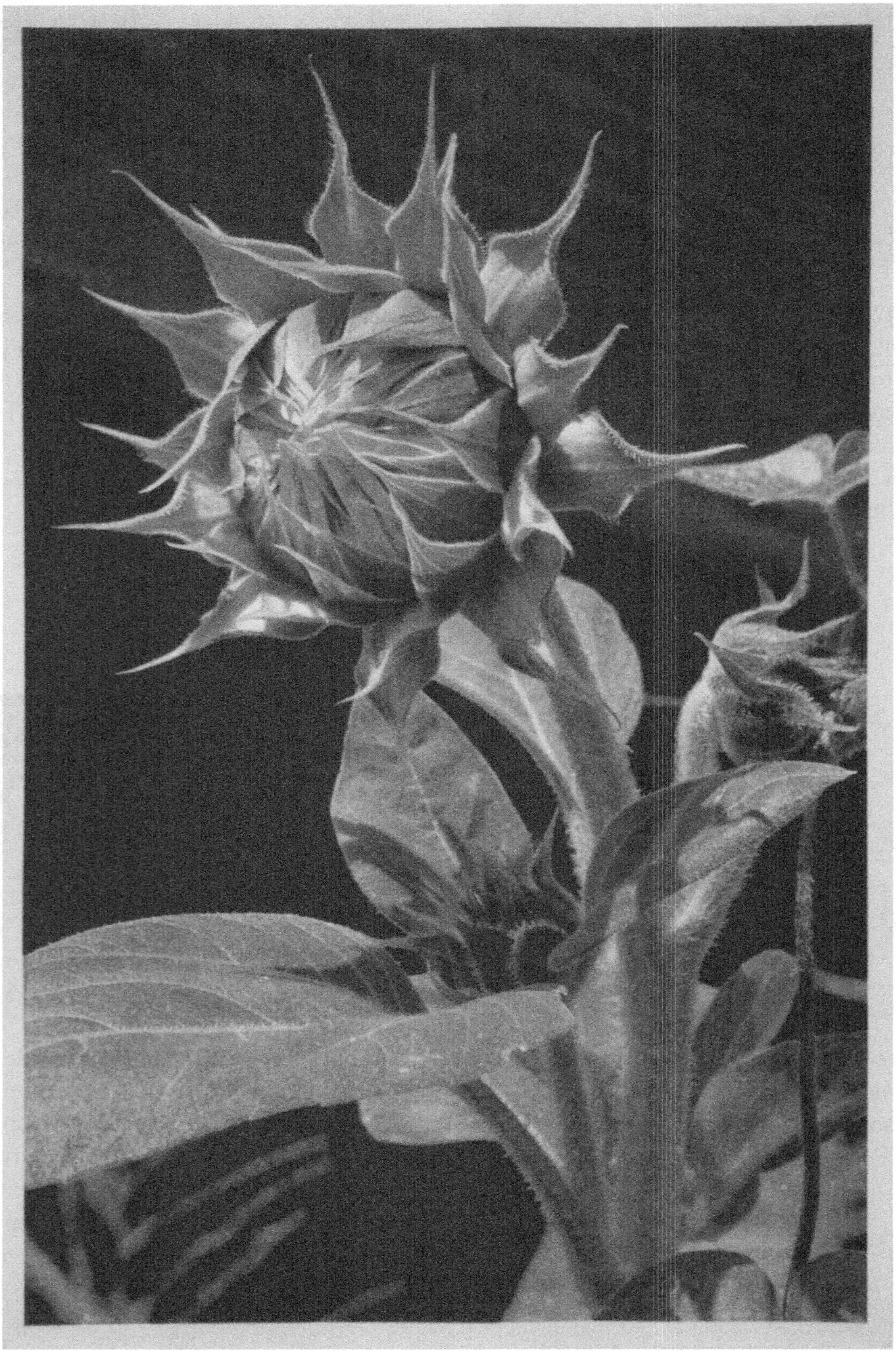

"Calyx"

photogravure

Scott Barnes

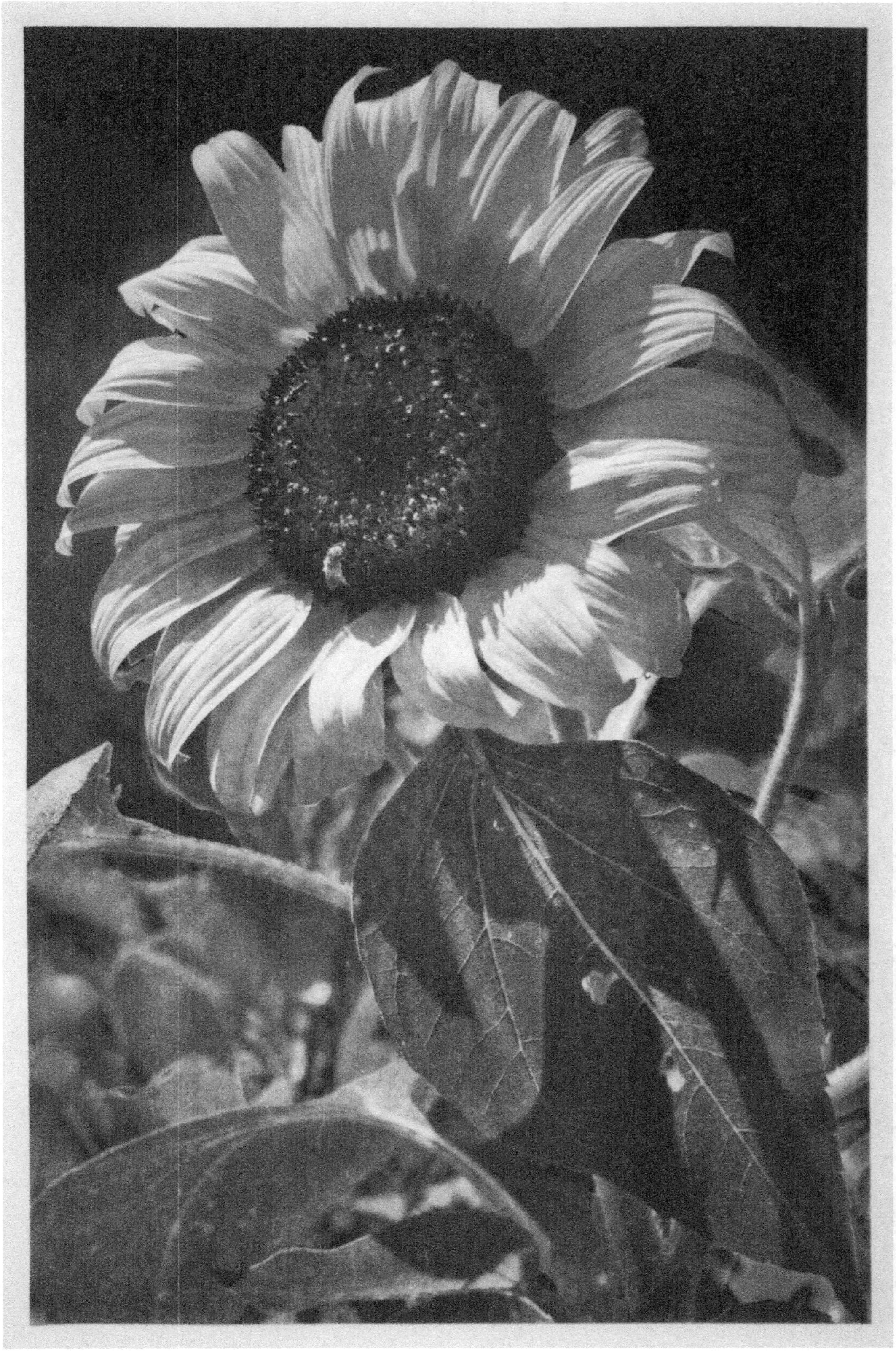

"Corolla"

photogravure

Scott Barnes

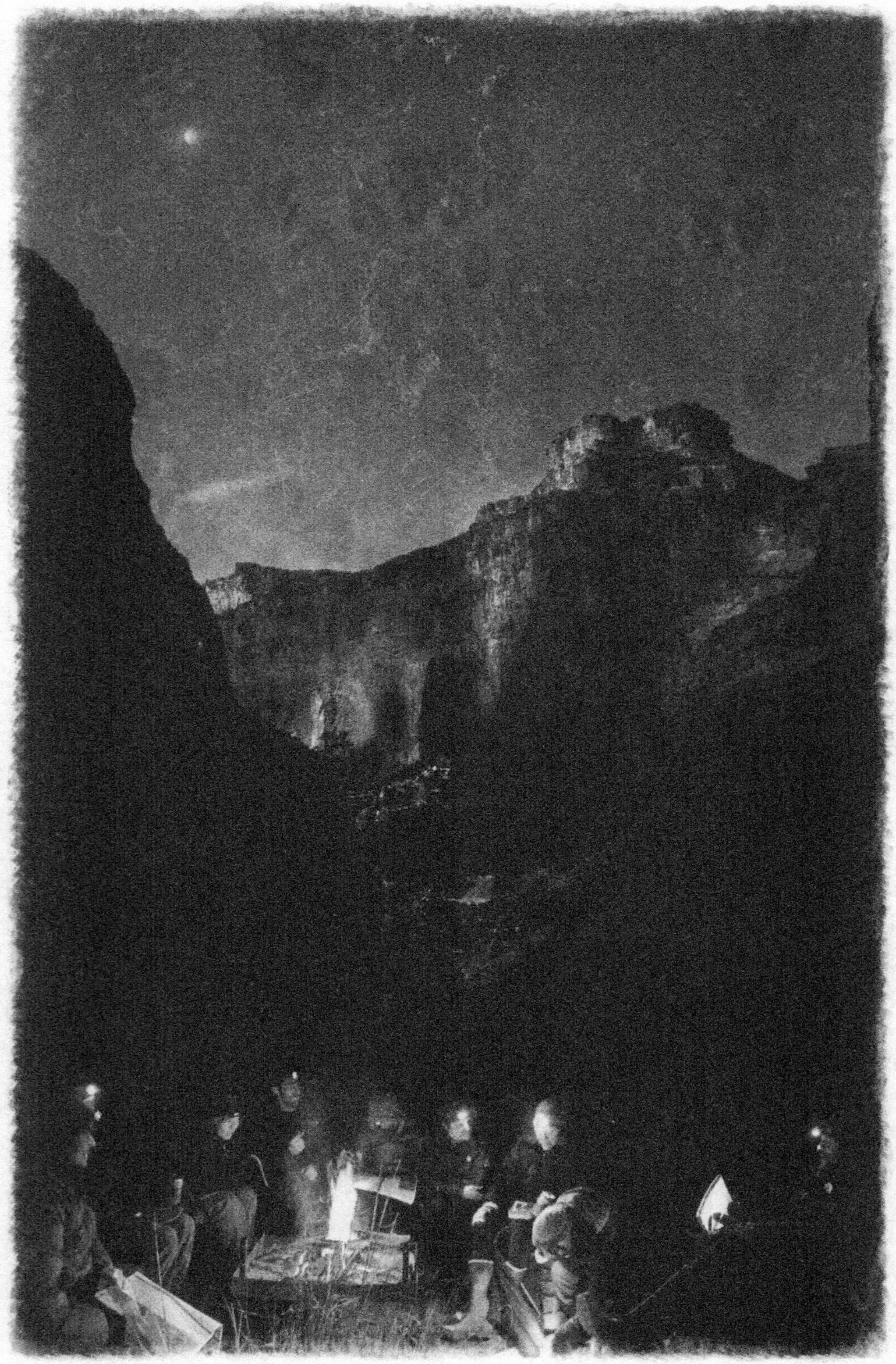

"Campsite Quanta'

photogravure

Scott Barnes

CPSIA information can be obtained
at www.ICGtesting.com
Printed in the USA
LVOW04s1718090417
530178LV00009B/79/P

9 780615 919218